Knitting with Icelandic Wool

Védís Jónsdóttir

ST. MARTIN'S GRIFFIN
NEW YORK

KNITTING WITH ICELANDIC WOOL. Pattern text copyright © 2011 by Ístex. Photographs copyright © 2011 by Gísli Egill Hrafnsson. All rights reserved. Printed in China. For information, address St. Martin's Press, 175 Fifth Avenue, New York, N.Y. 10010.

English translation: Ístex, Vigdís Þormóðsdóttir and Anna Cynthia Leplar
Editor: Oddný S. Jónsdóttir / Forlagið
Pattern advisor: Hulda Hákonardóttir / Ístex
Stylist: Alda G. Guðjónsdóttir
Design and layout: Anna Cynthia Leplar
This book has been typeset in Spectrum 12/15 pt. and Avenir 9.5/16 pt.

Special thanks to the staff at these photo locations:
Álafoss Outlet in Mosfellsbær, Hafnarfjörður Museum,
Laxnes Horse Rental, Reykjavik Zoo and Family Park
and Sigurjón Ólafsson Museum.

www.stmartins.com

The written instructions, photographs, designs, patterns, and projects in this volume are intended for personal use of the reader and may be reproduced for that purpose only.

Library of Congress Cataloging-in-Publication data available upon request

ISBN 978-1-250-02480-0 (paper-over-board)

Originally published in paper-over-board format by Vaka-Helgafell, an imprint of Forlagid, Iceland.

First U.S. Edition: January 2013

10 9 8 7 6 5 4 3 2 1

Contents

Introduction	1
The Origins of Icelandic Knitting	3
The Wool Industry in Iceland	15
1 x var	21
aftur	25
astrid	29
álafoss	33
ár trésins	37
árni	41
ása	45
bára	51
birta	55
bláklukka	59
dalur	63
dísa	66
dropar	69
endurreisn	73
faðmur	77
fiðrildaslóð and skotta	81
fjara and vormorgunn	87
frjáls	91
gefjun	95
gjöf	99
grein	103
handtak	107
hlökk and haddur	111
hosur	114
hraði	117
kambur	121
keðja	125
klukka	129
kría	133
kross	137
lamb and bjalla	140
land	143
lappi	147
leggur	150
leistar	152
ljúfa	155
mark	159
miðja	163
nost	171
nú	175
órói	179
prýði	183
ranga	187
regla	191
riddari	195
rjúpa	198
sigur	201
sjónvarpssokkar	204
stapi	207
strax	211
strik	214
strýta	217
toppur	220
upp	222
útjörð	225
varmi	228
verur	231
vetur	235
voff	238
vor	240
þel	242
æði	245
information	250
abbreviations	253
designers	254
picture credits	254

Introduction

Knitting with Icelandic Wool is a much-needed addition to Icelandic knitting literature, since it is the first book to not only chronicle the origins of knitting in Iceland and the history of the traditional lopi sweater but to also provide information about the Icelandic wool industry as well as a wide assortment of patterns for lopi sweaters and other garments knit with Icelandic wool. The oldest patterns in the book date to the late 1950s, around the time the traditional lopi sweater first emerged, while the most recent ones are brand-new.

The Icelandic wool industry experienced a downturn in the 1980s, but if one garment can be credited with the recent surge in Icelandic wool's popularity, it's the tradional Lopi sweater. For most of the twentieth century, Iceland's wool industry was booming, employing hundreds, if not thousands, of people all over the country. In the wake of the industry's crisis in the 1980s, the Gefjun wool factory in Akureyri and the Álafoss wool factory in Mosfellsbær merged under the name Álafoss, only to declare bankruptcy in 1991. At that point the country's entire wool industry was on the verge of collapse. Thankfully, due to the hard work and daring spirit of some Álafoss employees, a new wool-processing company, Ístex, was founded soon afterward. It is safe to say that this bold move rescued the Icelandic wool industry, and all of its invaluable knowledge, from oblivion. In recent years traditional handicrafts such as knitting have gone through a revival, both in Iceland and abroad, and thus the Lopi sweater is currently more popular than ever.

The team behind this book sincerely hopes that the book will both ignite the uninitiated's interest in Icelandic wool and prove to be a source of inspiration to those who already enjoy working with this unique material.

Elsa E. Guðjónsson
The Origins of Icelandic Knitting

The origins of knitting are not known for certain. The oldest known example of knitting is a stranded piece of silk found in the town of Fustat, now a part of the city of Cairo in Egypt. It is thought to be from the early Middle Ages, or the 7th to 9th centuries A.D. In the late Middle Ages knitting spread to northern Europe.

There is evidence of knitting in Britain, the Netherlands, and Germany from as early as the 15th century. It is thought that sea-faring traders introduced knitting to Iceland from one of these three countries. While it is not known precisely when this occurred, it was probably early in the 16th century or late in the 15th century.

Oldest Examples of Preserved Knitting

A single-thumbed, stockinette stitch mitten was excavated in 1981 at an archaeological dig at the Stóra-Borg farm just south of the Eyjafjallajökull glacier in southern Iceland. The mitten probably dates from the early 16th century, making it the oldest known piece of knitting in Iceland. More examples of early knitting were unearthed in 1987 at a dig in Viðey, including a stockinette stitch earflap hat, which may be even older than the mitten. The author of this article first thought that this hat was unique among preserved examples of old Icelandic knitting. However a similar hat, thought to date back to the 17th or 18th century, was found in 1977 during a dig in Dyrhólar in Mýrdalur.

This mitten from Stóra-Borg by Eyjafjöll is the oldest surviving example of Icelandic knitting. It was knitted at the beginning of the 16th century.

A considerable amount of knitting thought to be from the early 17th century was found at a dig in Bergþórshvoll in 1927. These were mostly small scraps in stockinette stitch whose purpose is unknown, along with a relatively undamaged single-thumbed mitten and part of a sock. More knitting has been found by the Stóra-Borg farm, including a child's sock and a stocking found in 1979. Both of these items were knitted in stockinette stitch and date from around 1650-1750. These are the only examples in Iceland of old socks that have been preserved, but a dig in Copenhagen unearthed a few adult-sized handknitted socks that are believed to have been exported from Iceland in the latter half of the 17th century.

It's interesting to note that the Bergþórshvoll mitten is quite different from the one found by the Stóra-Borg farm, in both the shape of the thumb and the rate of the decreases. No less than ten two-thumbed mittens, and one single-thumbed mitten, which are all thought to have been exported from Iceland, have been found at excavation sites in Copenhagen. These are thought to date back to around 1700 and are either knit from a thick single-ply yarn or a finer double-ply yarn. Other preserved examples of old Icelandic knitting are mostly from the 19th and 20th centuries.

Oldest Written Sources About Icelandic Knitting

Before the mitten from Stóra-Borg and the hat from the island of Viðey were known, the oldest written accounts of knitting date from the 1580s. These two previously mentioned examples seem to indicate, however, that knitting in Iceland started somewhat earlier.

The oldest written account of knitting is found in the collection of letters of Bishop Guðbrandur Þorláksson in Hólar, in the north of Iceland, which says that in 1582 and 1583 the bishop was paid rent for land he owned in knitted goods, which were most likely stockings, according to a source from 1581 in the same collection of letters. The first printed record of knitting is also connected to Bishop Guðbrandur because in the Bible printed in Hólar in 1584 the gown worn by Christ is described as being knitted, although it was said to be woven in the first translation of the New Testament by Oddur Gottskálksson, which was printed in Denmark in 1540. An earlier account of knitting in a letter from 1560 has sometimes been mentioned. Knitted sweaters are mentioned in this account, which may have been used to pay rent in Eyjafjörður in northern Iceland. This letter has only been preserved in a copy from 1703 and the sentence concerning the sweaters is considered to have been added at that time.

The oldest descriptions of knitting in this country, and the only accounts that exist from the 17th century, are said to come from the bailiff Skúli Magnússon. They exist among various descriptions of weaving in a manuscript from the island of Viðey from 1760-1770.

Production of Knitted Fabric

After its initial introduction, it seems that knitting spread quickly throughout Iceland, possibly because Icelanders soon came to realise that knitting was a faster way to make woolen products, than with the weaving looms used in Iceland at the time. The loom was difficult and slow, but its use was still widespread in the 18th and early 19th centuries.

Loom weaving was women's work only, but both men and women knitted. In fact, all able-bodied people were expected to produce a certain number of garments over certain periods of time. They were usually given a week at a time to complete their knitting tasks, but sometimes the deadline was longer or even as short as a day, depending on the project. This expectation also applied to children from as young as eight years old. Some say that Icelandic children were taught how to handle knitting needles as soon as they could crawl. Working women were expected to finish a pair of socks each day. Two women, knitting in tandem, facing each other, were expected to finish either six sweater bodies or four whole sweaters each week. Children were expected to

A 19th century drawing. A woman knits with five needles, another is spinning with a spindle and a third is using a foot loom.

finish a pair of two-thumbed mittens each week and the workload steadily increased as they got older and more proficient at knitting. It should come as no surprise that people were generally very fast knitters. People would knit whenever the opportunity presented itself, not only when taking a break from other work but also when outdoors, for example when herding farm animals or walking between farms, even in the wintertime. From the beginning of autumn until the new year was a busy time for knitters, mostly because everyone on the farm needed warm clothes for the winter, but also because knitted garments could be sold in town before Christmas. This was a time of wakeful nights when people's fingers became sore from all the knitting, so thimbles made from sheepskin came in handy.

Many different kinds of garments were produced for domestic use, but by the early 17th century socks and mittens had become an important source of export revenue for Icelanders and from the mid-18th century onward, Icelanders also exported handknitted sweaters. The oldest Icelandic export document that mentions knitted garments dates back to 1624. According to this document, Icelanders exported more than 72,000 pairs of socks and more than 12,000 pairs of two-thumbed mittens that year. The export of sweaters is first mentioned in export documents in 1743, when

Eyjafjörður, 1898. A woman spins with a spinning wheel while a girl cards the wool. Another woman and a girl are knitting.

more than 1,200 sweaters were exported, as well as more than 200,000 pairs of socks and 110,000 pairs of mittens. Sweater export peaked in 1849, when more than 8,000 sweaters were exported, socks peaked in 1753 when more than 360,000 pairs were exported, and mittens peaked in 1806 when more than 280,000 pairs were exported. The largest quantity of knitted goods came from the north of Iceland, along with Múlasýsla. They were also considered of the highest quality.

Garments knitted for domestic use, from the beginnings of knitting in Iceland and well into the 20th century, were quite varied depending on the style and tradition of each era. Commonly knitted garments included socks, stockings, riding stockings, shoe inserts, single- and double-thumbed mittens, gloves, wristwarmers, scarves, sweaters, hats, undergarments for both women and men, trousers and breeches, dickies, various hoods, slippers and suspenders for men, and sleeves, slips, shawls, garters and neckties for women. Other knitted items included kerchiefs, purses, pillowcases and bedclothes, tents for camping, and strainers (knit from coarse wool, horsehair, or hair from a cow's tail). There is documentation of knitted items being found among the possessions of three Icelandic churches in the 17th century.

Tools, Materials and Methods

The oldest mention of knitting needles in Icelandic documents can be found in Skarðsárannáll from 1615, where they are said to have caused someone's death. Knitting needles are described in an 18th century manuscript of an Icelandic dictionary by Jón Ólafsson from Grunnavík as being made of iron, thin and cylindrical, with points on both ends and measuring about 22.5cm in length. These needles were divided into two groups based on thickness. There are few preserved examples of these early knitting needles. Most date from the late

19th century, but in 1979 three needles from around 1700 were excavated at Stóra-Borg. Two of these are made of iron and the third one, broken, is made of copper. They are 2.5–3mm in diameter and about 20cm long, making them similar in length but larger in diameter than the 19th century needles housed in the National Museum of

A carved knitting needle box from 1842.

Iceland and the Borgarfjörður Museum. These later needles are all made of iron, are 0.75–2mm in diameter and 19.5–22.5cm long, fitting well with the description in the dictionary manuscript. The diameter, however, indicates that the Stóra-Borg needles are of the thicker variety used in early Icelandic knitting.

Women would traditionally keep their needles in long wooden boxes. They were often decorated with beautiful carved pictures and letters that indicated the owner's name, the year of manufacture, prayers, and descriptions of the case's contents.

Until wool factories emerged in Iceland in the late 19th century, nearly all knitting was produced from homespun wool yarn, usually in natural colors: white, gray, brown, and grayish-black. Dyed yarn was rare but existed in shades of black, navy, red, and green. Yellow was rarely ever seen. Knitted garments were usually felted and socks, mittens, and gloves were blocked on carved wooden blockers. Each home had as many as six to ten sock blockers. A 19th century woman's necktie, handknit from blue silk yarn, is a rare example of an older Icelandic garment knitted from a material other than wool that has been preserved.

Nearly all early Icelandic knitting was knitted in the round using five needles. More were used if the garment had a large diameter, such as a sweater body or men's undergarments. The stockinette stitch was the most commonly used stitch. The earliest example of Icelandic purling that this author is aware of is found in a brown, mostly stockinette stitch wool piece excavated at Stóra-Borg thought to be from around 1700. The earliest written mention of purling dates to 1760-1770 and is found in a headline describing a man's sweater in the aforementioned Viðey manuscript.

Judging from the known examples, early knitting

A man knitting, 1900.

A family in their sitting room in Reykjavík at the beginning of the 20th century.

techniques in Iceland were mostly similar to those still taught in Icelandic elementary schools, the so-called Continental or German knitting techniques where a knitting needle is held in each hand and the wool lies between them from the left around the index finger of the left hand. Icelandic knitting was usually done exclusively in the round, but stitches were knitted from the back of the loop for purl stitches and from the front for stocking stitches. If the garment was knitted back and forth, the opposite was done: stitches were knit into the back of the loop for stocking stitches and the front of the stitches for the wrong side. This does not, however, apply to purling, which was done by laying the yarn in front of the needles and pulling it through the stitch from the back. This method of purling is still used by some Icelandic women today. It's usually attributed to Eastern European and Asian countries and is referred to as the uncrossed eastern purl stitch. This is said to be faster than the usual Continenal purling and to result in a more even tension.

Shaped Knitting

Old, preserved, Icelandic body garments, dating from the late 18th century and the 19th century, are shaped to fit the body of the wearer. The garments in question

Leather shoes with garter stitch linings knitted in the eight-petal rose pattern.

are women's sweaters and men's vests, sweaters, breeches, and trousers. Such shaping in handknitting is now all but forgotten in Iceland, but the Viðey manuscript contains patterns for a man's and a woman's sweater, along with a pattern for underpants, where shaping is partially described. The manuscript also contains patterns for men's socks, two patterns for women's socks, and a pattern for a hat. These old patterns are difficult to understand compared to their modern equivalents, and despite a few honest attempts, no one has as yet managed to knit from them. However, two patterns based on old, preserved men's garments have recently been published: one is for a double-breasted cardigan and the other for a pair of breeches.

Color-patterned Knitting

A church document from Eyjafjörður in northern Iceland from 1695 contains the oldest known information on decorative knitting – in this case stranded knitting – in Iceland. It tells of a container for sacramental wafers that has been covered with red-and-white-patterned knitting. The document does not indicate, however, whether this container was built and decorated in Iceland or imported. Further mention of decorative knitting is not found in other docuumments until the late 18th century. The patterns found in the Viðey manuscript contain no mention of decorative knitting. However, this type of knitting was known at the time, as is verified by two manuscripts from 1776 and 1780 that contain drawings of various decorative patterns. The later manuscript stipulates that these drawings are meant for embroidery, picture weaving, and decorative knitting. The earlier manuscript contains ten charts, seven pattern repeats and three intarsia drawings that are said to be for embroidery on knitted fabric and for decorating men's undergarments. Unfortunately, no examples of decorated men's undergarments have survived, but the Brandsstaðaannáll manuscript from 1800 mentions that these garments were sometimes knitted with a two-colored pattern. The manuscript also reveals that most women possessed a number of written patterns to help them with their handicrafts, including decorative knitting.

An excavation in Reykholt in 1988 unearthed a piece of two-color patterned knitting that dates back to the 18th or perhaps even the 17th century. It contains a strip of a color-pattern repeat in two shades of brown on a gray background. A drawing for an identical pattern can be found in a manuscript from the 17th cen-

Handspun stranded mittens from the West Fjords.

tury. It's impossible to tell what this knitted piece was originally a part of, but a similar pattern is found on two-colored garters dating to the latter half of the 19th century, which is kept in a museum in the north of Iceland. A few documents dating from the late 18th century and the early 19th century mention decorative color-patterned knitting of hats and undergarments, but apart from the previously mentioned piece of two-colored knitting found in Reykholt, none dating further back than the 19th century has been preserved.

Examples of decorative color-patterned knitting are mostly found in mittens and shoe inserts. In the West

A family at the beginning of the 20th century. The woman is knitting and wearing the traditional Icelandic costume.

Fjords of Iceland, the tradition of knitting mittens with elaborate color patterns for special occasions became widespread in the early 20th century. This tradition cannot be traced back further than the late 19th century, however. The same can be said for two types of handknitted shoe inserts. One type was knit in the round, combining two inserts in one piece, and was decorated with stripes or a color pattern. The two inserts were then cut apart, lined, and stitched around the edges in a manner that was common in the north of Iceland. An eight-petaled rose pattern was usually used for these inserts, which were referred to as stitched-rose inserts. The other type of insert was knitted with a garter stitch and decorated with horizontal or vertical stripes, or both, or with a colorful garter stitch intarsia. The intarsia was usually a variant of the eight-petaled rose.

Knitted stranded gloves from the north of Iceland.

An elderly woman sits in front of a row of pack horses and knits. This photo was taken in the south of Iceland in 1898.

Decorative Single-colored Knitting

Decorative knitting with raised, purled stitches on a stockinette background was also known to have existed in Iceland in previous centuries, although to what extent remains uncertain. Only two examples of this kind of knitting exist. One is the previously-mentioned small, brown piece found at Stóra-Borg in 1980. This piece is decorated with two parallel diagonal lines of purled stitches and is thought to have been part of a sock, with the lines running up the back. The other example is a simple thirteen-stitch diamond-pattern repeat on the hem of a men's shaped sweater that dates to the late 18th century, and is now housed in the National Museum of Iceland. Two of the three previously mentioned pattern drawings for men's undergarments resemble purl-stitch patterns often found on Danish peasant women's nightshirts from the 19th century.

Around 1900 other forms of decorative single-colored knitting became popular in Iceland, including lace stitches such as old shale, feather and fan, and trellis lace, which were often seen in triangular shawls and mittens. Other lace stitches and cabling also gained popularity. Examples of some of these stitches can be seen in mittens and gloves housed in the National Museum of Iceland. Trellis lace was often used for wrist-warmers as well. Finishing schools, which began to be established in the late 19th century, probably had much to do with introducing decorative single-colored patterns to Icelandic knitting. The first book on Icelandic handicrafts, *Leiðarvísir til að nema ýmsar kvennlegar hannyrðir* (A Guide to Learning Various Feminine Crafts), written by Þóra Pjetursdóttir, Jarðþrúður Jónsdóttir and Þóra Jónsdóttir and published in 1886, contains fourteen knitting patterns, of which eight are for lace knitting. Furthermore, the first and second editions of Elín Briem's *Kvennafræðarinn* (The Woman's Educator), published in 1889 and 1891, contained patterns for a handknit lace scarf and two small lace shawls.

New trends in handknitting reached the general public through a variety of channels. For example, Gytha Thorlacius, the wife of a Danish official who lived in Iceland between 1801 and 1814, claims in her

A little girl knits in Reykjavik, photo from about 1921.

An elderly woman displaying socks at a craft show at a nursing home in Reykjavik in 1963.

autobiography to have taught the brioche stitch to Icelanders. In the 1886 handicrafts book mentioned before, the brioche stitch is the only stitch mentioned by name.

Knitting with Lopi

Before woolen mills began operating in Iceland in the late 19th century, the processing of wool took place within the home. During this time, the word *lopi* simply meant wool that had been washed and carded or combed and then stretched to make an unspun length of wool, which would then be spun on a spindle or, after the mid-18th century, a spinning wheel to make knitting yarn. The wheel became the dominant method of spinning in the 19th century. This unspun version of lopi was never used for handknitting since it was only seen as a stage the wool went through in the preparation for spinning.

When woolen mills began operating, the meaning of the word lopi expanded to include the lengths of wool that had been machine-combed but had not yet been machine-spun. At first, lopi was either spun in mills or, as was often the case, sent back to farms for domestic spinning. In such cases the wool would be spun on spinning wheels or on small spinning machines that were owned and operated by various local groups.

In the first half of the 20th century, knitting machines became common in Icelandic homes and spread throughout the countryside, and handknitting began to decline. In 1920 Elín Guðmundsdóttir Snæhólm, on a farm in northern Iceland, decided to try to machine-knit a scarf straight from plötulopi (unspun wool) instead of spinning the wool first, with good results. She wrote about her experiments machine-knitting various woolen garments in a women's magazine in 1923 and her methods soon spread.

It later emerged that two women in West Iceland had handknit mittens from unspun lopi some years earlier. Handknitting with lopi didn't become common until the 1930s, and knitting was considered women's work

A man and a woman in front of their house, around the middle of the 20th century.

and handknitting more of a leisure activity.

The lopi used for knitting was usually triple-stranded – one strand from each plate of unspun lopi. The three strands were often wound loosely together. A strand of stronger spun wool – such as Einband lace wool – was sometimes combined with the lopi to make it stronger. The lopi wool sold in skeins these days is lightly plied.

During and after the Second World War, two-colored handknit wool sweaters became popular in Iceland. These sweaters were primarily knit from Icelandic wool — yarn from other countries was a rare commodity in those days — and slowly lopi became the more popular yarn. The sweaters were usually worn for outdoor activities such as winter sports. They were knit in the round on circular needles, a novelty that was first imported to Iceland in the late 1930s.

A meeting at the beginning of the 20th century. Most of the women are wearing traditional costumes and are drinking coffee and doing handicrafts.

At first these Icelandic sweaters were modeled on foreign sweaters, most notably Norwegian two-colored, drop-shouldered ski sweaters. However, the wool manufacturer Íslenzk Ull (Icelandic Wool), which was in operation between 1939 and 1951, published a pattern for a two-colored Norwegian ski sweater in 1939 that was knit all in one piece using raglan decreases for the yoke. Customers could place orders with the company for sweaters handknit from Icelandic yarn, but not for sweaters knit with lopi. The author of this article received a gray sweater with a blue, red and white color pattern, knit from three-ply yarn from the above-mentioned pattern, as a Christmas present in 1939.

Raglan decreases never caught on as a method for knitting lopi sweaters, even though there are a few examples of sweaters knit this way. The drop-shouldered model was popular for many years, but from the mid-1950s onwards the Fair Isle round yoke, where decreases are evenly spaced throughout the yoke, gained in popularity and is still the dominant method of knitting lopi sweaters today. Sweaters knit from wool yarn using this construction method were already very popular elsewhere in the world by then, especially in Scandinavia. These were often referred to as Greenland sweaters, since the yoke patterns and decreases are reminiscent of the beaded collars on the Greenlandic women's national costume.

The origins of this particular type of yoke have been a source of considerable curiosity. However, in the year 2000, the author learned of a pattern and photograph of a stranded, round-yoked sweater, similar to the type mentioned above, in a Norwegian book of knitting patterns called *Strikkeopskrifter* (Oslo 1932), designed by Annichen Sibbern Bøhn. The sweater is called the Eskimo, and thus the designer was clearly inspired by the Greenlandic women's national costume. It's still unclear whether older models of this type of sweater exist anywhere. The pattern for the Eskimo sweater was re-

Teaching handicrafts at a school in Reykjavík in 1953.

This sweater, "Eskimo," was published as the Greenlandic Sweater in the magazine *Melkorka* in 1956.

sweaters, which have carried the reputation of Icelandic knitting far and wide.

Lopi sweaters made for commercial purposes, both domestic and foreign, were traditionally knit using natural colors. In more recent years, however, sweaters knit from dyed lopi have become increasingly popular. The charts used for the yoke patterning have various origins: some are adapted from traditional Icelandic charts borrowed from either old chart books or old knitted, woven or embroidered objects; others are based on foreign textile charts. In recent years, most yoke charts have been designed especially for lopi sweaters by textile designers and knitters alike.

printed in a Bøhn book of knitting patterns in 1939, and then again, using a different color scheme, in a Danish weekly magazine in 1955 or 1956. An Icelandic woman used that magazine pattern and some wool yarn to knit the sweater. She still has that sweater, which has the exact same yoke pattern and rate of decreases as the Norwegian Eskimo sweater. A pattern that uses the same yoke chart but different colors was published in *Melkorka* magazine in December 1956, where it was given the name "Grænlenzk peysa" (Greenlandic Sweater). Around the same time – and in the years that followed – patterns for similar sweaters could be found in Danish women's and knitting magazines and in Swedish knitting books, in which they were often referred to as Icelandic sweaters! Afterwards, this type of sweater was modified to be knit from lopi, and ever since the round yoke has been the signature look of Icelandic lopi

Children wearing handknitted lopi sweaters in the 1960s.

Magnús Guðmundsson
The Wool Industry in Iceland

Great strides were made in the development of Icelandic woolcrafts in the latter half of the 18th century as the protagonists of the industrial experiment imported the Danish loom, the spinning wheel and a comb for carding the fine inner wool fibres. Little by little people stopped using the old upright looms. Spindles and wool combs for outer fibres were mainly used to work the coarser wool. About 20 percent of the nation worked with wool for six months of the year and such work was the most common winter occupation of Icelanders. This handicraft activity flourished into the 19th century. Most woven wool fabric was used in the home and a great deal was knitted for private use as well as for selling on the market.

In the 19th century, the import of foreign handicrafts gradually took over the Icelandic market for woolen goods, as the European industrial revolution spread to Iceland. However, all over Iceland homes received assistance in the latter half of the 19th century when sewing and domestic knitting machines began to be imported. The market for home-made products was constantly diminishing at this time though. Shortly after 1900, woolen cloth was no longer exported and little was exported of woolen goods, but wool was still exported in considerable amounts. Although the handicraft industry had diminished substantially around this time, there were still some people who made their living by knitting and weaving for others and housewives still wove and knitted for their families.

Mechanisation of the wool industry began when Magnús Þórarinsson from Laxárdalur began operating wool machines in 1884. These were carding and spinning machines driven by water power. Soon, machine processing had spread all over the country. Five wool processing companies were founded over the following two decades, including Álafoss in 1896 and Gefjun in Akureyri in 1897. At the wool factories, wool was carded into lopi and yarn was spun.

The wool factories later branched out in two directions at the beginning of the 20th century. On the one hand they continued to card home-washed wool for farmers and spin it into yarn that was used within the home. On the other hand, they started weaving and manufacturing clothing. The whole processing cycle was gradually incorporated into the clothing factories: spinning workshops, weaving, knitting rooms and sewing rooms, as well as shops that sold their own production line. At this time, Álafoss and Gefjun towered over their competitors.

Farmers usually washed their wool at home in a

The weaving looms at the Álafoss factory around 1920.

stream, sometimes with old urine, before it was sent to be carded and spun into yarn. In the early days of the wool factories, the inner and outer layers of wool were often separated before they were sent for processing. The inner fibres, which are as soft as merino wool, were used for underwear that had to be next to the skin in fine weaving and in knitting. The outer fibres, which are long and strong, were used in protective and outer garments. Each and every craftswoman sent undyed wool, both inner and outer fibres, to wool processing factories, wanting to receive either yarn or lopi made from their own wool. As the 20th century progressed and the machines became larger, it became difficult to keep each shipment separate. Instead of getting back from the factory yarn made with their own wool, farmers had to accept receiving yarn, lopi, or textiles in keeping with the amount of wool that they had sent for processing. The companies Álafoss and Gefjun could not cope with the demand for separate carding for farmers and so four carding factories were operated in the country from the 1920s to the 1960s, including three operated by the cooperatives. Gradually the business developed from servicing farmers to bartering, until money transactions gained the upper hand. In recent decades, textile artists have been reviving the old tradition of separating the inner and outer fibres of the wool, thereby obtaining yarn with unique properties.

In the second decade of the 20th century, handicraft

Spinning machines at the Álafoss factory around 1920.

associations were founded to support knitting in the home. Handicraft-, women's-, and agricultural associations, together with the ceaseless battle of other interested parties, encouraged knitting and supported it widely in rural areas until the beginning of the Second World War. Halldóra Bjarnadóttir, consultant in matters connected to the handicrafts industry, was one of the leading campaigners for the revival of this old cultural heritage and published a book on weaving. But the import of cloth and the factory production of clothing meant that weaving in private homes had gradually stopped. While weaving and handknitting became less common within the home, the use of domestic knitting machines gained popularity. The handicrafts industry was strengthened during the First World War and in the Depression of the 1930s. During the Second World War, however, there was more paid work available in other sectors and so the handicrafts industry was not able to compete.

Knitters began using domestic knitting machines at the end of the 19th century and in the first decades of the 20th century. These machines were the first steps towards the mass-production of knitted goods for the general market. Although the handicrafts industry in general had declined substantially around 1950, knitting remained popular among the public. Those people who had been involved in wool processing within the country's homes also played a large role in the development of *hespulopi* and lace-weight yarn, which have been the main staple products manufactured by spinning factories in Iceland since the end of the 1960s. Lace-weight yarn became the staple for the machine knitting factories. Hespulopi came into existence at the Álafoss factory in 1967 when single lopi was successfully twisted slightly as it came out of the carding machine. Many varieties of this yarn have been manufactured since then and Hespulopi is without a doubt one of the best-known products of the Icelandic woolen industry. The term *lopi* has received international recognition as a trade name, but there is no patent on the

The cloth looms at the Álafoss factory around 1920.

A woman knitting in the 1950s.

production of lopi, in which the best properties of Icelandic wool are combined. The inner fibres give it a soft fullness while the outer fibres strengthen and hold the threads together. The Icelandic lopi jumper, designed by Icelandic knitters in the 1950s, was successfully marketed in in the early 1960s and played a large part in opening up a new market for Icelandic knitted goods overseas. Over the last 50 years, hundreds of Icelandic knitters have knitted jumpers, socks, gloves, shawls, and other items at home and sold them at shops in Iceland and abroad. In this way the handicrafts industry, the factories and the craft itself have developed side by side, rendering it highly unlikely that hand-knitting will ever be completely replaced by machine knitting, not least since the factories need the knowledge and creativity of craftspeople in order to develop new products.

The wool industry is divided into several fields, each of which has had its growth period, heyday and decline. Thus carding and spinning machines mostly manufactured lopi for the handicrafts industry before 1930. During the 1930s weaving increased substantially, together with yarn production for knitting firms. The lopi market collapsed in 1950, but not long afterwards production of carpet yarn began for the carpet industry. The carpet companies flourished in the 1960s, but in the 1970s they died off one by one in the face of competition from imported carpets. However, the production of machine-knit goods greatly increased in the same decade, so the 1970s could be called "the decade of the mechanised knitting industry". After considerable development and an increase in knitting companies, the overseas market began to decline in the 1980s, which resulted in the long-established, large companies going bankrupt.

The company Ístex was founded in 1981 on the Álafoss premises, and is owned by several of the workers together with 1,800 farmers. Their powerful spinning factory allows them to produce yarn from Icelandic wool for the handknitting market, including *Plötulopi, Álafoss Lopi, Bulky lopi* and *Létt-Lopi*.

icelandic
knitting patterns

1 x var

This pattern is new, but it still contains some nostalgic notes. The sweater is knitted with two strands of unspun Icelandic wool and its length can be easily altered.

SIZES S (M L XL XXL)
Chest: 92/36¼" (98/38½", 103/40½", 109/43", 115/45¼")cm
Length to armhole: 60/23¾" (62/24½", 64/25", 66/26", 66/26")cm
Sleeve length: 44/17¼" (45/17¾", 46/18", 47/18½", 48/18¾")cm

MATERIAL Plötulopi 100g plates (3.5oz)/300m (328yd)
A 0001 white 4, (4, 5, 5, 6)
B 1030 beige 1, (1, 1, 1, 1)
C 0005 black heather 1, (1, 1, 1, 1)

5.5mm (US 9) 40 and 80cm (16 and 30in) circular needles, 4.5mm (US 7) 80cm (30in) circular needle, 4.5mm and 5.5mm (US 7 and 9) double pointed needles, double-ended zipper

GAUGE
2 strands of plötulopi: 10 x 10cm (4 x 4in) = 14 sts and 19 rows in st st on 5.5mm (US 9) needles

NOTE
Cardigan is knitted with 2 strands of unspun Icelandic wool, *plötulopi*, held together. Body and sleeves are worked in the round from lower edge to underarms, then joined to work yoke in the round. Round begins and ends with a purl st at front of body. The front is cut open.

BODY

CO 127 (135, 143, 15,1 159) sts with B using 4.5mm circular needle. Work back and forth *k1, p1* rib, 5cm. Change to 5.5mm circular needle and CO 2 sts which count as first and last st of rnd, join in the round => 129 (137, 145, 153, 161) sts. Work st st patt from **Chart 1** (p first and last st of rnd). Cont with A until body measures 60 (62, 64, 66, 66) cm.-

SLEEVES

CO 34 (36, 38, 40, 40) sts with B using 4.5mm dpns. Join in the rnd and work *k1, p1* rib, 5cm. Change to 5.5mm needles and inc evenly spaced on rnd 6 (4, 6, 4, 4) sts => 40 (40, 44, 44, 44) sts. Work in st st rep from **Chart 1**. Cont with A. Inc in first rnd 1 st at beg and 1 st at end of rnd, then in every 10th (9th, 10th, 9th, 8th) rnd, total 6 (7, 6, 7, 8) times up sleeve => 52 (54, 56, 58 60) sts. Cont without further shaping until sleeve measures 44 (45, 46, 47, 48) cm from CO edge. Place 8 (9, 10, 11, 12) sts underarm on st holder => 44 (45, 46, 47, 48) sts. Work second sleeve.

YOKE

Join body and sleeves as follows: Using 5.5mm circular needle with A. Work 29 (30, 32, 33, 35) sts right front (beg with purl st), place next 8 (9, 10, 11, 12) sts of body on st holder. Knit 44 (45, 46, 47, 48) sts across first sleeve. Knit 55 (59, 61, 65, 67) sts across back, place next 8 (9, 10, 11, 12) sts of body on st holder. Knit 44 (45, 46, 47, 48) sts across second sleeve. Work 29 (30, 32, 33, 35) sts left front (end with purl st) => 201 (209, 217, 225, 233) sts. Work patt from **Chart 2+3+4** and dec as shown. Change to shorter needle when rnd gets smaller. When pattern is complete there are => 69 (71, 73, 75, 77) sts.

NECKBAND / COLLAR

Change to 4.5mm needle and cont with A. BO purl st, knit 1 rnd and dec evenly spaced on rnd 8 sts, BO end purl st => 61 (63, 65, 67, 69) sts. Work back and forth *k1, p1* rib, 3cm. Change to B and work until rib measures 10cm. BO.

FINISHING

Graft underarm sts together. Weave in loose ends but pull the ends by the purl st chain to RS. Sew across the ends at the same time as you sew by machine with straight, small stitches, twice into each chain of purl sts up body front. Rinse carefully by hand in lukewarm water and lay flat to dry.
Cut between sewn rows for front opening. Sew zipper under front edge twice with thread in matching color. First from RS where edge is folded, then slip stitch edge of zipper from WS.

S 92 cm
M 98 cm
L 103 cm
XL 109 cm
XXL 115 cm

S 60 cm
M 62 cm
L 64 cm
XL 66 cm
XXL 66 cm

S 44 cm
M 45 cm
L 46 cm
XL 47 cm
XXL 48 cm

NOTE: See sizes on page 21 for measurements in inches

Chart 4 – yoke

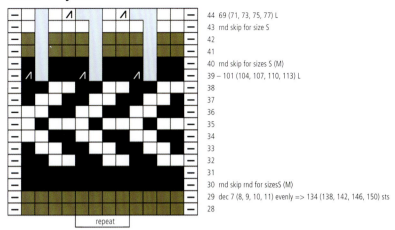

- 44 69 (71, 73, 75, 77) L
- 43 rnd skip for size S
- 42
- 41
- 40 rnd skip for sizes S (M)
- 39 – 101 (104, 107, 110, 113) L
- 38
- 37
- 36
- 35
- 34
- 33
- 32
- 31
- 30 rnd skip rnd for sizes S (M)
- 29 dec 7 (8, 9, 10, 11) evenly => 134 (138, 142, 146, 150) sts
- 28

Chart 3 – yoke

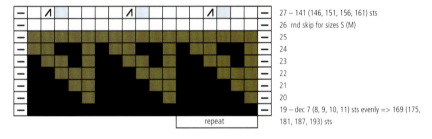

- 27 – 141 (146, 151, 156, 161) sts
- 26 rnd skip for sizes S (M)
- 25
- 24
- 23
- 22
- 21
- 20
- 19 – dec 7 (8, 9, 10, 11) sts evenly => 169 (175, 181, 187, 193) sts

Chart 2 – yoke

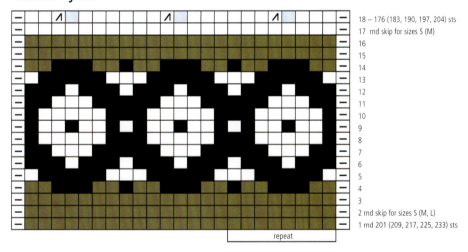

- 18 – 176 (183, 190, 197, 204) sts
- 17 rnd skip for sizes S (M)
- 16
- 15
- 14
- 13
- 12
- 11
- 10
- 9
- 8
- 7
- 6
- 5
- 4
- 3
- 2 rnd skip for sizes S (M, L)
- 1 rnd 201 (209, 217, 225, 233) sts

Chart 1 – body and sleeves

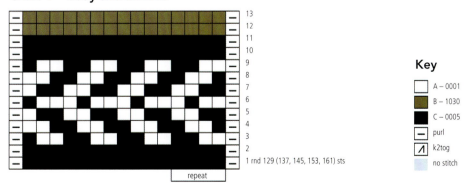

- 13
- 12
- 11
- 10
- 9
- 8
- 7
- 6
- 5
- 4
- 3
- 2
- 1 rnd 129 (137, 145, 153, 161) sts

Key

- ☐ A – 0001
- ▨ B – 1030
- ■ C – 0005
- – purl
- ∧ k2tog
- ▦ no stitch

aftur

A perfect example of how a careful choice of colors and a delicate yoke pattern can create a very special sweater.

SIZES XS (S, M, L, XL)
Chest: 91/35¾" (95/37½", 100/39½", 104/41", 108/42½")
Length to center front neck edge: 56/22" (57/22½", 58/22¾", 59/23¼", 60/23¾")
Sleeve length: 45/17¾" (46/18", 47/18½", 48/18¾", 49/19¼")

MATERIAL Létt-Lopi 50g balls (1.7oz) 100m (109yd)
A 0085 oatmeal heather 7 (8, 8, 9, 10)
B 0005 black heather 1 (1, 1, 1, 1)
C 0051 white 1 (1, 1, 1, 1)
D 9264 mustard 1 (1, 1, 1, 1)
E 9434 crimson red 1 (1, 1, 1, 1)
F 1410 orange 1 (1, 1, 1, 1)

4.5mm (US 7) 40 and 80cm (16 and 30in) circular needles, 4mm (US 6) 80cm (30in) circular needle, 4mm and 4.5mm (US 6 and 7) double pointed needles

GAUGE
10 x 10cm (4 x 4in) = 18 sts and 24 rows in st st on 4.5mm (US 7) needles.

NOTE
Body and sleeves are worked in the round from lower edge to underarms, then joined to work yoke in the round. Round begins at left side of body but on yoke at joining of body and sleeve on left side of back.

64, 66, 68) sts. Continue without further shaping until work measures 45 (46, 47, 48, 49)cm from CO edge. Place 11 (12, 13, 14, 15) sts underarm on st holder => 49 (50, 51, 52, 53) sts. Work second sleeve.

YOKE

Join sleeves to body as follows: With A and 4.5mm circular needle, place 6 (6, 7, 7, 8) last sts and 5 (6, 6, 7, 7) first sts of body on st holder. Knit 49 (50, 51, 52, 53) sts across first sleeve. Knit 71 (74, 77, 80, 83) sts across body (front). Place next 11 (12, 13, 14, 15) sts of body on st holder. Knit 49 (50, 51, 52, 53) sts across second sleeve. Knit 71 (74, 77, 80, 83) sts across body (back) => 240 (248, 256, 264, 272) sts. Work pattern from chart and dec as shown. Change to shorter needle as rnd gets smaller. When pattern is complete there are => 60 (62, 64, 66, 68) sts left.

NECKBAND

Change to 4mm needles. Work 1 rnd st st with A and dec evenly over rnd 0 (0, 0, 2, 4) sts = 60 (62, 64, 64, 64) sts. Work 7 rnds moss st. Work 1 rnd page Work 6 rnds st st. BO loosely.

BODY

CO 164 (172, 180, 188, 196) sts with A and 4mm circular needle. Join in the rnd and work 6 rnds moss st. Change to circular needle 4.5mm and work st st until body measures 33 (34, 35, 36, 37)cm from CO edge. Set aside and knit sleeves. Do not break yarn.

SLEEVES

CO 38 (40, 40, 42, 42) sts with A using 4mm dpn. Join in the rnd and work 6 rnds moss stitch. Change to 4.5mm circular needle and work st st. Inc 2 sts (1 st after first st and 1 st before last st in rnd) in every 9th (9th, 8th, 8th, 8th) rnd, 11 (11, 12, 12, 13) times up sleeve => 60 (62,

NOTE: See sizes on page 25 for measurements in inches

Chart – yoke

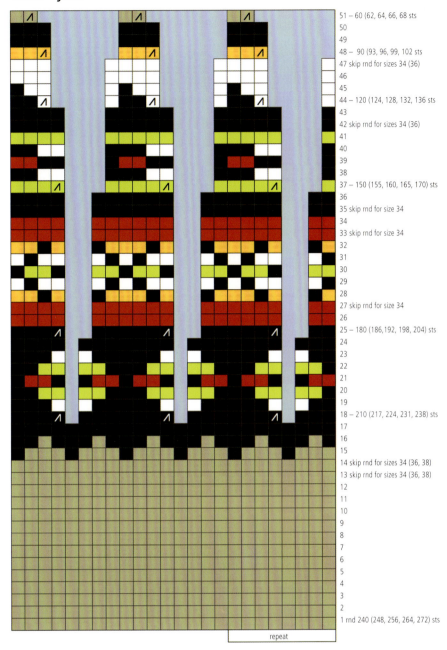

Key

- A – 0085
- B – 0052
- C – 0051
- D – 9264
- E – 9434
- F – 1410
- k2tog
- no stitch

FINISHING

Join underarm sts tog and weave in any loose ends.

Fold neckband in half to WS and slip stitch in position.

Rinse sweater and lay flat to dry.

astrid

This color pattern was designed by Astrid Ellingsen, one of the first designers to work with Álafoss factory from the 1960s onwards and this sweater is named after her. Here it's presented in a warm, modern coat.

SIZES S (M, L, XL)
Chest: 97/38" (101/39¾", 106/41¾", 111/43½")
Length to armhole: 72/28¼" (74/29", 76/30", 78/30¾")
Sleeve length: 46/18" (47/18½", 48/18¾", 49/19¼")

MATERIALS Álafoss Lopi 100g (3.5oz) balls, 100m (109yd)
Blue
A 9958 light indigo 7 (7, 8, 8)
B 0054 ash heather 3 (3, 3, 3)
C 0709 midnight blue 1 (1, 1, 1)
D 9969 fuchsia heather 1 (1, 1, 1)
E 9965 chartreuse green heather 1 (1, 1, 1)
F 9959 indigo 1 (1, 1, 1)

Brown
A 0053 acorn heather 7 (7, 8, 8)
B 9972 ecru heather 3 (3, 3, 3, 3)
C 0059 black 2 (2, 2, 2, 2)
D 0051 white 1 (1, 1, 1, 1)

6mm and 4.5mm (US 10 and 7) 40 and 80cm (16 and 30in) circular needles, 4.5mm and 6mm (US 7 and 10) double pointed needles, 7-8 snaps

GAUGE
10 x 10cm (4 x 4in) = 13 sts and 18 rows in st st on 6mm (US 10) needles.

NOTE
Body and sleeves are worked in the round from lower edge to underarms, then joined to work yoke in the round. Round begins and ends with a purl st at front of body. The front is cut open.

BODY

CO loosely 137 (143, 149,155) sts with B using 4.5mm circular needle. Work rib back and forth:
Row 1 WS: p1 *p1, k1* rep from *to*, p2 last sts.
Row 2 RS: k1*k1, p1* rep from *to*, k2 last sts.
Work rib for 2cm. Next row RS: Place 6 first sts on holder, knit to last 6 sts, place sts on st holder. Change to 6mm circular needle, CO 2 sts (p first and last st of rnd) and join in the rnd => 127 (133 ,139, 145) sts. Work in st st patt from **Chart 1**. When patt in complete cont with A until body measures 46 (48, 50, 52) cm from CO edge. Set aside.

Work pocket lining: CO 19 sts with A using 6mm needle, work back and forth in st st for 18cm, set aside. Work second pocket lining.

Pocket placement: Cont with body; p1, k11 (12, 14, 15) sts, place next 19 sts on st holder for rib border, knit first pocket lining to body, k 65 (69, 71, 75) sts, place next 19 sts on st holder, knit second pocket lining, k11 (12, 14, 15) sts, p1. Work until body measures 72 (74, 76, 78) cm from CO edge. Set aside and work sleeves.

SLEEVES

CO 30 (30, 32, 32) sts with B using 4.5mm dpns. Join in the rnd and work *k1, p1* rib for 5cm, in last rnd inc evenly spaced 6 (6, 4, 4) sts => 36 sts. Change to 6mm dpns and work in st st patt from **Chart 1**. When patt is complete cont with A. Inc 1 st after first st and 1 st before last st of rnd in every 8th rnd, 2 (3, 4, 5) times up sleeve => 40 (42, 44, 46) sts. Work without further shaping until sleeve measures 46 (47, 48, 49) cm from CO edge. Place 8 (9, 10, 11) sts underarm on st holder => 32 (33, 34, 35) sts. Work second sleeve.

YOKE

Join body and sleeves as follows: With A using 6mm circular needle, work right front (beg with purl st) 28 (29, 30, 31) sts, place next 8 (9, 10, 11) sts of body on st holder for underarm. Knit 32 (33, 34, 35) sts of first sleeve. Knit 55 (57, 59, 61) sts of back, place next 8 (9, 10, 11) sts of body on st holder for underarm. Knit 32 (33, 34, 35) sts of second sleeve. Work left front 28 (29, 30, 31) sts, (end with purl st) => 175 (181, 187,193) sts. Work patt and dec's from Chart 2 as indicated. Change to shorter circular needle when necessary. When chart is complete => 61 (63, 65, 67) sts.

FINISHING

Graft underarm sts tog. Weave in loose ends but pull the ends by the purl st chain to RS. Sew by machine using straight small stitches across the ends as you sew

S 97 cm
M 101 cm
L 106 cm
XL 111 cm

S 46 cm
M 47 cm
L 48 cm
XL 49 cm

S 72 cm
M 74 cm
L 76 cm
XL 78 cm

NOTE: See sizes on page 29 for measurements in inches

twice through each chain of purl sts up body front. Cut between the sewn rows at front.

Right band: RS: Slip 6 sts from holder to 4.5mm needle. With B CO 3 sts for facing at inner edge and work back and forth.

WS: P3 sts for facing, *p1, k1*, rep from *to*, p2 last sts.

RS: k2 *p1, k1*, rep from *to*, k3 last sts for facing.

Work as established until band, when slightly stretched, reaches neckline. BO 3 sts for facing and place rem 6 sts on st holder. Sew band and facing straight in place: Sew band between band st and facing st to knit st edge on front. Sew facing to WS, hiding the machine stitch.

Left band: WS: Slip 6 sts from holder to 4.5mm needle. With B CO 3 sts for facing at inner edge and work back and forth.

RS: k3 for facing, *k1, p1*, rep from *to*, k2 last sts.

WS: P2 sts *k1, p1*, rep from *to*, p3 last sts. Work as established until band, when slightly stretched, reaches neckline. BO 3 sts for facing and place rem 6 sts on st holder. Sew band and facing straight in place as before.

Neckband: RS: With B using 4.5mm needle, work rib from band as established, work yoke; knit 1 rnd and dec evenly spaced 6 sts, work rib from band as established => 65 (67, 69, 71) sts. Now work rib back and forth for 8 rows. BO in rib.

Pocket: Rib border: Slip sts from st holder at pocket opening to 4.5mm needle and with A work *k1, p1* rib for 4 rows. BO in rib. Work second border the same. Sew pocket lining to WS. Sew sides of rib to RS.

FINAL FINISHING

Rinse cardigan by hand in lukewarm water and lay flat to dry.
Sew snaps to front band.

Chart 1 – body and sleeves

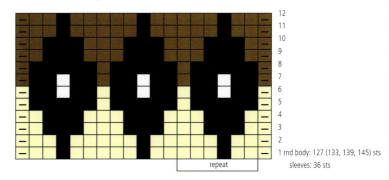

Chart 2 – yoke

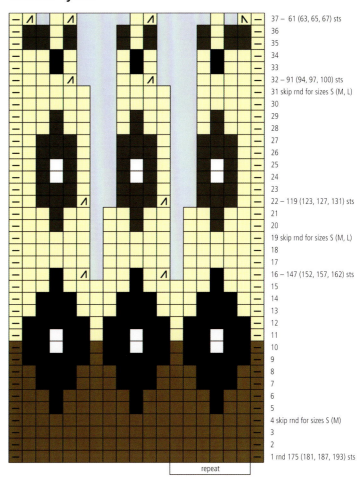

Key

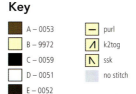

álafoss

The color pattern featured on this yoke was the first ever published by the Álafoss wool factory in the 1960s. A simple yet distinctive rose pattern that has long since become a classic.

SIZES SX (S, M, L, XL, XXL)
Chest: 93/36½" (97/38", 101/39¾", 106/41¾", 110/43¼", 115/45¼")
Length to armhole: 40/15¾" (41/16", 42/16½", 43/17", 44/17¼", 45/17¾")
Sleeve length: 48/18¾" (49/19¼", 50/19¾", 51/20", 52/20½", 53/21")

MATERIALS Álafoss Lopi 100g (3.5oz) balls, 100m (109yd)
A 0086 light beige heather 5 (5, 6, 6, 7, 7)
B 0085 oatmeal heather 1 (1, 1, 2, 2, 2)
C 0053 acorn heather 1 (1, 1, 2, 2, 2)
D 0867 chocolate heather 1 (1, 1, 2, 2, 2)
E 0052 black sheep heather 1 (1, 1, 2, 2, 2)

6mm and 4.5mm (US 10 and 7), 40 and 80cm (US 16 and 30in) circular needles, 6mm and 4.5mm (US 10 and 7) double pointed needles

GAUGE
10 x 10cm (4 x 4in) = 13 sts and 18 rows in st st on 6mm (US 10) needles.

NOTE
Body and sleeves are worked in the round from lower edge to underarms, then joined to work yoke in the round. Each round of the body begins on the left side of the sweater, but the yoke rounds begin where the back of the sweater meets the left sleeve.

BODY

Using A and longer 4.5mm circular needles, CO 114 (120, 126, 132, 138, 144) sts. Join and work 1x1 ribbing: *p1, k1*, rep from * to *, for 5cm. Switch to longer 6mm circular needle and knit one rnd, inc 6 sts evenly throughout => 120 (126, 132, 138, 144, 150) sts. Knit until body measures 40 (41, 42 43, 44, 45) cm from CO edge. Set the body aside and knit the sleeves.

SLEEVES

Using A and 4.5mm dpn, CO 34 (34, 36, 36, 38, 38) sts. Join and work 1x1 ribbing: *p1, k1*, rep from * to *, for 5cm. Switch to 6mm needles and knit one rnd, inc 4 sts evenly throughout => 38 (38, 40, 40, 42, 42) sts. Continue knitting with A and inc by 2 sts (inc 1 st after the first st in the rnd and 1 st before the last st in the rnd) every 8th rnd 6 (7, 7, 8, 7, 8) times => 50 (52, 54, 56, 56, 58) sts. Knit until sleeve measures 48 (49, 50, 51, 52, 53) cm from CO edge. Place 9 (8, 9, 10, 10, 9) underarm sts on a stitch holder or scrap yarn => 41 (44, 45, 46, 46, 49) sts. Knit the other sleeve.

YOKE

Join the body and sleeves on the longer 6mm circular needle as follows: Place last 4 (4, 4, 5, 5, 5) sts and first 4 (4, 5, 5, 5, 5) body sts on a stitch holder or scrap yarn. Knit left sleeve 41 (44, 45, 46, 46, 49) sts. Knit 52 (55, 57, 59, 62, 65) body sts (front). Place next 8 (8, 9, 10, 10, 10) body sts on a stitch holder or scrap yarn, knit right sleeve 41 (44, 45, 46, 46, 49) sts, knit 52 (55, 57, 59, 62, 65) body sts (back) => 186 (198, 204, 210, 216, 228) sts. Knit **Chart**, dec according to the chart. Switch to the shorter 6mm circular needle as the circumference of the yoke gets smaller. When the chart is complete, 70 (70, 77, 77, 84, 84) sts remain.

NECKLINE EDGING

Switch to 4.5mm shorter circular needle and knit one rnd, dec 10 (12, 12, 12, 12, 14) sts evenly throughout. Work 1x1 ribbing, * k1, p 1 *, for 6cm. BO.

FINISHING

Weave in all ends and graft underarm sts. Block the sweater into shape.

Chart – yoke

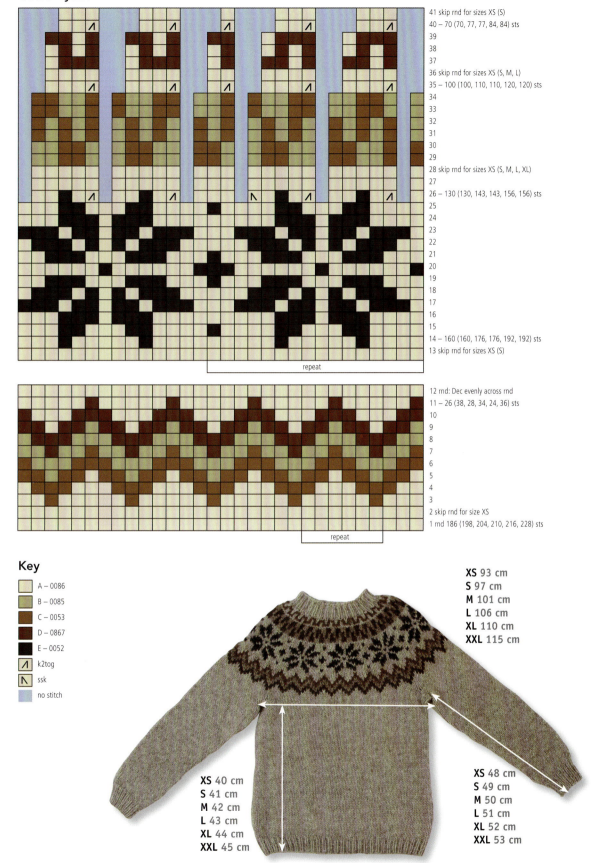

41 skip rnd for sizes XS (S)
40 – 70 (70, 77, 77, 84, 84) sts
39
38
37
36 skip rnd for sizes XS (S, M, L)
35 – 100 (100, 110, 110, 120, 120) sts
34
33
32
31
30
29
28 skip rnd for sizes XS (S, M, L, XL)
27
26 – 130 (130, 143, 143, 156, 156) sts
25
24
23
22
21
20
19
18
17
16
15
14 – 160 (160, 176, 176, 192, 192) sts
13 skip rnd for sizes XS (S)

12 rnd: Dec evenly across rnd
11 – 26 (38, 28, 34, 24, 36) sts
10
9
8
7
6
5
4
3
2 skip rnd for size XS
1 rnd 186 (198, 204, 210, 216, 228) sts

Key
- A – 0086
- B – 0085
- C – 0053
- D – 0867
- E – 0052
- k2tog
- ssk
- no stitch

XS 93 cm
S 97 cm
M 101 cm
L 106 cm
XL 110 cm
XXL 115 cm

XS 40 cm
S 41 cm
M 42 cm
L 43 cm
XL 44 cm
XXL 45 cm

XS 48 cm
S 49 cm
M 50 cm
L 51 cm
XL 52 cm
XXL 53 cm

NOTE: See sizes on page 33 for measurements in inches

ár trésins

This pattern was inspired by the United Nations' Year of the Tree. It was originally designed by Jóhanna Hjaltadóttir, who was a prolific knitwear designer in the 1960s and 1970s.

SIZES S (M, L, XL, XXL)
Chest: 92/36¼" (98/38½", 105/41¼", 111/43½", 117/46")
Length to armhole: 41/16" (42/16½", 43/17", 44/17¼", 45/17¾")
Sleeve length
Men's: 49/19¼" (50/19¾", 51/20", 52/20½", 53/21")
Women's: 45/17¾" (46/18", 47/18½", 48/18¾", 49/19¼")

MATERIAL Álafoss Lopi 100g (3.5oz) balls, 100m (109yd)
A 0051 white 4 (5, 6, 6, 7)
B 0057 gray heather 3 (3, 3, 3, 3)
C 0005 black heather 2 (2, 2, 2, 2)

4.5mm and 6mm (US 7 and 10) 80cm and 40cm (US 30 and 16in) circular needles, 4.5mm and 6mm (US 7 and 10) double pointed needles.

GAUGE
10 x 10cm (4 x 4in) = 13 st and 18 rows in st st on 6mm (US 10) needles.

NOTE
Body and sleeves are worked in the round from lower edge to underarms, then joined to work yoke in the round. Each round of the body begins on the left side of the sweater, but the yoke rounds begin where the back of the sweater meets the left sleeve.

BODY

CO 114 (122, 130, 138, 146) sts with B on the 4.5mm circular needle. Join in the rnd and knit the bottom ribbing: *k1,p1* for 3cm. Change to shorter 6mm circular needle and inc 6 sts evenly over the row => 120 (128, 136, 144, 152) sts. Knit **Chart 1**. Then knit with A until the body measures 41 (42, 43, 44, 45) cm from CO edge. Set the body aside on waste yarn or spare needles and knit the sleeves.

SLEEVES

CO 32 (34, 36, 36, 38) sts with B on 4.5mm dpn. Join in the rnd and knit the cuff ribbing: *k1,p1*, for 3cm. Change to 6mm needles and inc 4 (2, 4, 4, 2) sts evenly in the 1st rnd => 36 (36, 40, 40, 40) sts. Knit **Chart 1**. Knit with A, inc 2 sts (1 st after the 1st and 1 st before the last st in the rnd) every 13th (12th, 12th, 9th, 8th.) rnd 4 (6, 5, 8, 8) times => 44 (48, 50, 56, 56) sts. Knit until the men's sleeve length measures : 49 (50, 51, 52, 53) cm and the women's sleeve length measures 45 (46, 47, 48, 49) cm from the CO edge. Place the centre 8 (8, 9, 10, 10) sts at the arm holes on stitch holder/waste yarn =>36 (40, 41, 46, 46) sts. Knit the second sleeve.

YOKE

Join the stitches from the sleeves and the body together on the longer 6mm circular needle. Place the last 4 (4, 4, 5, 5) sts in the rnd and the first 4 (4, 5, 5, 5) sts of the rnd on a stitch holder/waste yarn. Knit 36 (40, 41, 46, 46) st of the 1st sleeve and the 52 52 (56, 59, 62, 66) sts of the front body. Place the next 8 (8, 9, 10, 10) sts on a stitch holder/waste band, knit second sleeve 36 (40, 41, 46, 46) sts and finally the 52 (56, 59, 62, 66) sts from the back => 176 (192, 200, 216, 224) sts. Knit Chart 2 and dec as shown on the chart. Change to a shorter needle when necessary. When the chart has been knit, 66 (72, 75, 81, 84) sts remain.

COLLAR

Change to 4.5mm needles and still with B, knit 1 row dec 4 (6, 5, 7, 8) sts evenly => 62 (66, 70, 74, 76) sts. Knit in rib *k1,p1* for 8cm (if the collar isn't folded then knit 4cm). BO loosely on the WS. Fold the collar in half and sew the collar fairly loosely down on the WS.

FINISHING

Weave in all ends and graft the underarm stitches. Wash and block the sweater.

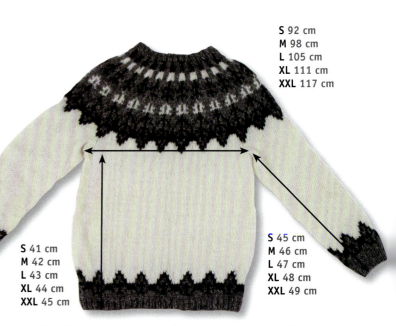

S 92 cm
M 98 cm
L 105 cm
XL 111 cm
XXL 117 cm

S 41 cm
M 42 cm
L 43 cm
XL 44 cm
XXL 45 cm

S 45 cm
M 46 cm
L 47 cm
XL 48 cm
XXL 49 cm

NOTE: See sizes on page 37 for measurements in inches

Chart 1 – body and sleeves

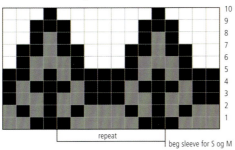

repeat

beg sleeve for S og M
(pattern doesn't fit all sizes, see page 258)

Key

- A – 0051
- B – 0057
- C – 0005
- k2tog
- no stitch

Chart 2 – yoke

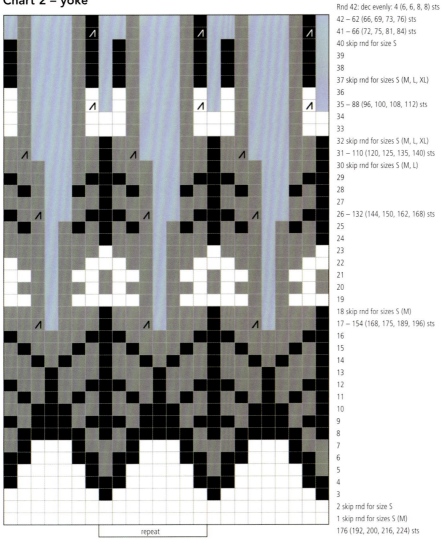

repeat

Rnd 42: dec evenly: 4 (6, 6, 8, 8) sts
42 – 62 (66, 69, 73, 76) sts
41 – 66 (72, 75, 81, 84) sts
40 skip rnd for size S
39
38
37 skip rnd for sizes S (M, L, XL)
36
35 – 88 (96, 100, 108, 112) sts
34
33
32 skip rnd for sizes S (M, L, XL)
31 – 110 (120, 125, 135, 140) sts
30 skip rnd for sizes S (M, L)
29
28
27
26 – 132 (144, 150, 162, 168) sts
25
24
23
22
21
20
19
18 skip rnd for sizes S (M)
17 – 154 (168, 175, 189, 196) sts
16
15
14
13
12
11
10
9
8
7
6
5
4
3
2 skip rnd for size S
1 skip rnd for sizes S (M)
176 (192, 200, 216, 224) sts

árni

Like many other traditional Icelandic sweater patterns, this one has been brought up to date. This zipped cardigan showcases the beautiful, diverse, gray tones found in the lopi wool color palette.

SIZES XS (S, M, L, XL, XXL)
Chest: 89/35" (94/37", 98/38½", 103/40½", 107/42", 112/44")
Length to armhole: 40/15¾" (42/16½", 43/17", 44/17¼", 45/17¾", 46/18")
Sleeve length: 47/18½" (49/19¼", 50/19¾", 51/20", 52/20½", 53/21")

MATERIALS Létt-Lopi 50g (1.7oz) balls, 100m (109yd)
A 0005 black heather 7 (8, 8, 9, 9, 10)
B 0054 ash heather 1 (1, 1, 2, 2, 2)
C 0056 light gray heather 1 (1, 1, 1, 1, 1)
D 0057 gray heather 1 (1, 1, 1, 1, 1)
E 0058 dark gray heather 1 (1, 1, 1, 1, 1)

4.5mm (US 7) 40 and 80cm (16 and 30in) circular needles, 3.5mm (US 4)
80cm (30in) circular needle, 3.5mm and 4.5mm (US 4 and 7) double pointed needles, zipper

GAUGE
10 x 10cm (4 x 4in) = 18 sts and 24 rows in st st on 4.5mm (US 7) needles.

METHOD
Body and sleeves are worked in the round from lower edge to underarms, then joined to work yoke in the round. Round begins and ends with a purl st at front of body. The front is cut open.

BODY

Using A and the 3.5mm circular needle, CO 161 (169, 177, 185, 193, 201) sts. Work 1x1 ribbing, *k1, p1*, rep from * to *, for 5cm. CO 2 sts (always purl these 2 sts) => 163 (171, 179, 187, 195, 203) sts. Join in the rnd and switch to the 4.5mm circular needle. Work st st until body measures 40 (42, 43, 44, 45, 46) cm from CO edge. Set the body aside and make the sleeves.

SLEEVES

Using A and 3.5mm dpn, CO 40 (42, 44, 46, 48, 48) sts. Join and work 1x1 ribbing, *k1, p1*, rep from * to *, for 5cm. Switch to 4.5mm needles and st st and immediately inc 2 sts (1 st after the first st in the rnd and 1 st before the last st in the rnd). Inc 2 sts every 7th (7th, 8th, 7th, 8th, 8th) rnd 13 (13, 13, 13, 13, 14) times => 66 (68, 70, 72, 74, 76) sts. After that, work without shaping until sleeve measures 47 (49, 50, 51, 52, 53) cm from CO edge. Place 9 (10, 11, 12, 13, 14) underarm sts on a stitch holder or scrap yarn => 57 (58, 59, 60, 61, 62) sts. Make the other sleeve.

YOKE

Join the body and sleeves on a 4.5mm circular needle as follows: knit 36 (38, 39, 41, 42, 44) sts (right front), place next 9 (10, 11, 12, 13, 14) sts on a stitch holder or scrap yarn, knit the right sleeve 57 (58, 59, 60, 61, 62) sts, knit next 73 (75, 79, 81, 85, 87) sts (back), place next 9 (10, 11, 12, 13, 14) sts on a stitch holder or scrap yarn, knit left sleeve 57 (58, 59, 60, 61, 62) sts, knit to end of rnd 36 (38, 39, 41, 42, 44) sts (left front) => 259 (267, 275, 283, 291, 299) sts. Work **Chart**, dec according to the chart. Switch to the shorter circular needle as the yoke's circumference gets smaller. When the chart is complete => 100 (103, 106, 109, 112, 115) sts rem.

NECKLINE EDGING

Switch to 3.5mm circular needle and knit 1 rnd, dec 28 (31, 30, 33, 32, 35) sts evenly throughout => 72 (72, 76, 76, 80, 80) sts. Work 1x1 ribbing, *k1, p1*, rep from * to *, for 5cm. BO.

FINISHING

Graft underarm sts. Weave in loose ends, except as follows: pull the loose ends at the front of the sweater out to the RS and lay them down on top of the purl sts. Using a sewing machine and a straight, small stitch, sew 2 lines into each of the purl sts up the front of the sweater, sewing into the loose ends as well along the way. Cut the sweater between the 2 purl sts. Work 1 row of sc along each cut edge, crocheting into every other k row. Stitch a zipper into place. Gently block the sweater into shape.

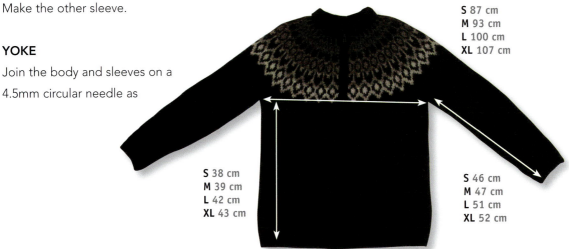

S 87 cm
M 93 cm
L 100 cm
XL 107 cm

S 38 cm
M 39 cm
L 42 cm
XL 43 cm

S 46 cm
M 47 cm
L 51 cm
XL 52 cm

NOTE: See sizes on page 41 for measurements in inches

Chart – yoke

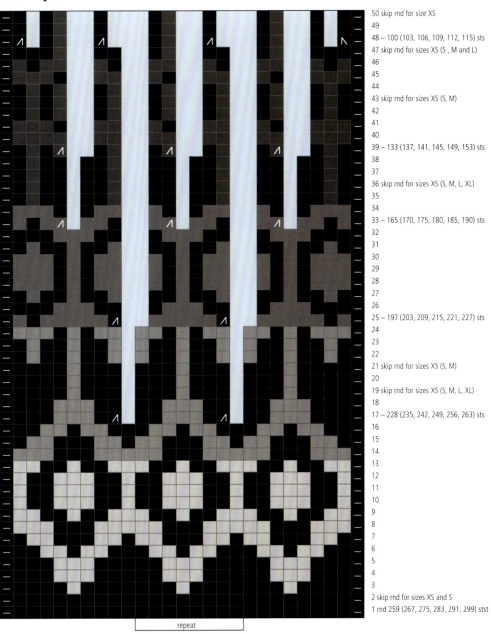

Key

- A – 0005
- B – 0054
- C – 0056
- D – 0057
- E – 0058
- k2tog
- ssk
- purl
- no stitch

ása

A hooded sweater can easily be turned into a pretty coat by adding length. This coat, with its playful color combination, was designed with fun-loving little girls in mind.

SIZES 6 (8, 10) years
Chest: 78/30¾" (84/33", 89/35")
Length to armhole: 36/14" (38/15", 41/16")
Sleeve length: 33/13" (35/13¾", 38/15")

MATERIAL Létt-Lopi 50g (1.7oz) balls, 100m (109yd)
A 0051 white 6 (7) 8
B 1413 lilac heather 1 (1, 1)
C 1412 pink heather 1 (1, 1)
D 1408 light red heather 1 (1, 1)
E 1410 orange 1 (1, 1)
F 1411 sun yellow 1 (1, 1)
G 1404 glacier blue heather 1 (1, 1)
H 1402 heaven blue heather 1 (1, 1)
I 1406 spring green heather 1 (1, 1)

3.5mm and 4.5mm (US 4 and 7) circular needles 60 and 80cm (US 24 and 30in), 3.5mm and 4.5mm (US 4 and 7) double pointed needles, 7 small buttons

GAUGE
10 x 10cm (4 x 4in) = 18 sts and 24 rows in st st on 4.5mm (US 7) needles.

NOTE
Body and sleeves are worked in the round from lower edge to underarms, then joined to work yoke in the round. Round begins and ends with a purl st at front of body. The front is cut open. Hood is knitted back and forth.

Key

- A – 0051
- B – 1413
- C – 1412
- D – 1408
- E – 1410
- F – 1411
- G – 1404
- H – 1402
- I – 1406
- — purl
- ⋀ k2tog
- no stitch

BODY

CO 149 (159, 169) sts with A using 3.5mm circular needle. Work moss st (First row: *k1, p1* next row: p1, k1*) back and forth, 5 rows.

Next row (RS): knit 5 sts in moss st and place these on a st holder. Work in st st to last 5 sts; moss and place on st holder. Change to 4.5mm circular needle. CO 2 sts which count as first and last st of rnd, join in the rnd => 141 (151, 161) sts. Work in st st (but purl first and last st of rnd) patt from **Chart 1** or until body measures 36 (38, 41) cm from CO edge.

Size 6 and (8): skip rnds that are indicated in chart. Set aside and work sleeves. Do not break yarn.

SLEEVES

CO 34 (36, 38) sts with A using 3.5mm dpn. Join in the rnd and work moss st for 5 rnds. Change to 4.5mm dpn and work in st st patt from **Chart 2**. Inc 1 st at beg and 1 st at end of rnd every 8th rnd 8 times => 50 (52, 54) sts.

Size 6 and (8): Skip rnds that are indicated in chart. Cont without further shaping until sleeve measures 33 (35, 38) cm from CO edge. Place 10 (11, 12) sts underarm on st holder => 40 (41) 42 sts. Work second sleeve.

YOKE

Join body and sleeves as follows: With A and 4.5mm circular needle, work 30 (32, 34) sts, right front (beg with purl st). Place next 10 (11, 12) sts of body on st holder. Knit 40 (41, 42) sts across first sleeve. Knit 61 (65, 69) sts across back, place next 10 (11, 12) sts of body on st holder. Knit 40 (41, 42) sts across second sleeve. Work 30 (32) 34 sts left front (end with purl st) => 201 (211, 221) sts. Work patt from **Chart 3** and dec as shown. Change to shorter needles when rnd gets smaller. When pattern is complete there are => 81 (85, 89) sts left. BO 2 purl sts at centre front.

6 78 cm
8 84 cm
10 89 cm

6 33 cm
8 35 cm
10 38 cm

6 36 cm
8 38 cm
10 41 cm

NOTE: See sizes on page 45 for measurements in inches

Chart 1 – body

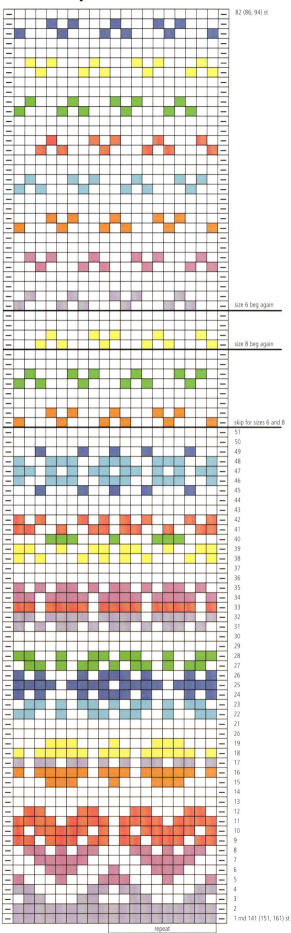

Chart 2 – sleeves

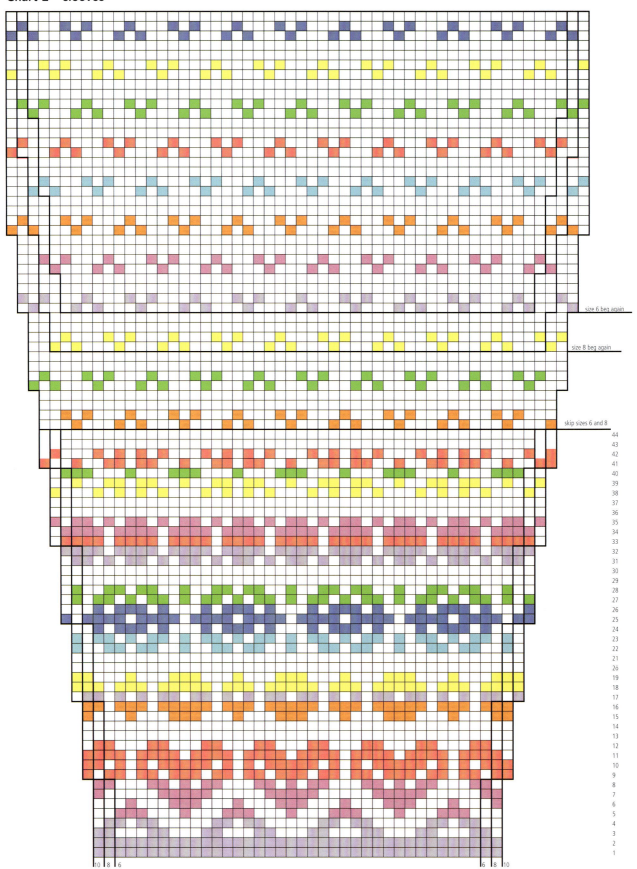

Chart 3 – yoke

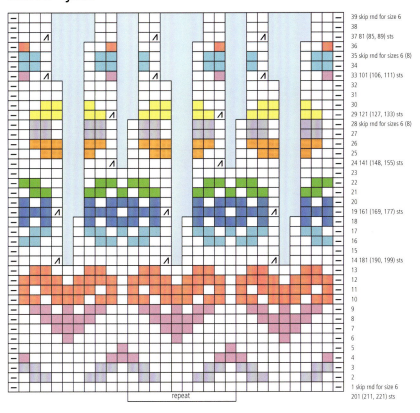

FINISHING

Graft underarm sts tog and weave in any loose ends. Sew by machine using straight small stitches twice into each chain of purl sts up body front.

Buttonband: RS: Slip 5 sts from holder onto 3.5mm needle, using A CO 3 sts for facing at inner edge. Cont in moss st as est but work facing in st st (RS) until band, when slightly stretched, reaches neckline. BO facing sts and slip rem 5 sts to holder. Mark position of 7 buttons, the first at band beg, last at centre of neckband, rem 5 buttons evenly spaced between.

Buttonhole band: Work to match buttonband, and work buttonholes:

Buttonhole (RS): k1, p1, k2tog, work till end of row. Work next row in moss st and CO 1 st in place of the BO on previous row.

Cut between sewn rows. Sew band and facing straight in place (the facing will hide the machine stitch).

NECKBAND/HOOD

RS: Using 3.5mm needles and A, knit 5 sts in moss st across band, knit st st and dec 18 (20, 22) sts evenly spaced across row, knit 5 sts in moss st as established across band => 71 (73, 75) sts. Work 5 rows moss st, working a buttonhole as before in 2nd row.

Hood: Work back and forth. Change to 4.5mm needles.

RS: knit 5 sts in moss st, then st st, inc 13 sts evenly across row, knit last 5 sts in moss st => 84 (86, 88) sts. Next row (WS): knit 5 sts in moss st, purl 74 (76, 78) sts, 5 sts in moss st. Work until hood measures 27 (28, 28) cm. Fold hood in half and graft sts together.

Rinse cardigan and lay flat to dry. Sew on buttons.

bára

A hooded sweater designed in the 1970s. The pattern has been revived with maximum comfort in mind.

SIZES 4 (5, 6, 7, 8) years
Chest: 63/24.5" (67/26.5", 71/28", 74/29", 81/32")
Length to armhole: 21/8" (23/9", 25/10", 27/10.5", 29/11.5")
Sleeve length: 23/9" (25/10", 27/10.5", 29/11.5", 31/12")

MATERIAL Létt-Lopi 50g (1.7oz) balls, 100m (109yd)
A 0051 white 3 (4, 4, 4, 5)
B 0085 oatmeal heather 2 (2, 2, 2, 3)
C 0867 chocolate heather 1 (1, 1, 1, 1)

3.5mm and 4.5mm (US 4 and 7) circular needles 40 and 60cm (US 16 and 24in) 3.5mm and 4.5mm (US 4 and 7) double pointed needles, 3.5mm crochet hook (E/4), 5 (5, 6, 7, 7) buttons

GAUGE
10 x 10cm (4 x 4in) = 18 st and 24 rows in st st on 4.5mm (US 7) needles.

NOTE
Body and sleeves are worked in the round from lower edge to underarms, then joined to work yoke in the round. The body and the hood are knitted in the round with 2 purl sts in the middle. Before the hood is closed at the top, the 2 purl sts are sewn up the length of the sweater and hood and then cut between them. The rounds start in the center front.

BODY

CO 113 (119, 125, 131, 143) sts with B with circular needle 3.5mm. Knit the bottom ribbing back and forth *k1, p1*, rep to end of row (starting and ending with a purl st for 3 (3, 4, 4, 5) cm. Change to circular needle 4.5mm, CO 2 sts and join in the rnd (these 2 sts are purl sts for the length of the body => 115 (121, 127, 133, 145) sts. Knit **Chart 1** (the chart has a purl stitch in the center front), and then with A inc 1 st each side of the chart (all sizes) => 117 (123, 129, 135, 147) sts. Knit until the body is 21 (23, 25, 27, 29) cm from the CO edge. Set aside on waste yarn or spare needles and knit the sleeves.

SLEEVES

CO 28 (30, 30, 32, 34) sts on 3.5mm dpns. Join in the rnd and knit the cuff *k1, p1* for 3 (3, 4, 4, 5) cm. Change to 4.5mm needles and knit 1 rnd inc 2 (4, 6, 8, 8) sts evenly over the rnd => 30 (34, 36, 40, 42) sts. Knit **Chart 1**. With A inc 1 st at beg and end of every 7th rnd 6 (5, 4, 3, 3) times => 42 (44, 44, 46, 48) sts. Knit until the sleeve measures 23 (25, 27, 29, 31) cm from CO edging. On the last rnd knit until til 3 (3, 3, 4, 4) are left of the rnd and then place the next 5 (6, 6, 7, 8) sts on stitch holder/waste yarn => 37 (38, 38, 39, 40) sts. Knit the second sleeve.

YOKE

Join the sts from the body and the sleeves: with A, knit 28 (28, 29, 30, 33) sts (right front), place next 5 (6, 6, 7, 8) sts on stitch holder/waste yarn for the armhole. Knit across 1st sleeve, 37 (38, 38, 39, 40) sts. Knit 51 (55, 59, 61, 65) sts (back), place next 5 (6, 6, 7, 8) sts on stitch holder/waste yarn. Knit across second sleeve, 37 (38, 38, 39, 40) sts. Knit last 28 (28, 29 30, 33) sts (left front) => 181 (187, 193, 199, 211).

Knit **Chart 2** and dec as shown in the chart. Change to shorter needles when necessary. When the chart is finished there are 61 (63, 65, 67, 71) sts. Change to 3.5mm needles and knit 1 row with A, dec evenly across the row 6 (6, 6, 6, 8) sts => 55 (57, 59, 61, 63) sts. Knit ribbing *k1,p1* for 3cm (2 purl sts in the centre).

Hood: The hood is knit in the rnd with 2 purl sts in the centre. Change to shorter 4.5mm needles and knit inc 12 (10, 14, 12, 10) sts evenly => 67 (67, 73, 73, 73) sts. Knit (2 purl sts in the centre) until the hood measures 19 (20, 21, 22, 23) cm from ribbing. Knit **Chart 3**. Before the hood is grafted together at the top sew 2 lines of stitches into the purl stitches in the centre and cut between them. Graft the hood together with B.

FINISHING

Crochet – Row 1: Crochet loosely with B over the seams, starting at the bottom of the right front. Crochet into every other stitch up the body and up and arnd the hood and down the left front to the CO edge.
Row 2: Turn with a chain stitch at the bottom edge and on the WS crochet fairly tightly into each stitch.
Row 3: Crochet as in Row 2 except make 5 (5, 6, 7, 7) buttonholes evenly spaced, on the left front for boys and the right front for. Mark for buttonholes, evenly

4 63 cm
5 67 cm
6 71 cm
7 74 cm
8 81 cm

4 21 cm
5 23 cm
6 25 cm
7 27 cm
8 29 cm

4 23 cm
5 25 cm
6 27 cm
7 29 cm
8 31 cm

NOTE: See sizes on page 51 for measurements in inches

spaced. The bottom one 1.5cm from CO edge and the top one at the middle of neck ribbing.

Buttonholes: Skip one dc stitch and make 1 chain st and catch the next DC stitch.

Row 4: Change to A and crochet the edge, 1 dc into each chain stitch for the buttonholes.

Weave in all ends and graft the underarm stitches. Wash and block the sweater. Sew on buttons

Chart 1 – body

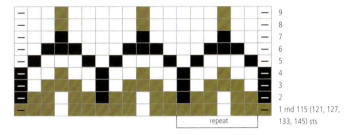

1 rnd 115 (121, 127, 133, 145) sts

Chart 1 – sleeves

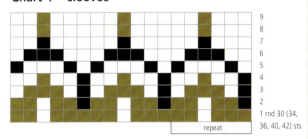

1 rnd 30 (34, 36, 40, 42) sts

Chart 2 – yoke

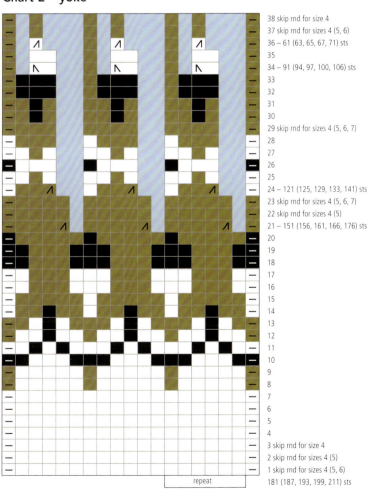

38 skip rnd for size 4
37 skip rnd for sizes 4 (5, 6)
36 – 61 (63, 65, 67, 71) sts
35
34 – 91 (94, 97, 100, 106) sts
33
32
31
30
29 skip rnd for sizes 4 (5, 6, 7)
28
27
26
25
24 – 121 (125, 129, 133, 141) sts
23 skip rnd for sizes 4 (5, 6, 7)
22 skip rnd for sizes 4 (5)
21 – 151 (156, 161, 166, 176) sts
20
19
18
17
16
15
14
13
12
11
10
9
8
7
6
5
4
3 skip rnd for size 4
2 skip rnd for sizes 4 (5)
1 skip rnd for sizes 4 (5, 6)
181 (187, 193, 199, 211) sts

Chart 3 – hood

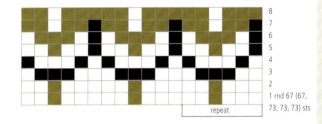

1 rnd 67 (67, 73, 73, 73) sts

Key

☐ A – 0051
▨ B – 0085
■ C – 0867
⟋ k2tog
⟍ ssk
▨ no stitch

birta

The beautiful yoke pattern seen in the sweater Dalur is shown here on a cardigan with a different pattern at the sleeves and bottom edging. Classically feminine, the shape is reminiscent of the fashion of the 1950s and 1960s.

SIZES XS (S, M, L, XL)
Chest: 92/36¼" (98/38½", 104/41", 110/43¼" ,116/45¾")
Length to armhole: 36/14" (38/15", 40/15¾", 42/16½", 44/17¼")
Sleeve length: 47/18½" (48/18¾", 49/19¼", 50/19¾", 51/20")

MATERIAL Álafoss Lopi 100g (3.5oz) balls, 100m (109yd)
A 0051 white 4 (5, 5, 6, 6)
B 0056 light ash heather 3 (3, 3, 3, 3)
C 0085 oatmeal heather 1 (1, 1, 1, 1)

6mm (US 10) circular needles 40 and 80cm (16 and 30in), 5mm (US 8) circular needle 80cm (30in), 5 and 6mm (US 8 and 10) double pointed needles, 6 hooks

GAUGE
10 x 10cm (4 x 4in) = 13 sts and 18 rows in st st on 6mm (US 10) needles.

NOTE
Body and sleeves are worked in the round from lower edge to underarms, then joined to work yoke in the round. Round begins and ends with a purl st at front of body. The front is cut open. The edging bands are knitted separately and sewn to the front.

BODY

CO 111 (119, 127, 135, 143) sts with color B with 5mm circular needles. Knit 8 rows back and forth in st.st (knit on RS, purl on WS). Purl 1 row. CO 2 sts These two sts are purled the length of the sweater => 113 (121, 129, 137, 145) sts. Join in the rnd. Work **Chart 1**. Change to the larger circular needle and knit with A until the body measures 36 (38, 40, 42, 44) cm from the purled row below the pattern. Remember to purl the 1st and last stitch of every row. Set the body aside on waste yarn or spare needles and knit the sleeves.

SLEEVES

With 5mm dpns (or circular needle) CO 32 (32, 36, 36, 36) sts with B. Join in the rnd and knit 8 rows and purl 1 row. Knit Work **Chart 1**. Change to 6mm needles and knit with A. Inc 2 st (1 st after the 1st sts and before the last stitch in the row) every 6th row 5 (7, 6, 8, 9) times => 42 (46, 48 52, 54) sts. Work until the sleeve measures 47 (48, 49, 50, 51) cm from the purl row below the patt. Place the centre 8 (8, 9, 9, 10) sts underarms on stitch holder/waste yarn => 34 (38, 39, 43, 44) sts.

YOKE

Join the body and arms together: With yarn A knit 23 (25, 26, 28, 30) sts (front). Place the next 8 (8, 9, 9, 10) sts on stitch holder/waste yarn. Knit 1st sleeve 34 (38, 39, 43, 44) sts. Knit 51 (55, 59, 63, 65) sts of the body (back). Place the next 8 (8, 9, 9, 10) sts on stitch holder/waste yarn, knit 2nd sleeve 34 (38, 39, 43, 44) sts and finally 23 (25, 26, 28, 30) sts (front) => 165 (181, 189, 205, 213) sts. Work Chart 2 and dec as shown on the graph, changing to shorter needles or dpns when necessary => 70 (76, 79, 85, 88) sts.

COLLAR

Changing to 5mm needles work **Chart 3** and dec evenly over the next 2 rows in the pattern 17 (19, 22, 24, 27) sts => 53 (57, 57, 61, 61) sts. Then with B p1 row and k7 rows. BO.

FINISHING

Weave in all ends and graft the underarm stitches. With a sewing machine sew a straight, tight stitches in the row of purled stitches on either side of the front centre stitch. Cut between these stitches. Fold edges to the WS and sew down.

Left edging band: CO 8 sts with B on 5mm needles. Work back and forth:

1. row (RS): knit
2. row: k1, p6, k1.
3. row: k4, sl1 purlwise (with yarn in back), k3.

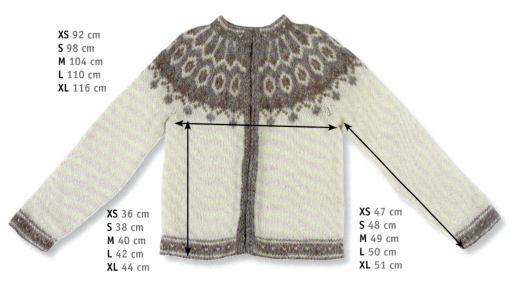

XS 92 cm
S 98 cm
M 104 cm
L 110 cm
XL 116 cm

XS 36 cm
S 38 cm
M 40 cm
L 42 cm
XL 44 cm

XS 47 cm
S 48 cm
M 49 cm
L 50 cm
XL 51 cm

NOTE: See sizes on page 55 for measurements in inches

Repeat rows 2–3 until the band, slightly stretched, reaches top of neckband..
With RS facing, BO purlwise. With RS facing, sew band into position. Fold band in half to cover the raw edge and slip stitch in position.

Right edging band: CO 8 sts with B on 5mm needles.
1. row (RS): knit
2. row: k1, p6, k1.
3. row: k3, sl1 purlwise (with yarn in back), k4.
Complete to match left front edging band. Sew hooks to edging bands.

Chart 1 – body and sleeves

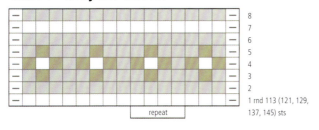

Chart 3 – collar

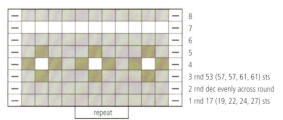

Chart 2 – yoke

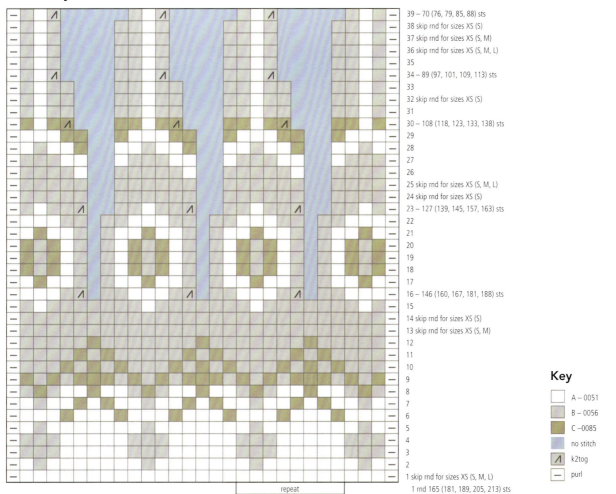

bláklukka

A pretty, colorful sweater decorated with a delicate flower pattern evokes blissful countryside living. It can be knitted with or without lace panels on the body and sleeves.

SIZES 1–2 (2–3, 4–5, 5–6) years
Chest: 56/22" (63/24¾", 70/27½", 76/30")
Width lower edge: 63/24¾" (70/27½", 77/30¼", 83/32¾")
Length to armhole: 25/9¾" (27/10½", 31/12¼", 33/13")
Sleeve length: 22/8¾" (24/9½", 28/11", 30/11¾")

MATERIALS Létt-Lopi 50g (1.7oz) balls, 100m (109yd)
Green
A 1406 spring green heather 3 (4, 4, 5)
B 0051 white 1 (1, 1, 1)
C 1402 heaven blue heather 1 (1, 1, 1)
D 1414 violet heather 1 (1, 1, 1)

White
A 1406 spring green 1 (1, 1, 1)
B 0059 black 1 (1, 1, 1)
C 0051 white 3 (4, 4, 5)
D 9434 crimson red 1 (1, 1, 1)

Both: 4.5mm (US 7) circular needles 40 and 60cm (16 and 24in), 3.5mm (US 4) circular needle 40cm (16in), 3.5mm and 4.5mm double pointed needles, small button. Green: 3.5mm circular needle 60cm White: 4mm (US 6) circular needle 60cm, markers

GAUGE
10 x 10cm (4 x 4in) = 18 sts and 24 rows in st st on 4.5mm (US 7) needles.

NOTE
Body and sleeves are worked in the round from lower edge to underarms, then joined to work yoke in the round. Each round of the body begins on the left side of the sweater, but the yoke rounds begin where the back of the sweater meets the left sleeve. Moss stitch: See page 250.

BODY

Green: CO 114 (126, 138, 150) sts with A using 3.5mm circular needle. Join in the rnd and work moss st for 4 rnds. Change to 4.5mm circular needle and work in st st until body measures 9 (10, 11, 12) cm from CO edge. Dec evenly spaced 6 sts => 108 (120, 132, 144) sts. Work until body measures 17 (19, 21, 23) cm, dec again evenly spaced 6 sts => 102 (114, 126, 138) sts. Work until body measures 25 (27, 31, 33) cm. Set aside and work sleeves.

White: CO 114 (126, 138, 150) sts with C using 4mm circular needle. Knit back and forth 5 rows (garter stitch). Change to 4.5mm circular needle and join in the rnd, work in st st 2 rnds.
Set Eyelet Pattern:
Knit 20 (23, 26, 29) sts, set patt from **Chart 1** at front, K 40 (46, 52, 58) sts, set patt from **Chart 1** for back, knit to end of rnd. Work patt as set up body.

At same time dec: Place marker on either side of body. Work 7 (8, 9, 9) cm from CO edge. Dec 2 sts on each side of marker: sl1, k1, psso, marker, k2tog. Work 13 (15, 17, 17) cm, dec on each side of marker. Work 19 (21, 24, 25) cm and dec again => 102 (114, 126, 138) sts.

Work until body measures 25 (27, 31, 33) cm. End patt with 1 knit rnd. Set aside and work sleeves.

SLEEVES

Green: CO 28 (30, 32, 34) sts with A using 3.5mm dpns. Join in the rnd and work moss st, 4 rnds. Change to 4.5mm needles and work in st st , inc evenly spaced 3 sts => 31 (33, 35, 37) sts. Then inc 1 st after first st and 1 st before last st of rnd in every 6th (6th 7th 8th) rnd, 7 times up sleeve => 45 (47, 49, 51) sts. Cont without further shaping until sleeve measures 22 (24, 28, 30) cm from CO edge. Place 6 (7, 8, 9) sts underarm on st holder => 39 (40, 41, 42) sts.
Work second sleeve.

White: CO 28 (30, 32, 34) sts with C using 3.5mm needle. Knit back and forth (garter st) 5 rows. Change to 4.5mm dpns. Join in the rnd and work in st st , inc evenly spaced 3 sts => 31 (33, 35, 37) sts, work total 2 rnds. Knit 13 (14, 15,16) sts, set patt sleeve from **Chart 1** (5 sts), knit to end of rnd. Work patt as set.

At same time: Inc 1 st after first st and 1 st before last st of rnd in every 6th (6th 7th 8th) rnd 7 times up sleeve => 45 (47, 49, 51) sts. Cont without further shaping until sleeve measures 22 (24, 28, 30) cm from CO edge, end patt with 1 knit rnd. Place 6 (7, 8, 9) sts underarm on st holder => 39 (40, 41, 42) sts.
Work second sleeve.

YOKE

Join body and sleeves as follows: With A using 4.5mm circular needle, place the last 3 (4, 4, 5) sts and the first 3 (3, 4, 4) sts of body on st holder for underarm. Knit 39 (40, 41, 42) sts of first sleeve. Knit 45 (50, 55, 60) sts for front, place next 6 (7, 8, 9) sts of body on st holder for underarm. Knit 39 (40, 41, 42) sts of second sleeve. Knit 45 (50, 55, 60) sts for back => 168 (180, 192, 204) sts.

Green: knit 2 rnds.

White: Purl 1 rnd, knit 1 rnd, purl 1 rnd.
Work patt and dec's from Chart 2 as indicated. Change to shorter circular needle or dpns when necessary. When chart is complete => 56 (60, 64, 68) sts.

NECKBAND

Change to 3.5mm needles.

Green: With A, **White:** With C, dec evenly spaced 4 (6, 6, 8) sts => 52 (54, 58, 60) sts.

Green: Work back and forth moss st, 4 rows.

White: Knit back and forth (garter stitch), 4 rows. BO loosely from WS.

FINISHING

Graft underarm sts tog and weave in loose ends. Make small button loop on left side of neckband.

White: Sew garter st ridges at edges together on the inside.

For tighter neckline: Skim elastic thread through WS. Rinse sweater by hand in lukewarm water. Carefully lay flat to dry and smooth gently into right shape and measurements. Fasten button to neckband.

Chart 1 – body and sleeves

Chart 2 – yoke

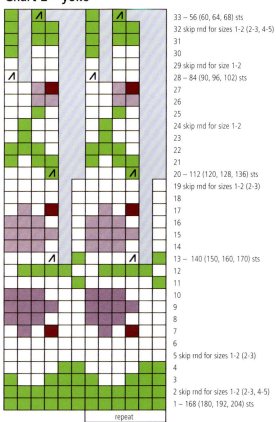

Key Green / White

- A – 1406 / 1406
- B – 0051 / 0059
- C – 1402 / 9434
- D – 1414 / 9434
- – purl
- ⁄ k2tog
- \ ssk
- O yo
- no stitch

1-2 56 cm
2-3 63 cm
4-5 70 cm
5-6 76 cm

1-2 22 cm
2-3 24 cm
4-5 28 cm
5-6 30 cm

1-2 25 cm
2-3 27 cm
4-5 31 cm
5-6 33 cm

NOTE: See sizes on page 59 for measurements in inches

dalur

A classic yoke design that forms a decorative chain pattern across the shoulders. The sleeves and bottom edge mirror the yoke pattern. This design was first published in the 1960s.

SIZES XS (S, M, L, XL)
Chest: 92/36¼" (98/38½", 105/41¼", 111/43½", 117/46")
Length to armhole: 41/16" (42/16½," 43/17", 44/17¼", 45/17¾")
Sleeve length
Men's: 49/19¼" (50/19¾", 51/20", 52/20½", 53/21")
Women's: 45/17¾" (46/18", 47/18½", 48/18¾", 49/19¼")

MATERIAL Álafoss Lopi 100g (3.5oz) balls, 100m (109yd)
A 0056 light ash heather 4 (5, 6, 6, 7)
B 0059 black 3 (3, 3, 3, 3)
C 0051 white 2 (2, 2, 2, 2)

6mm (US 10) 40 and 80cm (16 and 30in) circular needles, 4.5mm (US 7) 80cm (30in) circular needle, 4.5mm and 6mm (US 7 and 10) double pointed needles

GAUGE
10 x 10cm (4 x 4in) = 13 st and 18 rows in st st on 6mm (US 10) needles.

NOTE
Body and sleeves are worked in the round from lower edge to underarms, then joined to work yoke in the round. Each round of the body begins on the left side of the sweater, but the yoke rounds begin where the back of the sweater meets the left sleeve.

BODY

CO 114 (122, 130, 138, 146) sts with B on the 4.5mm circular needle. Join in the rnd and knit the bottom ribbing: *k1,p1* for 4cm. Change to shorter 6mm circular needle and inc 6 sts evenly over the row => 120 (128, 136, 144, 152) sts. Place marker at the centre of the front (the rnds beg at the left front), i.e. 31, (33, 35, 37 og 39) sts from the beg. Knit patt 1 and count where the best place is to start depending on where the centre marker is. Then knit with A until the body measures 41 (42, 43, 44, 45) cm from CO edge. Set the body aside on waste yarn or spare needles and knit the sleeves.

SLEEVES

CO 32 (34, 36, 36, 38) sts with B on 4.5mm dpn. Join in the rnd and knit the cuff ribbing: *k1,p1*, for 4cm. Change to 6mm needles and inc 4 (2, 4, 4, 2) sts evenly in the 1st rnd => 36 (36, 40, 40, 40) sts. Knit pattern 1. Knit with A, inc 2 sts (1 st after the 1st and 1 st before the last st in the rnd) every 13th (12th, 12th, 9th, 8th.) rnd 4 (6, 5, 8, 8) times => 44 (48, 50, 56, 56) sts. Knit until the men's sleeve length measures : 49 (50, 51, 52, 53) cm and the women's sleeve length measures 45 (46, 47, 48, 49) cm from the CO edge. Place the centre 8 (8, 9, 10, 10) sts at the arm holes on stitch holder/waste yarn =>36 (40, 41, 46, 46) sts. Knit the second sleeve.

YOKE

Join the stitches from the sleeves and the body together on the longer 6mm circular needle. Place the last 4 (4, 4, 5, 5) sts in the rnd and the first 4 (4, 5, 5, 5) sts of the rnd on a stitch holder/waste yarn. Knit 36 (40, 41, 46, 46) st of the 1st sleeve and the 52 52 (56, 59, 62, 66) sts of the front body. Place the next 8 (8, 9, 10, 10) sts on a stitch holder/waste band, knit second sleeve 36 (40, 41, 46, 46) sts and finally the 52 (56, 59, 62, 66) sts from the back => 176 (192, 200, 216, 224) sts. Knit pattern 2 and dec as shown on the chart. Change to a shorter needle when necessary. When the pattern has been knit 66 (72, 75, 81, 84) sts remain.

COLLAR

Change to 4.5mm needles and still with B, knit 1 row dec 4 (6, 5, 7, 8) sts evenly => 62 (66, 70, 74, 76) sts. Knit in rib *k1,p1* for 4cm. BO loosely.

FINISHING

Weave in all ends and graft the underarm stitches. Wash and block the sweater.

Chart 2 – yoke

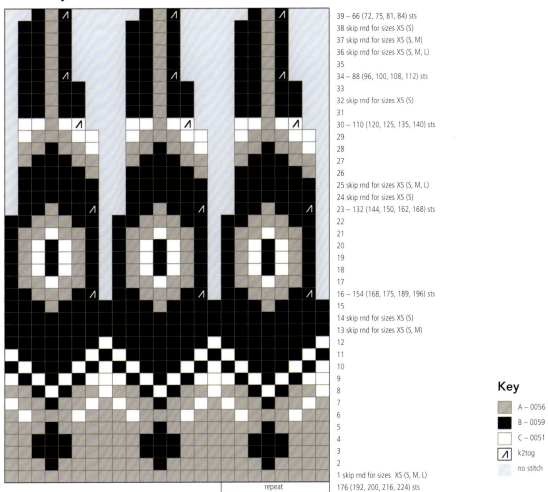

39 – 66 (72, 75, 81, 84) sts
38 skip rnd for sizes XS (S)
37 skip rnd for sizes XS (S, M)
36 skip rnd for sizes XS (S, M, L)
35
34 – 88 (96, 100, 108, 112) sts
33
32 skip rnd for sizes XS (S)
31
30 – 110 (120, 125, 135, 140) sts
29
28
27
26
25 skip rnd for sizes XS (S, M, L)
24 skip rnd for sizes XS (S)
23 – 132 (144, 150, 162, 168) sts
22
21
20
19
18
17
16 – 154 (168, 175, 189, 196) sts
15
14 skip rnd for sizes XS (S)
13 skip rnd for sizes XS (S, M)
12
11
10
9
8
7
6
5
4
3
2
1 skip rnd for sizes XS (S, M, L)
176 (192, 200, 216, 224) sts

Key

- A – 0056
- B – 0059
- C – 0051
- ∧ k2tog
- no stitch

Chart 1 – body and sleeves

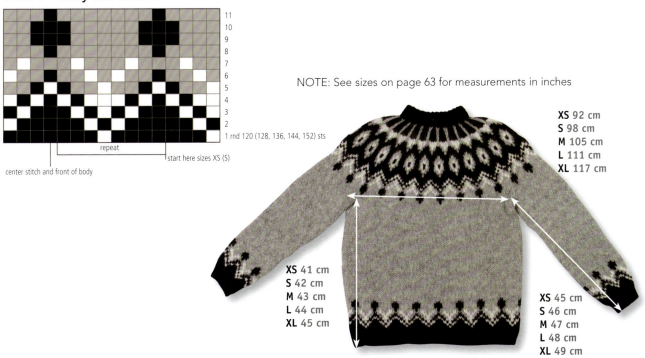

11
10
9
8
7
6
5
4
3
2
1 rnd 120 (128, 136, 144, 152) sts

center stitch and front of body
start here sizes XS (S)

NOTE: See sizes on page 63 for measurements in inches

XS 92 cm
S 98 cm
M 105 cm
L 111 cm
XL 117 cm

XS 41 cm
S 42 cm
M 43 cm
L 44 cm
XL 45 cm

XS 45 cm
S 46 cm
M 47 cm
L 48 cm
XL 49 cm

dísa

When knitting lopi sweaters for your family, don't forget about the favorite doll.

BODY

CO 72 sts. with D on 3.5mm needles. Join in the rnd and knit the ribbing for 3 rows. Change to 4.5mm needles. Knit **Chart 1** and then change to A in st st until the body is 11cm from the beg. Slip the last 3 sts in the rows. Put the body aside and knit the sleeves.

SLEEVES

CO 18 st with D on 3.5mm needles. Join in the rnd and knit the ribbing to match the body. Change to 4.5mm needles and knit **Chart 1** increasing 2 sts in the last pattern row (1 st after the first st and 1 st before the last stitch). Change to A and inc 2 sts as before in the middle of the underarm every 4th row, 2 more times => 24 sts. Knit until the sleeves measure 10cm from the CO edge. Slip the last 3 sts of the rows.

YOKE

Join the body and the sleeves: Place the last 3 sts and the 1st 3 sts of the row on stitch holder/ waste yarn. With A knit 18 sts of the 1st sleeve. Knit 29 sts of the front of body, place next 6 sts on a stitch holder/ waste yarn. Then knit the 18 sts of the second sleeve and then the final 31 of the back of the body => 96 sts. Knit **Chart 2** and dec as shown on the chart => 32 L.

NECK EDGING

Change to 3.5mm needles and knit 1 row with B. Turn and knit 2 rows of ribbing back and forthith B and 1 row with C. BO on the RS with C. With C crochet 8 chainstitches to make a button loop on the left side of the neck. If the neck opening is too tight make 2 tight seams 6cm long and 1 row apart on either side of the neck opening. Cut between the stitching and finish with double crochet along the neck edge and along the cut edge.

FINISHING

Weave in all ends and graft the underarm stitches. Sew a button on the neck edge.

SIZE 40cm (16in) tall doll
Chest: 40 cm/15¾"
Length: 17cm/6¾"
Sleeve length: 10cm/4"

MATERIALS Létt-Lopi 50g (1.7oz) balls, 100m (109yd)
A 0051 white 1
B 0085 oatmeal heather 1
C 0053 acorn heather1
D 0052 black sheep heather1

3.5mm and 4.5mm (US 4 and 7) double pointed needles, 3mm (C/2) crochet hook, 1 button

GAUGE
10 x10cm (4 x 4in) = 18 sts x 24 rows in st.st on 4.5mm (US 7) needles.

NOTE
Body, yoke and sleeves are knitted in the round. The cuffs are sewn down later to avoid the sweater being stretched. The yoke is knitted in the round and cut at the neck to make it wide enough for the doll's head. The rounds begin on the left side of the body but the yoke rounds begin at the left side on the back.

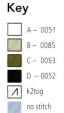

Key
A – 0051
B – 0085
C – 0053
D – 0052
k2tog
no stitch

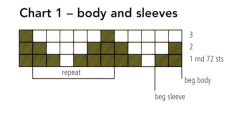

Chart 1 – body and sleeves

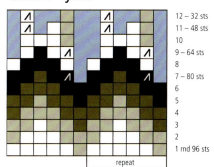

Chart 2 – yoke

dropar

This beautiful, old, color pattern has been used in many different garments through the years, but here it's an integral part of a lovely sweater for either men or women.

SIZES XS (S, M, L, XL, XXL)
Chest: 92/36¼" (96/37¾", 100/39½", 104/41", 110/43¼", 114/44¾")
Length to armhole: 40/15¾" (41/16", 43/17", 44/17¼", 45/17¾", 45/17¾")
Sleeve length:
Men's: 47/18½" (49/19¼", 51/20", 53/21", 55/21¾", 55/21¾")
Women's: 45/17¾" (46/18", 47/18½", 48/18¾", 50/19¾", 50/19¾")

MATERIALS Álafoss Lopi 100g (3.5oz) balls, 100m (109yd)
Black sweater
A 0059 black 6 (7, 7, 8, 8, 9)
B 0051 white 2 (2, 2, 2, 2, 2)
C 0056 light ash heather 1 (1, 1, 1, 1, 1)

Brown sweater
A 0085 oatmeal heather 6 (7, 7, 8, 8, 9)
B 0051 white 2 (2, 2, 2, 2, 2)
C 0053 acorn heather 1 (1, 1, 1, 1, 1)

4.5mm and 6mm (US 7 and 10) circular needles 40 and 80cm (16 and 30in), 4.5mm and 6mm (US 7 and 10) double pointed needles

GAUGE
10 x 10cm (4 x 4in) = 13 sts and 18 rows in st st on 6mm (US 10) needles.

NOTE
Body and sleeves are worked in the round from lower edge to underarms, then joined to work yoke in the round. Each round of the body begins on the left side of the sweater, but the yoke rounds begin where the back of the sweater meets the left sleeve.

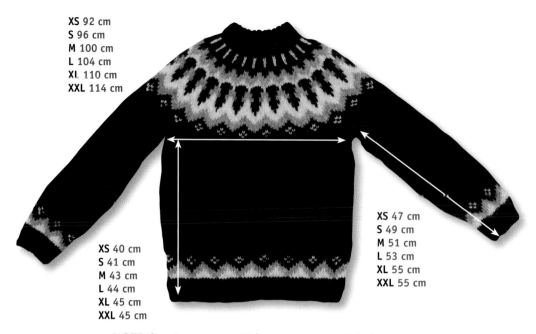

NOTE: See sizes on page 69 for measurements in inches

BODY

Using A and 4.5mm circular needle, CO 112 (120, 120, 126, 132, 138) sts. Join in the rnd and work 1x1 ribbing, *k1, p1*, rep from * to *, until piece measures 5 (5, 6, 6, 6, 6) cm. Switch to 6mm circular needle and knit 1 rnd, inc 8 (8, 8, 10, 12, 14) sts evenly throughout => 120 (128, 128, 136, 144, 152) sts. Work **Chart 1**. Once chart is complete, knit using A until piece measures 40 (41, 43, 44, 45, 45) cm from CO edge. Do not knit the last 4 (4, 4, 4, 5, 5) sts in the last rnd. Set the body aside and make the sleeves.

SLEEVES

Using A and 4.5mm dpn, CO 32 (32, 32, 36, 36, 36) sts. Join in the rnd and work 1x1 ribbing, *k1, p1*, rep from * to *, until piece measures 5 (5, 6, 6, 6, 6) cm. Switch to 6mm needles and knit 1 rnd, inc 8 (8, 8, 4, 4, 8) sts evenly throughout => 40 (40, 40, 40, 40, 44) sts. Please note that for size XXL the color patt doesn't add up. Work **Chart 1**. Once chart is complete, knit using A, inc immediately 2 sts (1 st after the first st in the rnd and 1 st before the last st in the rnd) and then every 8th (8th, 6th, 6th, 6th, 5th) rnd 4 (4, 6, 7, 8, 7) times => 48 (48, 52, 54, 56, 58) sts. Knit without shaping until piece measures 47 (49, 51, 53, 55, 55) cm from CO edge. Place 8 (8, 8, 9, 10, 11) underarm sts on a stitch holder or scrap yarn => 40 (40, 44, 45, 46, 47) sts. Make the other sleeve.

YOKE

Using A and the longer 6mm circular needle, combine the body and sleeve sts to form the yoke as follows: place next 8 (8, 8, 9, 10, 11) sts on a stitch holder or scrap yarn, knit first sleeve 40 (40, 44, 45, 46, 47) sts, knit 52 (56, 56, 59, 62, 65) sts (back), place next 8 (8, 8, 9, 10, 11) sts on a stitch holder or scrap yarn, knit second sleeve 40 (40, 44, 45, 46, 47) sts, knit 52 (56, 56, 59, 62, 65) sts (front) => 184 (192, 200, 208, 216, 224) sts. Work **Chart 2** and dec accordingly. Switch to a shorter circular needle as the yoke's circumference becomes smaller. Once chart is complete => 69 (72, 75, 78, 81, 84) sts rem.

Neckline edging: Switch to 4.5mm needles. Using A, work 1x1 ribbing, *k1, p1*, rep from * to *, dec 17 (18, 19, 20, 23, 24) evenly throughout the first rnd => 52 (54, 56, 58, 58, 60) sts. Work ribbing for 7 (8, 8, 8, 8, 8) cm. BO.

FINISHING

Graft underarm sts and weave in loose ends. Fold the neckline ribbing in half and stitch to the WS of the neckline. Gently block the sweater into shape.

Chart 2 – yoke

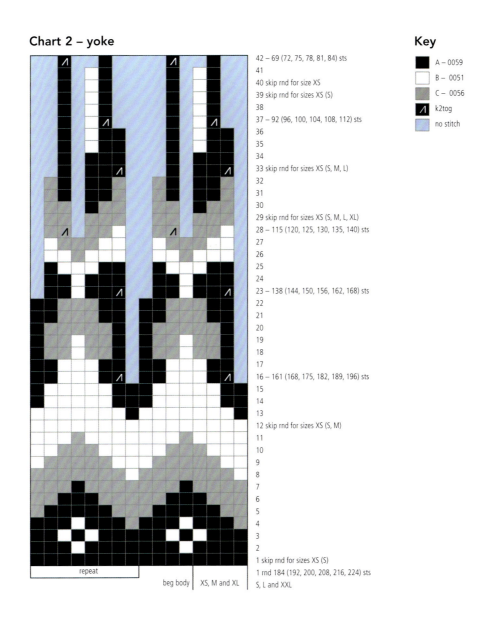

Chart 1 – body and sleeves

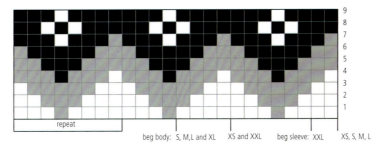

endurreisn

This colorful, patterned sweater was designed in 2009. Its name means "renaissance". The design includes two types of yarn: Létt-Lopi, held double, and a single strand of Álafoss Lopi.

NOTE: There is no US equivelant for 7MM needle

SIZES S (M, L)
Chest: 93/36½" (101/39¾", 110/43¼")
Length to armhole: 55/21¾" (57/22½", 59/23¼")
Sleeve length to underarm: 46/18" (48/19", 50/19¾")

MATERIALS Álafoss Lopi 100g (3.5oz) balls, 100m (109yd)
A 0059 black 3 (4, 5)
L 9962 fire red 1 (1, 1)
N 1234 monet blue 1 (1, 1)

Létt-Lopi 50g (1.70oz) balls, 100m (109yd)
B 9423 lagoon heather 2 (2, 2)
C 1404 glacier blue heather 2 (2, 2)
D 1402 heaven blue heather 1 (1, 1)
E 1413 lilac 1 (1, 1)
F 1414 violet heather 1 (1, 1)
G 1412 pink heather 1 (1, 1)
H 9434 crimson red 1 (1, 1)
I 1410 orange 1 (1, 1)
J 9426 golden heather 1 (1, 1)
K 9264 mustard 1 (1, 1)
M 9421 celery green heather 1 (1, 1)

7mm (See NOTE) circular needles 40 and 80cm (16 and 30in), 6mm (US 10) circular needle 80cm, 5mm (US 8) circular needle 40cm, 6mm and 7mm (US 10, and see NOTE below) double pointed needles, 6mm (US J/10) crochet hook, 7 buttons

GAUGE
10 x 10cm (4 x 4in) = 12 sts and 14 rows in st st on 7mm needles.

NOTE
Body and sleeves are worked in the round from lower edge to underarms, then joined to work yoke in the round. Round begins and ends with a purl st at front of body. The front is cut open.

BODY

CO 115 (125, 135) sts with one strand of Létt-Lopi F, using 6mm circular needle. Work back and forth in st st for 5 rows. Change to Álafoss Lopi A, knit 1 row, WS: knit 1 row, work 5 rows in st st . Change to 7mm circular needle, CO 2 sts (p first and last st of rnd) and join in the rnd => 117 (127, 137) sts. Work in st st patt from **Chart 1**. Rnd marked 45: dec evenly spaced 15 sts => 102 (112, 122) sts. Cont patt as set. Rnd marked 67: inc evenly spaced 10 sts => 112 (122, 132) sts. Cont patt as set for total 71 (75, 78) rnds, body measures 55 (57, 59) cm from purl row. Set aside and work sleeves.

SLEEVES

CO loosely 31 (35, 35) sts with one strand of Létt-Lopi, H, using 6mm dpns. Join in the rnd and work in st st for 5 rnds. Change to Álafoss Lopi A, knit 1 rnd, purl 1 rnd, knit 5 rnds. Change to 7mm needles and work in st st patt from **Chart 2**. Inc 1 st after first st and 1 st before last st of rnd in every 10th (12th 10th) rnd, total 5 (4, 5) times up sleeve => 41 (43, 45) sts. When chart is complete 60 (63, 65) rnds, sleeve measures 46 (48, 50) cm from purl row. Place 8 (9, 10) sts underarm on st holder => 33 (34, 35) sts.
Work second sleeve.

YOKE

Join body and sleeves as follows: With A using 7mm circular needle, work right front (beg with purl st) 24 (26, 28) sts, place next 8 (9, 10) sts of body on st holder for underarm. Knit 33 (34, 35) sts of first sleeve. Knit 48 (52, 56) sts of back, place next 8 (9, 10) sts of body on st holder for underarm. Knit 33 (34, 35) sts of second sleeve. Work left front 24 (26, 28) sts (end with purl st) => 162 (172, 182) sts. Work patt and dec's from **Chart 3**. Change to shorter needle when necessary. When chart is complete => 66 (70, 74) sts.

NECKBAND

Change to 5mm needle and cont with A. Dec evenly spaced 11 (15, 15) sts => 55 (55, 59) sts. Work patt from **Chart 4**. When chart is complete change to B+C, BO purl st, knit and BO end purl st. Now work back and forth, knit 1 row from WS. Cont with one strand B, work in st st for 6 rows. BO loosely.

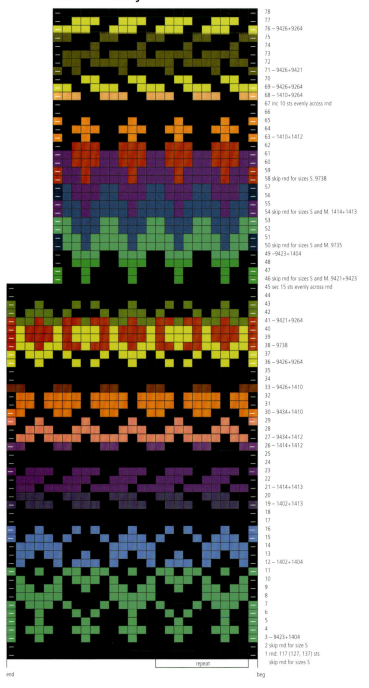

Chart 1 – body

FINISHING

Graft underarm sts tog and weave in loose ends but pull the ends next to the purl st chain to RS. Sew by machine using straight small stitches twice through each chain of purl sts up body front. Cut carefully between the sewn rows.

NOTE: See sizes on page 73 for measurements in inches

Front border right

Row 1 RS: With A using 6 mm crochet hook beg at lower edge, work loosely sc over machine stitch and single stitch, into every other row up front, work to end of neckline, turn. Row 2 WS: Ch1. Mark position of 7 button loops, first at neckline, last above st st border, the others spaced evenly between. Now sc in each sc, ch4-5 for button loop (depending on button size). Fasten off.

Front border left

Row 1 RS: With A, beg at top and work loosely sc over machine stitch and single stitch, into every other row to lower edge, work to end, turn. Row 2 WS: Ch1. Sc in each sc. Fasten off. Fold hem on body, sleeves and neck in half to inside at p row and slip stitch in place. Rinse jacket by hand in lukewarm water. Carefully lay flat to dry and smooth gently into right shape and measurements. Fasten buttons.

Chart 2 – sleeves

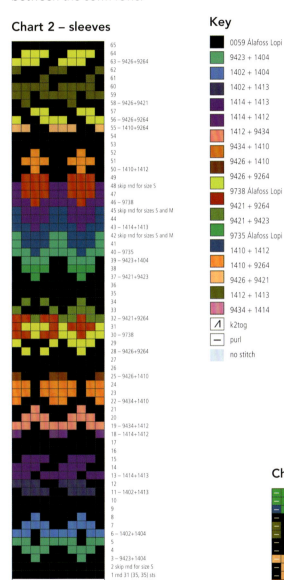

Key

- ■ 0059 Álafoss Lopi
- 9423 + 1404
- 1402 + 1404
- 1402 + 1413
- 1414 + 1413
- 1414 + 1412
- 1412 + 9434
- 9434 + 1410
- 9426 + 1410
- 9426 + 9264
- 9738 Álafoss Lopi
- 9421 + 9264
- 9421 + 9423
- 9735 Álafoss Lopi
- 1410 + 1412
- 1410 + 9264
- 9426 + 9421
- 1412 + 1413
- 9434 + 1414
- ⋀ k2tog
- — purl
- no stitch

Chart 4 – collar

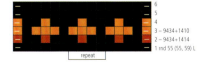

Chart 3 – yoke

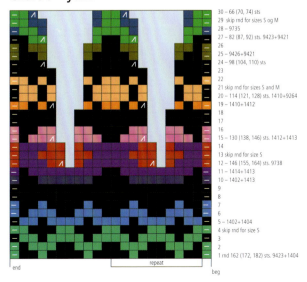

faðmur

Originally this lovely shawl-sweater was intended to be a bed-jacket worn at a leasurely weekend brunch, but since ideas are often transformed during the design phase, the result turned out to be a glamorous top that looks equally good with jeans or a dress.

SIZES after blocking S/M (L/XL)
Length: 178/70" (187/73½")cm
Width: 48/18¾" (57/22½")cm

MATERIALS Einband 50g (1.7oz) balls, 225m (245yd)
A 0851 white 5 (7)
B 1038 ivory beige 1 (1)
C 0886 light beige 1 (1)
D 0885 oatmeal 1 (1)

4mm and 5mm (US 6 and 8) circular needles 80cm (30in), 4mm (US 6) double pointed needles, 3.5mm (US E/4) crochet hook

BLOCKED GAUGE
1 patt rep: 9.5cm x 1.5cm (3.75 x .6in) = 25 sts and 4 rows on 4mm needles (US 6).

NOTE
The wrap cardigan is worked back and forth. Sleeves are worked in the round from armhole down. The work will stretch when washed and blocked.

WRAP CARDIGAN

With D using 5mm needle CO very loosely 131 (156) sts. Change to 4mm needle and work **feather and fan chart,** each patt rep consists of 25 sts and 4 rows:

1st row WS: knit.

2nd row RS: knit.

3rd row WS: knit first 3 sts, purl 128 (153), knit 3 last sts.

4th patt row RS: k3, k2tog 4 times => 4 sts. *k1, yo, 8 times, k1=> 17 sts. ssk 4 times, k2tog 4 times => 8 sts*. Rep from *to* until last 11 sts: ssk 4 times, k3 last sts.

Now work patt 3 times, last patt row: change to C.

Work patt 3 times, last patt row: change to B.

Work patt 2 times, last patt row: change to A.

Work patt 27 (29) times, or as long as preferred.

Next row WS: Work st st .

Size S/M only: dec 1 st at end of row => 130 sts.

Now work lace and ridges:

Lace pattern:

**1st row RS: knit

2nd row WS: k3, purl row, k3 last sts.

3rd lace row RS: k3, *yo, k2tog *, k3 last sts.

4th row WS: k3, purl row, k3 last sts.

Ridges:

Work 8 rows garter st, (knit on RS and WS, forming 4 ridges)**.

Rep from **to** once.

Work lace patt once.

Work garter st 4 rows (2 ridges).

Armhole: From RS, knit 46 (50) sts. Knit 36 (49) sts on to piece of scrap yarn in different color, slip these sts back to left needle and work again, work to end of row. Work garter st 4 rows.

Rep from **to** 12 (13) times, rep second armhole between last 4 ridges (2 ridges armhole 2 ridges). Now work lace patt, 4 ridges and again lace pat.

Size S/M only: Inc 1 st at end of row => 131 sts.

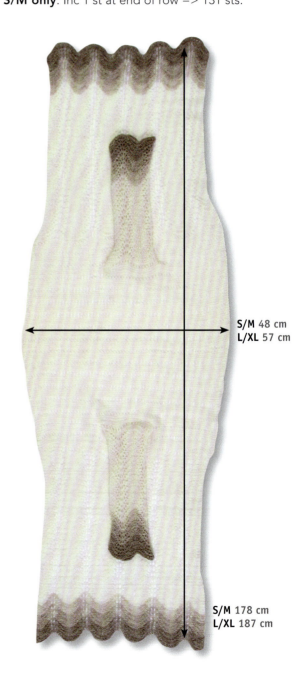

S/M 48 cm
L/XL 57 cm

S/M 178 cm
L/XL 187 cm

Next: Work patt as before, 27 (29) times, last patt row: change to B.
Work patt 2 times, last patt row: change to C.
Work patt 3 times, last patt row: change to D.
Work patt 3 times.
Next: Work rows 1-3.
Using 5mm needle, BO very loosely purlwise.

SLEEVES

With A using four 4mm dpns, start at lower edge of armhole. Pick up 1 (1) st from the strand between the rows, knit and pick up sts from scrap yarn and 2 (1) sts between the rows at top of armhole (between 2nd and 3rd needle), work to end of rnd, total 75 (100) sts.
Work garter st in the rnd: *knit 1 rnd, purl next rnd*, 2 ridges.
Knit 2 rnds.
Work lace row: *k2tog , yo*.
Knit 2 rnds.
Work **feather and fan chart** in the rnd:
1st rnd: purl.
2nd rnd: knit.
3rd rnd: knit.

4th patt rnd: *k2tog 4 times => 4 sts. k1, yo, 8 times, k1=> 17 sts. ssk 4 times*. Rep from *to* to end of rnd.
Work patt 16 (18) times or as long as preferred, last patt rnd: change to B.
Work patt 2 times, last patt rnd: change to C.
Work patt 3 times, last patt rnd: change to D.
Work patt 3 times.
Next: Work rnds 1-3.
Using 5mm needle, BO very loosely purlwise.

FINISHING

Back of cardigan, lower edge of "lace and ridges": With A, using 3.5mm crochet hook work sc into edge, to keep the back straight. Fasten off.

Weave in loose ends. Rinse by hand in lukewarm water, squeeze out excess water with towel. Lay flat to dry and stretch carefully.

NOTE: See sizes on page 77 for measurements in inches

Feather and fan chart

Key

—	p on RS, k on WS
	K on RS, p on WS br á röngu
/	k2tog
\	ssk
O	yo

fiðrildaslóð and skotta

This warm, comfortable dress features a lace-edged hem and butterflies on the bodice.

The beautiful cardigan decorated with even more butterflies is perfect for any special occasion.

SIZES – Skotta-dress 2 (3, 4, 6, 8) years
Chest: 55/21¾" (61/24", 67/26½", 72/28¼", 78/30¾")
Width at lower edge: 78/30¾" (83/32¾", 89/35", 94/37", 100/39½")
Length: 45/17¾" (50/19¾", 55/21¾", 63/24¾", 70/27½")

MATERIALS
Létt-Lopi 50g (1.7oz) balls, 100m (109yd)

Blue dress
A 1403 lapis blue 2 (3, 3, 4, 4)
B 0051 white 1 (1, 1, 1, 1)
C 1410 orange 1 (1, 1, 1, 1)
D 9434 crimson red 1 (1, 1, 1, 1)
E 9420 navy blue 1 (1, 1, 1, 1)
1406 spring green and 1402 heaven blue for embroidery

Red dress
A 9434 crimson red 3 (4, 4, 5, 5)
B 0059 black 1 (1, 1, 1, 1)
C 1411 sun yellow 1 (1, 1, 1, 1)
D 0051 white 1 (1, 1, 1, 1)
small amount of golden yarn for embroidery

4.5mm (US 7) circular needles 40 and 60cm (16 and 24in), 3.5mm (US E/4) crochet hook, 3-4 small buttons, markers

GAUGE
10 x 10cm (4 x 4in) =18 sts and 24 rows in st st on 4.5mm (US 7) needles.

NOTE
The dress is worked in the round to armhole, then back and front are worked separately. Crochet around neck and armholes.

SKOTTA dress

CO very loosely 140 (150, 160, 170, 180) sts, **blue** with A, **red** with D, using 4.5mm circular needle. Join in the rnd and work single eyelet rib:
Rnd 1: *p2, k3*, rep from *to* to end.
Rnd 2: *p2, k2tog, yo, k1*, rep from *to* to end.
Rnd 3: Work as rnd 1.
Rnd 4: *p2, k1, yo, Sl1, k1, psso*, rep from *to* to end.
All sizes: Rep rnd 1-4, 1 (2 ,2, 3, 3) times.
Size 2 and 4: Rep rnd 1-2, once, (vertical row of 5 (6, 7, 8) 8 holes).
When rib is complete:
Red: knit 1 rnd, change to A.
Both blue and red: knit until piece measures 7 (8, 9, 10, 11) cm from CO edge. Divide the piece into 6 sections as follows and place marker after each:
Size 2: 23, 24, 23, 23, 24, 23 sts in each section.
Size 3: 25 sts in each section.
Size 4: 27, 26, 27, 27, 26, 27 sts in each section.
Size 6: 28, 29, 28, 28, 29, 28 sts in each section.
Size 8: 30 sts in each section.
Cont in st st and dec 2 sts (ss, k2tog) on each side of marker, then in every 16th (18th, 20st, 22nd, 25th) rnd 2 times, finally dec only in sides (4 sts) => 100 (110, 120, 130, 140) sts. Work until piece measures 27 (31, 35, 42, 48) cm from CO edge. (Work more/less rnds between dec's if you like the dress longer/shorter).
Work patt from chart.
When chart is complete, knit 3 rnds: **blue** with E, **red** with A. Do not work last 3 (4, 4, 5, 5) sts of last rnd. BO 6 (8,8, 10, 10) sts, knit 44 (47, 52, 55, 60) sts (front), BO 6 (8, 8, 10, 10) sts, knit 44 (47, 52, 55, 60) sts (back). Now work back and forth.

Armhole shaping back: BO 2 sts at beg of next 2 rows. Dec 1 st at beg and end of next 3 (3, 4, (4, 4) rows, then every other row 2 times. => 30 (33, 36, 39, 44) sts. Work until armhole measures 10 (11, 12, 13, 14) cm.
Neck shaping RS: Work 8 (9, 10, 11, 13) sts, BO center 14 (15, 16, 17, 18) sts, work to end. Work both sides, dec 1 st at each neck edge every other row, 2 times => 6 (7, 8, 9, 11) sts. Work 1 row. BO.
Armhole shaping front: BO 2 sts at beg of next 2 rows. Dec 1 st at beg and end of next 3 (3, 4, 4, 4) rows, then every other row 2 times. => 30 (33, 36, 39, 44) sts. Work until armhole measures 6 (7, 7, 7, 7) cm.
Neck shaping RS: Work 10 (11, 12, 13, 15) sts, BO center 10 (11, 12, 13, 14) sts, work to end. Work both sides, BO 2 sts at each neck edge, dec 1 st at end of next row and end of foll row => 6 (7, 8, 9, 11) sts. Work without further shaping 12 (13, 14, 15, 16) cm and front measures the same as back. BO left shoulder.

FINISHING

Graft right shoulder tog from RS.
Armhole and neck: With 3.5mm crochet hook, **blue** E, **red** A, sc 2 rnds around right armhole. Sc around neck, left shoulder and armhole. Mark evenly position of 3-4 buttonholes on front shoulder. *Sc in each sc to 1 sc before marker, buttonhole: ch 1, skip 1 sc, sc in next sc*. Rep until all buttonholes have been made, work to end.

Chart

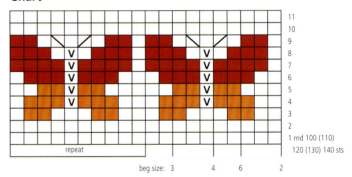

Key Blue / Red
- B – 0051 / 0059
- C – 1410 / 1411
- D – 9434 / 0051

Embroidery
- V   duplicate stitch
- ╱   backstitch to the right
- ╲   backstitch to the left

2 55 cm
3 61 cm
4 67 cm
6 72 cm
8 78 cm

2 45 cm
3 50 cm
4 55 cm
6 63 cm
8 70 cm

2 78 cm
3 83 cm
4 89 cm
6 94 cm
8 100 cm

EMBROIDERY

Blue: Split the wool into two strands. With one strand embroider the body of the butterfly with duplicate stitch and the antenna with backstitch (see page 258), alternate green and blue bodies.

Red: With golden yarn: Embroider butterfly body with duplicate stitch and the antenna with backstitch. Weave in loose ends. Rinse dress by hand in lukewarm water and lay flat to dry. Sew on buttons.

NOTE: See sizes on page 81 for measurements in inches

FIÐRILDASLÓÐ – cardigan

BODY

CO very loosely 122 (132, 147, 157) sts with A using 4.5mm circular needle.

Work single eyelet rib back and forth:

Row 1 WS: *k2, p3*, rep from *to*, end k2.

Row 2 RS: *p2, k2tog, yo, k1*, rep from *to*, end p2.

Row 3: Work as row 1.

Row 4: *p2, k1, yo, Sl1, k1, psso*, rep from *to*, end p2.

All sizes: Rep row 1-4, 2 (2, 3, 3) times (vertical row of 6 (6) 8 (8) holes). CO 2 sts (p first and last st of rnd) and join in the rnd => 124 (134, 149, 159) sts. Work in st st until body measures 21 (24, 27, 30) cm from CO edge. Dec evenly spaced 11 (11, 16, 16) sts => 113 (123, 133, 143) sts.

Set aside and work sleeves.

SLEEVES

CO loosely 30 (30, 35, 35) sts with A using 4.5mm dpns. Join in the rnd and work single eyelet rib:

Rnd 1: *p2, k3*, rep from *to* to end.

Rnd 2: *p2, k2tog, yo, k1*, rep from *to* to end.

Rnd 3: Work as rnd 1.

Rnd 4: *p2, k1, yo, Sl1, k1, psso*, rep from *to* to end.

All sizes: Rep rnd 1-4, 1 (1, 2, 2) times (vertical row of 4 (4, 6, 6) holes).

NOTE: See sizes on page 84 for measurements in inches

2 63 cm
3-4 68 cm
6 74 cm
8 79 cm

2 21 cm
3-4 24 cm
6 27 cm
8 30 cm

2 24 cm
3-4 27 cm
6 30 cm
8 33 cm

SIZES – Fiðrildaslóð – cardigan 2 (3-4, 6, 8) years
Chest: 63/24¾" (68/26¾", 74/29", 79/31")
Width at lower edge: 69/27" (74/29", 82/32¼", 88/34¾")
Length to armhole: 21/8¼" (24/9½", 27/10½", 30/11¾")
Sleeve length: 24/9½ (27/10½", 30/11¾", 33/13")cm

MATERIALS Létt-Lopi 50g (1.7oz) balls, 100m (109yd)
A 9434 crimson red 3 (4, 5, 5)
B 0059 black 1 (2, 2, 2)
C 1411 sun yellow 1 (1, 1, 1)
D 0051 white 1 (1, 1, 1)
small amount of golden yarn for embroidery

4.5mm (US 7) circular needles 40 and 60cm (16 and 24in), 3.5mm (US 4) circular needle 40cm, 4.5mm (US 7) double pointed needles 3.5mm (US E/4) crochet hook, 5-7 small buttons

GAUGE
18 sts and 24 rows = 10 x 10cm (4 x 4in) in st st on 4.5mm (US 7) needles.

NOTE
Body and sleeves are worked in the round from lower edge to underarms, then joined to work yoke in the round. Round begins and ends with a purl st at front of body. The front is cut open.

Key – Blue / Red	Embroidery
A – 1403 / 9434	V duplicate stitch
B – 0051 / 0059	╱ backstitch to the right
C – 1410 / 1411	╲ backstitch to the left
D – 9434 / 0051	
E – 1406 / 1411	
F – 1402 / 0051	
∕ k2tog	
∖ ssk	
— purl	
no stitch	

Work in st st and inc evenly spaced 0 (2, 1, 1) sts. Next rnd inc 1 st after first st and 1 st before last st of rnd, then every 8th (9th, 9th, 9th) rnd up sleeve, total 6 (6, 6, 7) times => 42 (44, 48, 50) sts. Cont without further shaping until sleeve measures 24 (27, 30, 33) cm from CO edge. Place 6 (7, 9, 10) sts underarm on st holder => 36 (37, 39, 40) sts.
Work second sleeve.

YOKE
Join body and sleeves as follows: With A and 4.5mm circular needle, work right front (beg p1) 25 (27, 29, 31) sts, place next 6 (7, 9, 10) sts of body on st holder for underarm. Knit 36 (37, 39, 40) sts of first sleeve. Knit 51 (55, 57, 61) sts of back, place next 6 (7, 9, 10) sts of body on st holder for underarm. Knit 36 (37, 39, 40) sts of second sleeve. Work left front 25 (27, 29, 31) sts (end p1) => 173 (183, 193, 203) sts. Work patt and dec's from chart as indicated. Change to shorter circular needle when necessary. When chart is complete => 70 (74, 78, 82) sts.

NECKBAND
Change to 3.5mm needle and A. BO purl st, knit 1 rnd and dec evenly spaced 13 (15, 17, 19) sts, BO end purl st => 55 (57, 59, 61) sts. Now work back and forth. Work 4 rows *p1, k1* rib. BO in rib.

FINISHING

Graft underarm sts tog and weave in loose ends. Sew by machine using straight small stitches twice through each chain of purl sts up body front. Cut carefully between the sewn rows.

Front border right: Row 1 RS: With A using 3.5mm crochet hook beg at lower edge, work loosely sc over machine stitch and single stitch, into every other row up front. Switch to B when color changes at yoke. Work to end, turn.
Row 2: Ch1. Mark position of 5-7 button loops, first at end of yoke, last 2cm above lower edge, the others spaced evenly between. Now sc in each sc, ch3 for button loop. Switch back to A at yoke. Fasten off.
Front border left: Row 1 RS: With B, beg at top and work loosely sc over machine stitch and single stitch, into every other row to lower edge. Change colors at yoke. Work to end, turn.
Row 2: Ch1. Sc in each sc and change colors as before. Fasten off.

EMBROIDERY

Blue: Split the wool into two strands. With one strand embroider the body of the butterfly with duplicate stitch (see page 258) and the antenna with backstitch. In first and third row; butterflies with green and blue bodies, second row with red and orange bodies (see photo).

Red: With golden yarn: Embroider butterfly body with duplicate stitch and the antenna with backstitch. Weave in loose ends. Rinse cardigan by hand in lukewarm water and lay flat to dry. Sew on buttons.

Chart – yoke

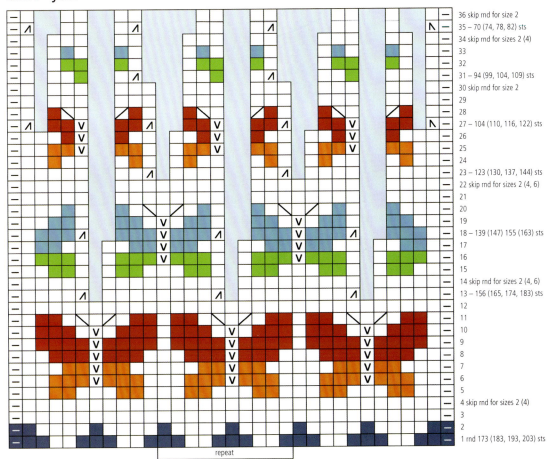

fjara and vormorgunn

This skirt is worked from the waist down. It can also be worn reversed, so that the wrong side faces out. This will make the ripples in the bottom edging more noticable.
And why not use a traditional Icelandic sweater pattern to knit a pullover shaped to give it a feminine silhouette?

SIZES – Fjara Skirt XS (S, M, L, XL, XXL)
Waist: 60/23¾" (63/24¾", 66/26", (70/27½", 73/28¾ ", 76/30")
Length: 58/22¾" (59/23¼", 59/23¼", (60/23¾", 61/24", (62/24½")

MATERIAL Létt-Lopi 50g (1.7oz) balls, 100m (109yd)
A 0059 black 4 (4, 5, 5, 6, 6)
B 0005 black heather 1 (1, 1, 1, 1, 1)
C 0058 dark gray 1 (1, 1, 1, 1, 1)
D 0057 gray 1 (1, 1, 1, 1, 1)
E 0056 light gray 1 (1, 1, 1, 1, 1)
F 0054 ash heather 1 (1, 1, 1, 1, 1)

4.5mm (US 7) circular needles 60cm (24in), 80–100cm (30–40in), elastic for waist

GAUGE
10 x 10cm (4 x 4in) = 18 sts and 24 rows in st st on 4.5mm (US 7) needles.

NOTE
The skirt is worked in the round from the waist down and is reversible. It can be worked in one color or add colored stripes at lower edge. Add rounds to make the skirt longer.
The waist may seem small but the skirt is very stretchy.

FJARA – skirt

CO 108 (114, 120, 126, 132, 138) sts with A using 4.5mm circular needle. Join in the rnd and work in st st. Divide the skirt into 6 sections by placing a marker after every 18 (19, 20, 21, 22, 23) sts. Inc 2 sts in each section (1 st after first st and 1 st before last st of rnd) a total of 12 sts, 8 times. Inc in every 10th rnd in sizes 34 (36), rep rnds see chart for bigger sizes. => 204 (210, 216, 222, 228, 234) sts. Change to longer needle when rnd gets bigger.

Now work triple yo sts:

1st rnd: Work st st.

2nd rnd: Change color as shown *yo 3 times, k1* rep from *to* to end of rnd.

3rd rnd: Work st st, dropping the triple yo off the needle, making a long st.

4th rnd: Work 1 rnd st st and inc as before. => 216 (222, 228, 234, 240, 246) sts.

Rep these 4 rnds, 5 times: First with A, then B, C, D and E => 276 (282, 288, 294, 300, 306) sts. Work with F till 4th rnd. Work 1 rnd P, 1 rnd K, 1 rnd page BO loosely in st st.

FINISHING

Weave all loose ends in carefully. Rinse skirt and lay flat to dry. Measure elastic and sew close to CO so the skirt can be used from both sides.

VORMORGUNN—pullover
BODY

Using color A and the longer 3.5mm circular needle, CO 140 (148, 156, 164, 172) sts. Join in the rnd and knit 5 rnds moss st. Switch to 4.5mm circular needle and begin working in stockinette st. Place markers in the sides of the body and dec 2 sts on each side 7cm, 12cm and 17cm from the CO edge; 12 sts decreased => 128 (136, 144, 152, 160) sts. Inc 2 sts on each side of the body 22cm, 27cm and 30 (31, 32, 33, 34) cm from the CO edge => 140 (148, 156, 164, 172) sts. Knit until body measures 32 (34, 36, 38, 39) cm from the CO edge. Do not knit the last 5 (5, 6, 6, 7) sts of the rnd.

YOKE

BO 9 (10, 11, 12, 13) sts, knit front piece 61 (64, 67, 70, 73) sts, BO next 9 (10, 11, 12, 13) sts, knit back piece 61 (64, 67, 70, 73) sts.

Next rnd: CO, using the same method as for the body, 44 (45, 46, 47, 48) sts (left shoulder), knit front piece, CO 44 (45, 46, 47, 48) sts, knit back piece => 210 (218, 226, 234, 242) sts. Work moss stitch for 3 rnds on only those stitches that were CO above the armholes, but keep the front and back pieces in stockinette stitch. Inc 3 sts above each armhole as follows: *k11 (11, 11, 11, 12) sts, inc 1 st, k11 (11, 12, 12, 12) sts, inc 1 st, k11 (12, 12, 12, 12) sts, inc 1 st*. Knit to the right armhole (72, 75, 78, 82, 85) sts and rep the increases from * to *. Finish the rnd => 216 (224, 232, 240, 248) sts. Now work the chart and dec accordingly. Switch to a shorter needle as the circumference of the yoke gets smaller. When the chart is complete, 81 (84, 87, 90, 93) sts remain.

NECKLINE EDGING

Switch to the 3.5mm circular needle and knit 1 rnd, dec 13 (14, 15, 16, 17) evenly throughout => 68 (70, 72, 74, 76) sts. Work moss st for 3 rnds. BO in moss st.

FINISHING

Weave in loose ends. Gently block the vest into shape.

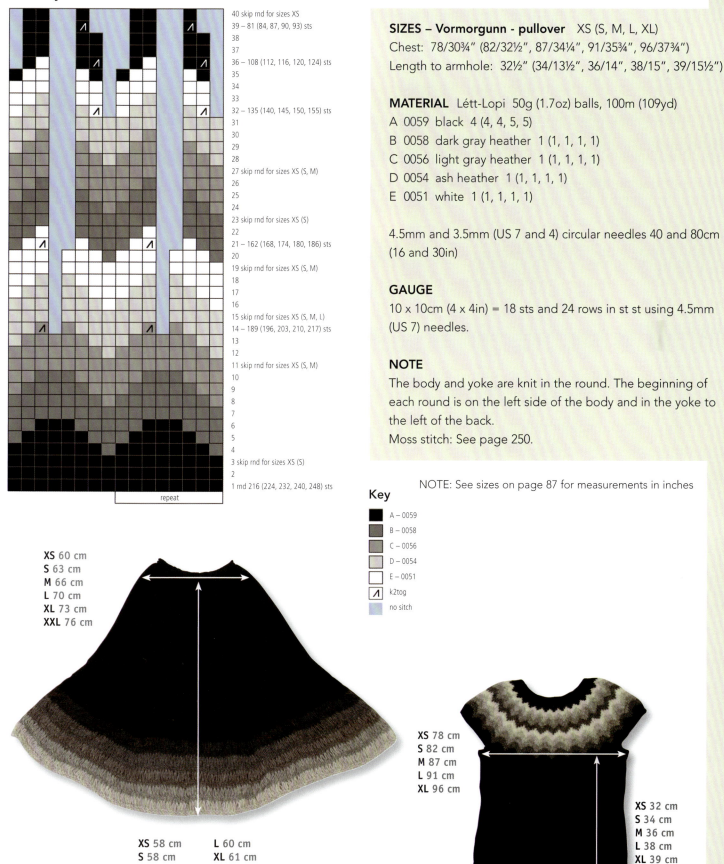

frjáls

A pretty short-sleeved, lace sweater knitted using lace weight wool. This sweater can be dressed up by threading a ribbon through the bodice.

SIZES after blocking S/M (M/L, L/XL)
Chest: 90/35½" (97/38", 105/41¼")
Width lower edge: 102/40" (110/43¼", 119/46¾")
Length to armhole: 36/14" (39/15½", 42/16½")

MATERIALS Einband 50g (1.7oz) balls 225m (245yd), 1026 ash heather 3 (4, 5)

4mm (US 6) circular needle 60 or 80cm (24 or 30in), 2.5mm (US 1½) circular needle 40cm (16in), 4mm (US 6) double pointed needles, markers, ribbon

BLOCKED GAUGE
Pattern 1 (one rep): 8.5cm x 3cm = 16 sts and 8 rnds on 4mm (US 6) needles.
Pattern 2 (one rep): 7.5cm x 3cm = 14 sts and 8 rnds on 4mm (US 6) needles.

NOTE
Body and sleeves are worked in the round from lower edge to underarms, then joined and yoke is worked in the round. Round begins on back. Add repeats of pattern rounds for a longer sweater. The sweater will stretch when washed and blocked.

BODY

Using 4mm needle, CO 192 (208, 224) sts. Work back and forth in garter st for 5 rows (3 ridges). Join in the rnd and place marker at beg of rnd, work **patt 1** (8 rnds) from chart total 9 (10, 1 times, or as long as preferred. **Chart** shows every other rnd, even rnds are all knitted in the round.

1st decrease: Dec 2 sts in every rep as shown on chart => 168 (182) 196 sts.

Work **patt 2** (8 rnds) total 3 (3) 4 times.

Set aside and work sleeves.

SLEEVES

Using 4mm dpns, CO 80 sts. Work back and forth in garter st for 5 rows (3 ridges). Join in the rnd and place marker at beg of rnd, work **patt 1** (8 rnds) from chart total 3 (3, 4) times.

1st decrease: Dec 2 sts in every rep as shown on chart => 70 sts.

Work **Patt 2** once.

S/M: Left sleeve: Place last 14 sts on holder for underarm.

Right sleeve: Place first 14 sts on holder.

M/L: Left sleeve: Place 10 first and 4 last sts on holder for underarm.

Right sleeve: Place 4 first and 10 last sts on holder.

L/XL: Place 7 last and 7 first sts on holder for underarm. Work second sleeve.

YOKE

Join body and sleeves as follows: Using 4mm circular needle, cont patt 2, work 28 (38, 35) sts for back, place 14 sts of body on st holder for underarm. Work 56 sts of first sleeve. Work 70 (78, 84) sts for front, place next 14 sts of body on st holder for underarm. Work 56 sts of second sleeve. Work 42 (38, 49) sts for back => 252 (266, 280) sts on needle.

Work **patt 2** total 2 (2, 3) times.

2nd decrease: Dec 2 sts in every rep as shown on chart => 216 (228, 240) sts.

Work **patt 3** once.

3rd decrease: Dec 4 sts in every rep as shown on chart => 144 (152, 160) sts.

Purl 1 rnd.

Knit 1 rnd.

Purl 1 rnd.

Work patt 4 from chart.

4th decrease: Dec 1 st in every rep as shown on chart => 126 (133, 140) sts.

Neckline: Change to 2.5mm needle. Knit 8 rnds. BO knitwise.

FINISHING

Graft underarm sts carefully together and weave in loose ends. Rinse sweater by hand in lukewarm water and squeeze excess water out with towel. Lay flat to dry in right shape and measurements.

Draw ribbon through holes under bust for decoration, see photo.

Chart

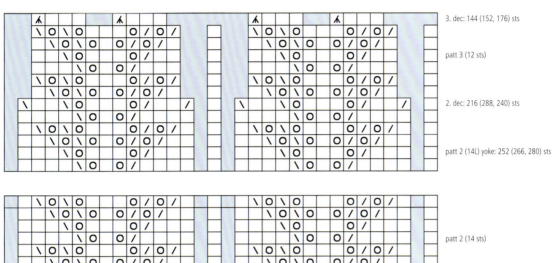

4. dec: 126 (133, 154) sts

skip rnd for sizes S (M)

patt 4 (8 sts)

3. dec: 144 (152, 176) sts

patt 3 (12 sts)

2. dec: 216 (288, 240) sts

patt 2 (14L) yoke: 252 (266, 280) sts

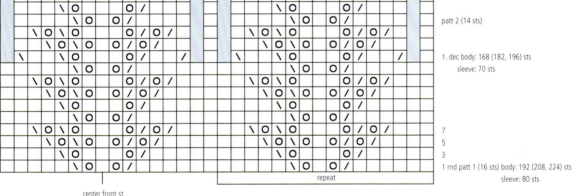

patt 2 (14 sts)

1. dec body: 168 (182, 196) sts
sleeve: 70 sts

7
5
3
1 rnd patt 1 (16 sts) body: 192 (208, 224) sts
sleeve: 80 sts

repeat

center front st

Chart shows every other row: 1, 3, 5, ….
Rows 2, 4, 6, … are knit on the WS: k3, p33, k3.

Key

- ☐ knit
- O yo
- / k2tog
- \ ssk
- ⋀ s1, k2tog, psso
- ▨ no stitch

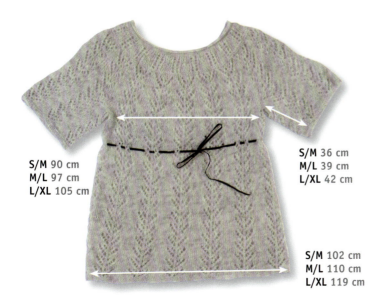

S/M 90 cm
M/L 97 cm
L/XL 105 cm

S/M 36 cm
M/L 39 cm
L/XL 42 cm

S/M 102 cm
M/L 110 cm
L/XL 119 cm

NOTE: See sizes on page 91 for measurements in inches

93

gefjun

The color pattern used for this sweater's yoke first appeared in around 1970 in pattern books published by the yarn manufacturer Gefjun from Akureyri.

SIZES S (M, L, XL, XXL)
Chest: 92/36¼" (98/38½", 105/41¼", 111/43½", 117/46")
Length to armhole: 41/16" (42/16½", 43/17", 44/17¼", 45/17¾")
Sleeve length
Men's: 48/18¾" (49/19¼", 51/20", 52/20½", 53/21")
Women's: 45/17¾" (46/18", 47/18½", 48/18¾", 49/19¼")

MATERIALS Álafoss Lopi 100g (3.5oz) balls, 100m (109yd)
A 0058 dark gray heather 6 (7, 8, 8, 9)
B 0051 white 2 (2, 2, 2, 2)
C 0059 black 1 (1, 1, 1, 1)

6mm and 4.5mm (US 10 and 7) circular needles 40 and 80cm (16 and 30in), 6mm and 4.5mm (US 10 and 7) double pointed needles

GAUGE
10 x 10cm (4 x 4in) = 13 sts and 18 rows in st st on 6mm (US 10) needles.

NOTE
Body and sleeves are worked in the round from lower edge to underarms, then joined to work yoke in the round. Each round of the body begins on the left side of the sweater, but the yoke rounds begin where the back of the sweater meets the left sleeve.

BODY

CO 114 (122, 130, 138, 146) sts with A using 4.5mm circular needle,. Join in the rnd and work *k1, p1* rib for 5cm. Change to 6mm circular needle inc evenly spaced 6 (4, 8, 6, 4) sts => 120 (126, 138, 136, 144, 150) sts. Work in st st patt from **Chart 1**. When patt is complete, continue with A until body measures 41 (42, 43, 44, 45, 45) cm from CO edge. Do not work the last 4 (4, 5, 5, 5, 5) sts in the last rnd. Set the body aside and work the sleeves.

SLEEVES

CO 32 (34, 36, 36, 38) sts with A using 4.5mm dpn. Join in the rnd and work *k1, p1* rib for 5cm. Change to 6mm needles, work in st st and inc evenly spaced 4 (2, 6, 6, 4) sts => 36 (36, 42, 42, 42) sts. Work patt from **Chart 1**. When chart is complete, continue with A, inc 1 st after the first st and 1 st before the last st in the rnd, and then

Men's: every 13th (12th, 12th, 9th, 8th) rnd, Women's: every 12th (11th, 11th, 8th, 7th) rnd, total 5 (6, 5, 7, 8) times up sleeve –> 46 (48, 52, 56, 58) sts. Continue without further shaping until sleeve measures Men's: 49 (50, 51, 52, 53) cm, Women's: 45 (46, 47, 48, 49) cm from CO edge. Place 8 (7, 9, 10, 11) underarm sts on a stitch holder => 38 (41, 43, 46, 49) sts. Work second sleeve.

YOKE

Join the body and sleeves as follows: with A using 6mm circular needle, place the last 4 (4, 4, 5, 5) sts and the first 4 (4, 4, 5, 5) sts of body on a stitch holder for underarm, knit 38 (41, 43, 46, 49) sts of first sleeve, knit 52 (55, 59, 62, 65) sts for front, place next 8 (8, 10, 10, 10) sts on a stitch holder for underarm, knit 38 (41, 43, 46, 49) sts of second sleeve, knit 52 (55, 59, 62, 65) sts from back => 180 (192, 204, 216, 228) sts. Work **Chart 2** as indicated. Change to a shorter circular needle when necessary. When chart is complete => 63 (69, 72, 78, 81) sts rem.

NECKBAND

Change to 4.5mm needles, continue with A and dec evenly spaced 5 (9, 10, 14, 15) sts => 58 (60, 62, 64, 66) sts. Work *k1, p 1* rib forl 5cm. BO loosely.

FINISHING

Graft underarm sts tog and weave in loose ends. Fold the neckband in half and stitch to the WS. Rinse sweater by hand in lukewarm water. Carefully lay flat to dry and smooth gently into right shape and measurements.

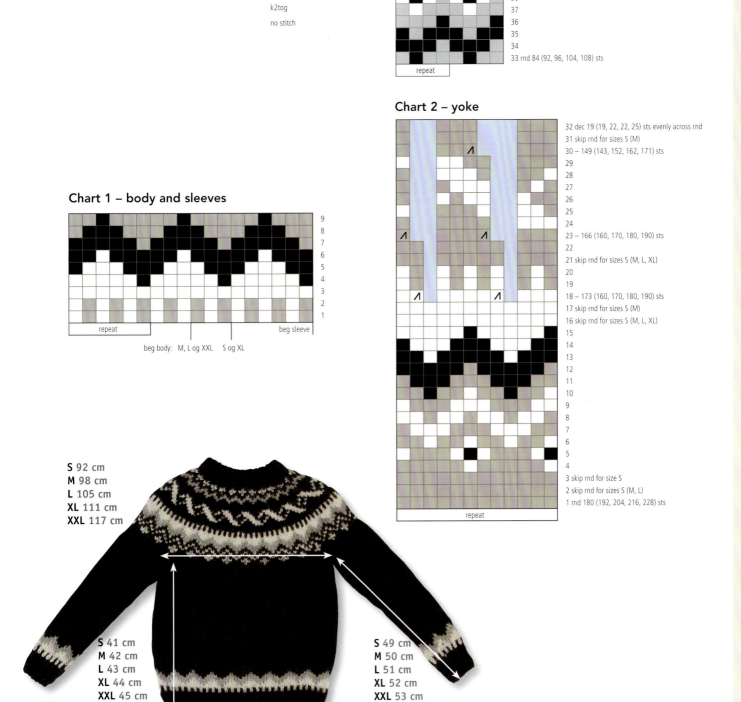

gjöf

Bands of simple repeat patterns frame the traditional rose design on this sweater's yoke. The buttonband and buttonhole band are knitted separately and sewn on.

SIZES S (M, L, XL, XXL)
Chest: 94/37" (99/39", 104/41", 110/43¼", 115/45¼")cm
Length to armhole: 39/15½" (40/15¾", 41/16", 42/16½", 43/17")
Sleeve length: 47/18½" (48/18¾", 49/19¼", 50/19¾", 51/20½")

MATERIALS Álafoss Lopi 100g (3.5oz) balls, 100m (109yd)
A 0051 white 5 (6, 6, 6, 7)
B 0053 acorn heather 1 (1, 1, 2, 2)
C 0086 light beige heather 1 (1, 1, 2, 2)
D 0085 oatmeal heather 1 (1, 1, 1, 1)

6mm (US 10) circular needles 40 and 60cm (16 and 24in), 5mm (US 8) circular needle 60cm, 5mm and 6mm (US 8 and 10) double pointed needles, 6 (6, 6, 7, 8) buttons

GAUGE
10 x 10cm (4 x 4in) = 13 sts and 18 rows in st st on 6mm (US 10) needles.

NOTE
All ribbing is knit back and forth, while the body and the sleeves are knit in the round. At the armholes, the sleeve and body stitches are joined on one needle and the yoke is knit in the round. The front is cut open and edgings added.

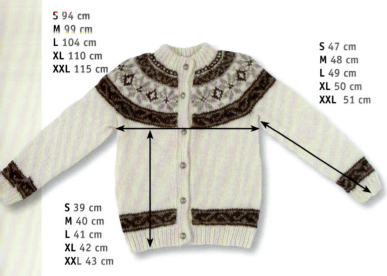

S 94 cm
M 99 cm
L 104 cm
XL 110 cm
XXL 115 cm

S 47 cm
M 48 cm
L 49 cm
XL 50 cm
XXL 51 cm

S 39 cm
M 40 cm
L 41 cm
XL 42 cm
XXL 43 cm

NOTE: See sizes on page 99 for measurements in inches

BODY

Using A and 5mm circular needle, CO 127 (133, 139, 145, 151) sts. Work in rib back and forth as follows: Row 1 (RS): k1, *k1, p1*, rep from * to *, k2. Row 2: k1, *p1, k1*, rep from * to *. The first and last stitch of every row are worked in garter st (k on every row). Repeat rows 1 and 2 until the ribbing measures 2cm. End with a WS row. Next row (buttonhole): Work first 4 sts as before, yo, k2tog, work to end of row as before. Work ribbing until it measures 6cm from CO edge. End with a WS row. Next row: Work 8 sts as before and then place them on a stitch holder or scrap yarn. Continue in st st, inc 1 (2, 3, 4, 5) sts evenly over the next 111 (117, 123, 129, 135) sts. Place the last 8 sts of the row on a stitch holder/scrap yarn => 112 (119, 126, 133, 140) sts. Switch to a 6mm circular needle and CO 2 sts; these will count as the 1st and last stitches in the rnd when working in the rnd => 114 (121, 128, 135, 142) sts. Join and work **Chart 1** and then continue in st st using A. Note that the 1st and last sts of the rnd are purled up the body of the sweater. Knit until body measures 44 (45, 46, 47, 48) cm from the CO edge. Set body aside and make the sleeves.

SLEEVES

Using A and 5mm needles, CO 32 (32, 34, 36, 36) sts. Join and work in rib, *k1, p1*, rep from * to *, for 6cm. Switch to 6mm needles and knit one rnd, inc 3 (3, 1, 6, 6) evenly in the rnd => 35 (35, 35, 42, 42) sts. Work **Chart 1**. Once chart is complete, inc 2 sts (1 st after the 1st st in the row and 1 st before the last st in the row) every 6th row 4 (6, 6, 5, 6) times => 43 (47, 47, 52, 54) sts. Knit until sleeve measures 47 (48, 49, 50, 51) cm from CO edge. Place 7 (7, 7, 8, 9) underarm sts on a stitch holder/scrap yarn => 36 (40, 40, 44, 45) sts.

YOKE

Combine the body and sleeve sts on 6mm circular needle: with A, knit the first 24 (26, 28, 29, 30) body sts (right front). Place next 8 (8, 8, 9, 10) sts on a stitch holder/scrap yarn. Knit the right sleeve, 35 (39, 39, 43, 44) sts. Knit the next 50 (53, 56, 59, 62) (back). Place next 8 (8, 8, 9, 10) sts on a stitch holder or scrap yarn. Knit the left sleeve, 35 (39, 39, 43, 44) sts. Knit rem 24 (26, 28, 29, 30) (left front) => 168 (183, 190, 203, 210) sts (including the 2 purled sts on the front). Work **Chart 2** and dec 1 st for size S, 3 sts for size XXL and inc 1 st for size M (omit decreasing or increasing for sizes L and XL) => 167 (184, 190, 203, 207) sts. Dec according to the chart and switch to a shorter needle as the stitches become fewer => 88 (95, 103, 108, 112) sts.

FINISHING

Weave in loose ends and graft underarm sts. Using a sewing machine and a small, straight stitch, sew 2 lines into the 2 purled stitches up the front of the sweater.
Buttonband: Starting with a RS row, transfer the 8 sts from the stitch holder/scrap yarn onto a 5mm needle. Using A, CO 3 sts (edge sts) on the side facing the steek. Work the 8 held sts as before, but work the 3 edge sts in st st. Work buttonband until it is the same length as the sweater (gently stretched), BO the edge sts and transfer the rem 8 sts to a stitch holder/scrap yarn. Carefully cut the sweater up the front in between the 2 purled stitches. Sew the buttonband to the left cut edge from the RS, stitching into a knit st on the sweater front and in between a knit st and an edge st on the buttonband. Stitch the edge sts to the WS of the cardigan so that they cover the cut edge.

Chart 1 – body and sleeves

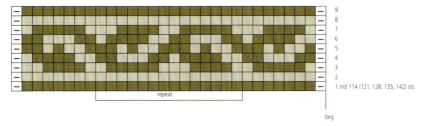

Chart 2 – yoke

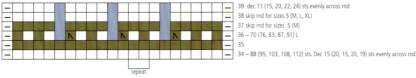

Key

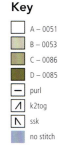

- A – 0051
- B – 0053
- C – 0086
- D – 0085
- — purl
- ∕ k2tog
- ∖ ssk
- no stitch

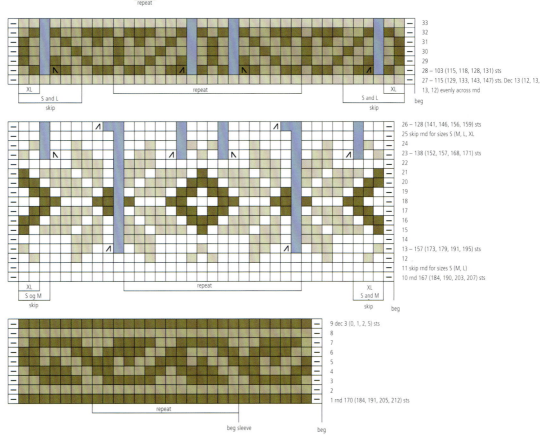

Buttonhole band: Mark the placement of buttons on the band. The lowest buttonhole has already been made and the top one will be placed on the neckline edging (2cm above the band). Work this band in the same manner as the buttonband, but making buttonholes that correspond with the markings on the buttonband. Sew the band to the right cut edge and stitch the edge sts to the WS of the cardigan to cover the cut edge.

Neckline edging

Starting with a RS row, using A and 5mm needles, work the 8 sts as before, *k1, p1*, rep from * to *, dec 10 sts evenly over the next 59 (61, 63, 65, 67) sts, work the rem 8 sts as before => 65 (67, 69, 71, 73) sts. Work 3 rows ribbing, make a buttonhole in the next row, work 4 more rows in rib. BO 8 sts at the beg of the next 2 rows. Work 9 more rows in rib BO. Fold in half and stitch to the WS of the neckline. Sew on buttons.

grein

This sweater uses a vintage yoke pattern. Well-designed, classic patterns never go out of fashion.

SIZES XS (S, M, L, XL, XXL)
Chest: 92/36¼" (96/37¾", 100/39½", 104/41", 110/43¼", 114/44¾")
Length to center front neck edge: 62/24½" (64/25", 66/26", 68/26¾", 70/27½", 70/27½")
Sleeve length: 47/18½" (49/19¼", 51/20", 53/21", 55/21¾", 55/21¾")

MATERIALS Álafoss Lopi 100g (3.5oz) balls, 100m (109yd)
A 9959 indigo 5 (5, 6, 6, 7, 7)
B 9958 light indigo 1 (1, 1, 1, 1, 1)
C 0008 light denim heather 1 (1, 1, 1, 1, 1)
D 0005 black heather 1 (1, 1, 1, 1, 1)
E 0054 ash heather 1 (1, 1, 1, 1, 1)

6mm (US 10) circular needles 40cm and 80cm (16 and 30in), 4.5mm (US 6) circular needle 80cm, 4.5mm (US 6) double pointed needles

GAUGE
10 x 10 cm (4 x 4in) = 13 sts and 18 rows in st st on 6mm (US 10) needles.

NOTE
Body and sleeves are worked in the round from lower edge to underarms, then joined to work yoke in the round. Each round of the body begins on the left side of the sweater, but the yoke rounds begin where the back of the sweater meets the left sleeve.

BODY

CO 112 (120, 120, 126, 132, 138) sts with A, and 4.5mm circular needle. Join in the rnd and work in k1, p1 rib until work measures 5 (5, 6 6, 6, 6) cm. Change to 6mm, 80cm circular needle, cont in st st and inc 8 (8, 8, 10, 12, 14) sts evenly spaced in first rnd (=>120 (128, 128, 136 144, 152) sts). Work in st st patt from **Chart 1**. Cont in st st with A until work measures 40 (41, 43, 44, 45, 45) cm from CO edge. Place 8 (8, 8, 9, 10, 11) sts on each side to stich holder for underarms. Set body aside.

SLEEVES

CO 32 (32, 32, 36, 36, 36) sts with A, using 4.5mm dpn. Join in the rnd and work in k1, p1 rib until work measures 5 (5, 6, 6, 6, 6) cm. Change to 6mm dpn needles cont in st st and inc 8 (8, 8, 4, 4, 8) sts evenly spaced in first rnd (=> 40 (40, 40, 40, 40, 44) sts). Work in st st patt from **Chart 1**. Cont in st st with A and at the same time inc 1 st at beg and end of every 8th (8th, 6th, 6th, 6th, 5th) rnd, 4 (4, 6, 7, 8, 7) times (=> 48 (48, 52, 54, 56, 58) sts and 47 (49, 51, 53, 55, 55) cm. Place 8 (8, 8, 8, 9, 10, 11) sts underarm on st holder. Work second sleeve.

YOKE

Note: Beg and end of rnds are at left side on back. Join sleeves to body as follows:

Using A and the longer 6mm circular needle, knit sts from left sleeve, front of body, right sleeve and back of body (=> 184, 192, 200, 208, 216, 224) sts). Work in st st patt from **Chart 2** until 69 (72, 75, 75, 78, 81, 84) sts remain. Dec evenly in next rnd with A until 52 (54, 56, 58, 58, 60) sts remain.

NECKBAND

Change to 4.5mm needles and work k1, p1 rib, for 7 (8, 8, 8, 8, 8) cm. BO loosely.

FINISHING

Join underarm sts together and weave in any loose ends. Fold neckband in half inside and stitch in position. Rinse sweater and lay flat to dry.

Chart 1 – body and sleeves

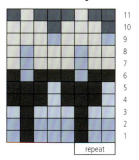

Chart 2 – yoke

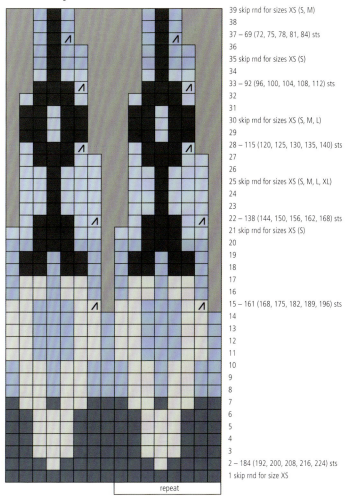

39 skip rnd for sizes XS (S, M)
38
37 – 69 (72, 75, 78, 81, 84) sts
36
35 skip rnd for sizes XS (S)
34
33 – 92 (96, 100, 104, 108, 112) sts
32
31
30 skip rnd for sizes XS (S, M, L)
29
28 – 115 (120, 125, 130, 135, 140) sts
27
26
25 skip rnd for sizes XS (S, M, L, XL)
24
23
22 – 138 (144, 150, 156, 162, 168) sts
21 skip rnd for sizes XS (S)
20
19
18
17
16
15 – 161 (168, 175, 182, 189, 196) sts
14
13
12
11
10
9
8
7
6
5
4
3
2 – 184 (192, 200, 208, 216, 224) sts
1 skip rnd for size XS

Key

A – 9959
B – 0054
C – 9958
D – 0008
E – 0005
k2tog
no stitch

XS 92 cm
S 96 cm
M 100 cm
L 104 cm
XL 110 cm
XXL 114 cm

XS 47 cm
S 49 cm
M 51 cm
L 53 cm
XL 55 cm
XXL 55 cm

XS 62 cm
S 64 cm
M 66 cm
L 68 cm
XL 70 cm
XXL 70 cm

NOTE: See sizes on page 103 for measurements in inches

handtak

Beautiful, traditionally patterned mittens. The thumb is placed so that each mitten can be worn on either the right or left hand. The double thickness of these mittens makes them especially warm.

SIZE Women's

MATERIALS
Létt Lopi 50g (1.7oz) balls, 100m (109yd) – use leftover yarn

A 0059 black
B 0054 ash heather
C 1420 murky
D 9264 mustard
E 1417 frostbite
F 1416 moor
G 9427 rust
H 9418 stone blue
I 0086 light beige

3.5mm and 4.5mm (US 4 and 7) double pointed needles

GAUGE
10 x 10cm (4 x 4in) = 18 sts and 24 rows in st st on 4.5mm (US 7) needles

NOTE
The mittens are worked in the round and are identical.

MITTENS

CO 36 sts with A using 3.5mm dpns. Join in the rnd and work *k1, p1* rib for 5cm. Change to 4.5mm dpns work in st st and inc evenly spaced 4 sts => 40 sts. Now work patt from **Chart 1** and inc 2 sts (k1, right-lifted inc, knit around, left-lifted inc) in every other rnd up to beg of thumb, total 8 times => 56 sts.

Place 16 sts on piece of scrap yarn for thumb and work later.

Work patt for total 38 rnds or as long as desired.

Dec: *k1, k2tog, k15, sl1, k1, psso*, rep from *to* around. Dec every other rnd total 8 times. Break yarn and pull through rem 8 sts.

Thumb: Begin where rnd ended: Pick up 2 sts from mitten and stitches from scrap yarn => 18 sts. Work patt from **Chart 2** for 14 rnds or as long as desired.
Dec 1: *k1, k2tog, k4, sl1, k1, psso*, rep from *to*.
Dec 2: *k1, k2tog, k2, sl1, k1, psso*, rep from *to*.
Dec 3: *k1, k2tog, sl1, k1, psso*, rep from *to*. Break yarn and pull through rem 6 sts.
Work second mitten.

FINISHING

Rinse mittens by hand in lukewarm water. Lay flat to dry and smooth into shape.

Chart 1 – mitten

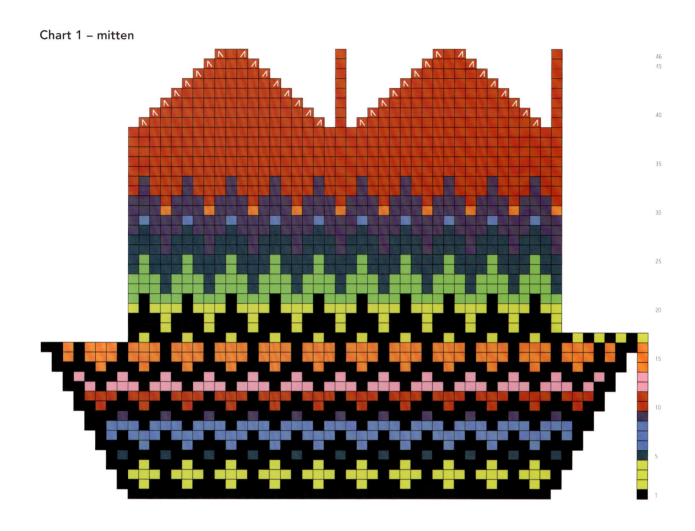

Chart 2 – thumb

Key Black – red / Black – green

- A – 0059 / 0059
- B – 9264 / 0054
- C – 9423 / 1420
- D – 1402 / 9264
- E – 1414 / 1417
- F – 9434 / 1416
- G – 1412 / 9427
- H – 1410 / 9418
- I – 1406 / 0086
- ⟋ k2tog
- ⟍ ssk

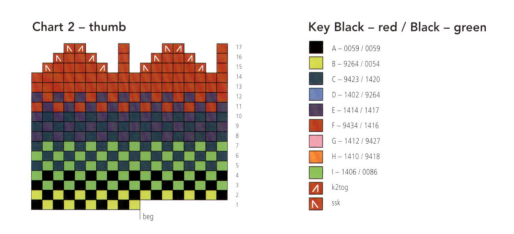

hlökk and haddur

This cute children's sweater is worked top-down so it can easily be lengthened as the child grows. The stylish hat matches the sweater and generous ribbing keeps it snug and warm over the ears.

SIZES 6 (8, 10) years
Chest: 80/31½" (86/33¾", 92/36¼")cm
Length to shoulder: 45/17¾" (50/19¾", 54/21½")cm
Sleeve length: 33/13" (37/14½", 40,5/16")cm

MATERIAL Álafoss Lopi 100g (3.5oz) balls, 100m (109yd)
A 0159 orchid 1 (1, 2)
B 1242 burgundy 2 (2, 3)
C 0163 soft purple 1 (1, 2)
D 9964 ochre 1 (1, 1)
E 1236 orange rust 1 (1, 1)

4.5mm and 6mm (US 7 and 10) circular needles 60cm (24in), zipper 45 (55, 60)cm, 18 (22, 24)in

GAUGE
10 x 10cm (4 x 4in) = 13 stitches and 18 rows in st st on 6mm (US 7) needles.

NOTE
The sweater is knitted from the top down. Front and back are knitted separately back and forth in stocking stitch to armholes then all stitches are joined on one needle. Stitches are picked up in armhole for the sleeves which are knitted in the round When the color is changed, bind off from the right side and pick up stitches behind the bound off stitches in a new color.

HLÖKK – cardigan

BACK
CO 48 (52, 56) sts with A using 6mm needles. Purl first row (WS). Knit 28 (30, 32) rows st st. BO in next row from the RS.

LEFT FRONT
With RS of back towards you and CO edge (neckline) up. Pick up stitches at the BO edge, from right edge with A, 15 (16, 18) stitches.
Purl first row (WS). Work 4 rows st st. CO 1 st at end of next row (RS). Purl back. CO 1 st in beg of next row. Purl back. CO 3 sts at end of next row. Purl back and CO 4 (5, 5) sts in next row. (=> 24 (26, 28) sts). Cont with 3 sts at edge of front in moss sts. Next row (WS) k1, p1, k1 and purl to end of row. Work 16 (18, 20) rows st st and note that on the RS knit until 2 sts are left of row, p1, k1. BO from RS.

RIGHT FRONT
With front of back towards you, pick up stitches in the BO edge, from left edge with A, 15 (16, 18) stitches. Purl first row (WS). Work 5 rows st st. CO 1 stitch at end of next row (WS). Work 2 rows st st and CO 1 stitch at end of row 2. Work 2 rows again and CO 1 stitch at end of row 2. Work 2 rows and CO 3 sts at end of row 2. Work 2 rows and CO 4 (5, 5) sts at end of row 2. (=> 24 (26, 28) sts). Work next row from RS: p1, k1, p1 and knit to end of row. Work 15 (17, 19) rows st st. Note: From WS; purl until 2 sts are left of row, k1, p1. BO from RS.

BODY
Begin with left front. With RS facing, pick up stitches in back of BO edge with B (top of purl stitches from previous row). Pick up 24 (26, 28) sts on front, CO 4 sts for armhole, pick up 48 (52, 56) sts on back, CO 4 sts for armhole and pick up 24 (26, 28) sts on right front. (=> 104 (112, 120) sts). Purl back. Work 40 (44, 48) rows st st, but note that first 3 and last 3 sts of row are worked in moss stitch. BO from RS. Pick up as many sts as before from the RS of work. Purl back. Work 5 (7, 7) rows st st. BO from RS. Pick up sts again with E, the same way using 4.5 needles. Knit rib (k1, p1) but cont in moss stitch for the first 3 and last 3 sts of rows. Work 5 (7, 7) rows rib. BO.

SLEEVES
Pick up 44 (46, 50) sts in armhole with A using 6mm needles, thus: Position beg of rnd in middle of armhole. Pick up 2 sts in every 3 rnd and pick up 4 sts under arms. Knit 11 (13, 16) rnds, and dec 1 stitch in the beg and end of 3rd, 9th, 10th and 16th rnd (=> 40 (44, 46) sts). BO. Pick up 40 (42, 46) sts with C at back of CO edge as for body. Dec 1 stitch in beg and end of 2nd (5th, 3rd) rnds and in every 6th rnd, 5 (5, 6) times. (=> 28 (30, 32) sts). Knit 2 rnds (total 34 (37) 41) rnds) BO. Pick up 28 (30, 32 sts as before with D. Knit 5 (7, 7) rnds and then BO. Pick up 26 (28, 30) sts with E using 4.5mm needles and work 5 (7, 7) rnds rib.
BO.

NECKBAND
Pick up 50 (54, 54) sts at neckline with C using 4.5 needles. Knit 3 rows with C, 8 rows with E and 2 rows with C. BO.

FINISHING
Weave in all loose ends. Wash the sweater and lay flat to dry. Sew zip to the front edge with thread in similar color. Fold collar double and slip stitch in place on WS. Hide edge of zip in collar.

SIZE – Haddur – hat 6–10 years

MATERIAL Álafoss Lopi 100g (3.5oz) balls, 100m (109yd)
Less than one ball of each
A 9210
B 0163
C 0159
D 9988
E 0065

6mm (US 10) circular needle or 1 pair straight needles

GAUGE
10 x 10cm (4 x 4in) = 12 stitches and 17 rows in brioche stitch on 6mm (US 10) needles.

NOTE
The hat is knitted back and forth in brioche stitch:
Brioche stitch: See page 250.

HADDUR – hat

CO 48 sts with A using 6mm needles. Work pattern for 14 rows with A, 10 rows with B, 8 rows with C, 4 rows with A, 6 rows with D, 6 rows with E and 10 rows with B.
Next row (RS): Knit 2 tog out row => 24 sts.
Next row: Purl.
Next row (RS): Knit 2 tog out row => 12 sts. Break off yarn, thread through rem sts. Weave in loose ends and sew sides together.

Pom-pom

Draw a circle 8cm (3in) in diameter on thick cardboard. Draw another ring in the middle 2cm (¾in) in diameter. See further information on making pom-poms on page 252.

6 33 cm
8 37 cm
10 40½ cm

6 80 cm
8 86 cm
10 92 cm

6 45 cm
8 50 cm
10 54 cm

NOTE: See sizes on page 111 for measurements in inches

hosur

Soft children's socks. The same method is used for shaping both the heel and the toe.

SOCK

CO 24 (32, 36) sts with 3.5mm needles. Join in the rnd and work *k1, p1* rib 10 (12,14) rnds.

Knit 8 (10, 12) rnds.

Divide the sts equally on 1st, 2nd and 3rd, 4th needle.

Position heel: Knit first 12 (16, 18) sts to holder, slip these sts back to left needle and work again to end of rnd.

Knit 18 (22, 24) rnds.

Toe next rnd dec: *1st and 3rd needle: k1, sl1, k1, psso, work to end of rnd. 2nd and 4th needle: knit until 3 sts are left of rnd, k2tog, k1.* Knit 2 rnds. Rep from *to*. Knit 1 rnd.

Repeat from *to* until 8 sts are left. Break yarn and pull through rem sts.

Heel: Using 3.5mm needles slip sts from holder and pick up 24 (32, 36) sts.

Divide the sts equally on 1st, 2nd, 3rd and 4th needle. Knit 2 rnds. Next rnd work dec as before: *1st and 3rd needle: k1, sl1, k1, psso, work to end of rnd. 2nd and 4th needle: Knit until 3 sts are left of rnd, k2tog, k1.* Knit 2 rnds. Repeat from *to*. Knit 1 rnd.

Repeat from *to* until 8 sts are left. Break yarn and pull through rem sts. Work second sock.

FINISHING

Weave in any loose ends. Rinse by hand in lukewarm water and lay flat to dry.

SIZES 2 (4, 6) years

MATERIAL Létt-Lopi 50g (1.7oz) balls, 100m (109yd)
Yellow socks
1411 sun yellow 1 (1, 2)

Green socks
1406 spring green 1 (1, 2)

Turquoise socks
1404 glacier blue 1 (1, 2)

3.5mm (US 4) double pointed needles

NOTE
Socks are worked in the round.

hraði

A quick knit using lace-weight wool and big knitting needles. The simple design accentuates the colors and texture of the yarn, while the eyelets at the hem and sleeve cuffs add visual interest.

SIZES after blocking XS (S, M, L, XL)
Chest: 80/31½" (84/33", 88/34¾", 92/36¼", 96/37¾")
Length to armhole: 39/15½" (40/15¾", 41/16", 42/16½", 43/17")
Sleeve length: 44/17¼" (45/17¾", 46/18", 47/18½", 48/18¾")

MATERIALS Einband 50g (1.7oz) balls 225m (245yd)
A 0151 black heather 2 (2, 2, 2, 2)
B 9076 tawny 1 (1,1, 1, 1)
C 1026 ash heather 1 (1,2, 2, 2)
D 9102 dark gray 1 (1,1, 1, 1)

6mm (US 10) circular needles 40 and 60–80cm (16 and 24–30in), 4mm (US 10) circular needle 40cm, 6mm (US 10) double pointed needles

BLOCKED GAUGE
10 x 10cm (4 x 4in) =15 sts and 24 rnds in st st on 6mm (US 10) needles.

NOTE
Body and sleeves are worked in the round from lower edge to underarms, then joined to work yoke in the round. Each round of the body begins on the left side of the sweater, but the yoke rounds begin where the back of the sweater meets the left sleeve.

BODY

With two strands of A using 6mm circular needle, CO 120 (126, 132, 138, 144) sts and join in the rnd. Cont with one strand, knit 5 rnds.

Work holes (2 rnds): *1st rnd: *k1, k2tog, yo twice, ssk, k1*, rep from *to* to end of rnd. 2nd rnd: *K2, knit into 1st yo, purl into 2nd yo, k2*, rep from *to* to end of rnd.

Knit 5 rnds.

1: Change to B, knit 2 rnds. Work holes (2 rnds). Knit 6 rnds.

2: Change to C, work holes (2 rnds). Knit 29 (30, 31, 32, 33) rnds.

3: Change to D, knit 10 (10, 11, 11, 11) rnds.

4: Change to A, knit 25 (26, 26, 27) 28) rnds.

5: Change to C, knit 8 (8, 9 ,(9, 9) rnds, or until body measures 39 (40, 41, 42, 43) cm from CO edge. Do not work last 4 (5, 5, 4, 5) sts of last rnd. Set aside and work sleeves.

SLEEVES

With two strands of A using 6mm needles, CO 36 (36, 42, 42, 42) sts. Join in the rnd and cont with one strand, knit 5 rnds. Work holes (2 rnds) as before.
Knit 5 rnds.

1: Change to B, knit 2 rnds. Work holes (2 rnds). Knit 6 rnds.

2: Change to C and work holes (2 rnds). Knit 35 (36, 37, 38, 39) rnds, at same time- Inc right after holes, 1 st after first st and 1 st before last st of rnd, then in 13th (11th, 16th, 14th, 12th) rnd, total 5 (6, 4, 5, 6) times up sleeve => 46 (48, 50, 52, 54) sts.

3: Change to D, work 12 (12, 13, 13, 13) rnds.

4: Change to A, work 29 (30, 30, 31, 32) rnds.

5: Change to C, work 8 (8, 9, 9, 9) rnds, or until sleeve measures 44 (45, 46, 47, 48) cm from CO edge.
Place 8 (9, 8, (8, 9) sts underarm on st holder => 43 (44, 45, 46, 47) sts.
Work second sleeve.

YOKE

Join body and sleeves as follows: With C using 6mm circular needle, place 4 (5, 5, 4, 5) last sts and 4 first sts of body on st holder for underarm. Knit 38 (39, 42, 44, 45) sts of first sleeve. Knit 52 (54, 57, 61, 63) sts for front, place next 8 (9, 8, 8, 9) sts of body on st holder for underarm. Knit 38 (39, 42, 44, 45) sts of second sleeve. Knit 52 (54, 57, 61, 63) sts for back => 180 (186, 198, 210, 216) sts on needle. Work color changes and dec's from chart as indicated. Change to shorter circular needle when necessary. When chart is complete => 60 (62, 66, 70, 72) sts.

Neck edge: Change to 4mm needle and BO knitwise with two strands of A. Neck should be wide.

FINISHING

Graft underarm sts carefully together, as the stitches are big, and weave in loose ends. Rinse sweater by hand in lukewarm water and squeeze out excess water with towel. Lay flat to dry in right shape and measurements.

Chart – yoke

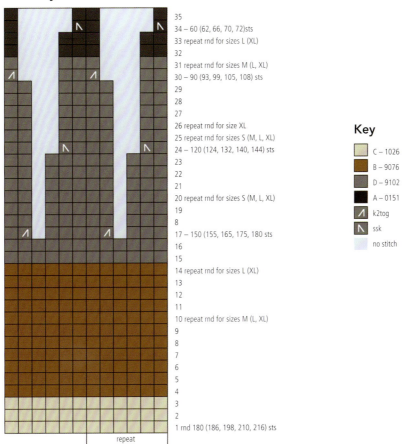

Key
- C – 1026
- B – 9076
- D – 9102
- A – 0151
- ⃫ k2tog
- ⃪ ssk
- no stitch

XS 80 cm
S 84 cm
M 88 cm
L 92 cm
XL 96 cm

XS 39 cm
S 40 cm
M 41 cm
L 42 cm
XL 43 cm

XS 44 cm
S 45 cm
M 46 cm
L 47 cm
XS 48 cm

NOTE: See sizes on page 117 for measurements in inches

kambur

A traditional, patterned sweater for busy kids. The yoke is decorated with a lovely chain-like pattern and the hat is designed to stay put on small heads.

SIZES – Sweater 1 (2, 3, 4) years
Chest: 58/22¾" (62/24½", 66/26", 71/28")
Length to armhole: 20/7¾" (22/8¾", 24/9½", 26/10¼")
Sleeve length: 22/8¾" (24/9½", 26/10¼", 28/11")

MATERIALS Létt-Lopi 50g (1.7oz) balls, 100m (109yd)
gray
A 0056 light gray 3 (3, 3, 4)
B 9418 stone blue 1 (1, 1, 2)
C 0051 white 1 (1, 1, 1)
D 0005 black heather 1 (1, 1, 1)

Green
A 1417 frostbite 3 (3, 3, 4)
B 1416 moor 1 (1, 1, 2)
C 0051 white 1 (1, 1, 1))
D 0052 black sheep 1 (1, 1, 1)

4.5mm and 3.5mm (US 7 and 4) circular needles 40 and 60cm (16 and 24in), 3.5mm and 4.5mm (US 4 and 7) double pointed needles

GAUGE
10 x 10cm (4 x 4in) = 18 sts and 24 rows in st st on 4.5mm (US 7) needles.

NOTE
Body and sleeves are worked in the round from lower edge to underarms, then joined to work yoke in the round. Each round of the body begins on the left side of the sweater, but the yoke rounds begin where the back of the sweater meets the left sleeve.

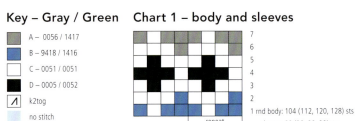

Key – Gray / Green

▨	A – 0056 / 1417
▨	B – 9418 / 1416
☐	C – 0051 / 0051
■	D – 0005 / 0052
╱	k2tog
	no stitch

Chart 1 – body and sleeves

1 rnd body: 104 (112, 120, 128) sts
sleeves: 28 (32, 32, 32) sts

BODY

CO 104 (112, 120, 128) sts with B using 3.5mm circular needle, join in the rnd and work *k1, p1* rib for 2 (2, 3, 3) cm. Change to 4.5mm circular needle and work in st st patt from **Chart 1**. When patt is complete cont with A until body measures 20 (22, 24, 26) cm from CO edge. Do not work last 3 (4, 4, 5) sts of body. Set aside and work sleeves.

SLEEVES

CO 28 (30, 32, 32) sts with B using 3.5mm dpns. Join in a cirlce and and work *k1, p1* rib for 2 (2, 3, 3) cm, size (2): inc 2 sts in last rnd. Change to 4.5mm dpns. Work in st st patt from **Chart 1** and inc 4 (2) 4 (4) sts in first rnd. Cont with A and inc 1 st after first st and 1 st before last st of rnd, then in every 5th (5th, 6th, 6th) rnd, 6 (6, 6, 7) times up sleeve => 44 (46, 48, 50) sts. Cont without further shaping until sleeve measures 22 (24, 26, 28) cm from CO edge. Place 6 (7, 8, 9) sts underarm on st holder => 38 (39, 40, 41) sts. Work second sleeve.

YOKE

Join body and sleeves as follows: With A using 4.5mm circular needle, place the last 3 (4, 4, 5) sts and the first 3 (3, 4, 4) sts of body on st holder for underarm. Knit 38 (39, 40, 41) sts of first sleeve. Knit 46 (49, 52, 55) sts for front, place next 6 (7, 8, 9) sts of body on st holder for underarm. Knit 38 (39, 40, 41) sts of second sleeve. Knit 46 (49, 52, 55) sts for back => 168 (176, 184, 192) sts. Work patt and dec's from Chart 2 as indicated. Change to shorter needle/dpns when necessary. When chart is complete => 63 (66, 69, 72) sts.

NECKBAND

Change to 3.5mm dpns and cont with B, dec evenly spaced 7 (8, 7, 8) sts => 56 (58, 62, 64) sts. Work *k1, p1* rib for 4 (4, 4, 5) cm. BO loosely.

FINISHING

Graft underarm sts tog and weave in loose ends. Fold neckband in half to inside and slip stitch in place. Rinse sweater by hand in lukewarm water and lay flat to dry.

1 22 cm
2 24 cm
3 26 cm
4 28 cm

1 58 cm
2 62 cm
3 66 cm
4 71 cm

1 20 cm
2 22 cm
3 24 cm
4 26 cm

NOTE: See sizes on page 121 for measurements in inches

Chart 2 – yoke

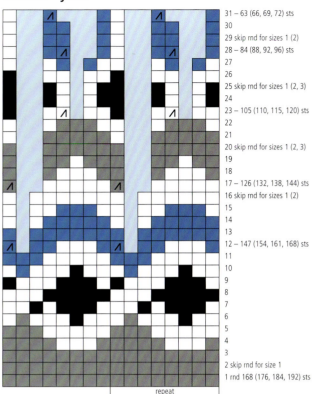

31 – 63 (66, 69, 72) sts
30
29 skip rnd for sizes 1 (2)
28 – 84 (88, 92, 96) sts
27
26
25 skip rnd for sizes 1 (2, 3)
24
23 – 105 (110, 115, 120) sts
22
21
20 skip rnd for sizes 1 (2, 3)
19
18
17 – 126 (132, 138, 144) sts
16 skip rnd for sizes 1 (2)
15
14
13
12 – 147 (154, 161, 168) sts
11
10
9
8
7
6
5
4
3
2 skip rnd for size 1
1 rnd 168 (176, 184, 192) sts

repeat

Chart – Hat

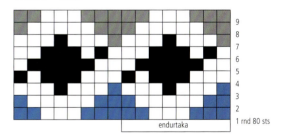

9
8
7
6
5
4
3
2
1 rnd 80 sts

endurtaka

HAT

CO 80 sts with B using 3.5mm circular needle. Join in the rnd and work *k1, p1* rib for 20 rnds. Change to 4.5mm circular needle and knit 2 rnds. Work in st st patt from chart for 9 rnds. Cont with A for 12 rnds.

SIZE – Hat 2–4 years

MATERIALS Létt-Lopi 50g (1.7oz) balls, 100m (109yd)

gray
A 0056 light gray 1
B 9418 stone blue 1
C 0051 white 1
D 0005 black heather 1

Green
A 1417 frostbite 1
B 1416 moor 1
C 0051 white 1
D 0052 black sheep 1

4.5mm and 3.5mm (US 7and 4) circular needles 40cm (16in), 4.5mm (US 7) double pointed needles

GAUGE

10 x 10cm (4 x 4in) = 18 sts and 24 rows in st st on 4.5mm (US 7) needles.

Shape top:
1st dec rnd: *k8, k2tog*, rep around.
Knit 1 rnd.
2nd dec rnd: *k7, k2tog*, rep around.
Knit 1 rnd.
3rd dec rnd: *k6, k2tog*, rep around.
4th dec rnd: *k5, k2tog*, rep around.
5th dec rnd: *k4, k2tog*, rep around.
6th dec rnd: *k3, k2tog*, rep around.
7th dec rnd: *k2, k2tog*, rep around.
8th dec rnd: *k1, k2tog*, rep around.
Break yarn and pull through rem sts.

FINISHING

Weave in loose ends. Rinse by hand in lukewarm water, fold rib in half and lay flat to dry.

keðja

The pattern for this dress includes instructions for two lengths. The classic Keðja color pattern is incorporated in a unique, modern garment.

SIZES S (M, L, XL)
Chest: 82/32¼" (91/35¾", 100/39½", 109/43")
Width lower edge: 115/45¼" (124/48¾", 133/52½", 142/56")
Length to armhole short: 58/22¾" (60/23¾", 62/24½", 64/25")
Length to armhole long: 68/26¾" (70/27½" 72/28¼", 74/29")
Sleeve length to underarm: 44/17½" (46/18", 48/19", 49/19¼")

MATERIALS Létt-Lopi 50g (1.7oz) balls, 100m (109yd)
A 0059 black short: 9 (10, 10, 11)
             long: 10 (11, 11, 12)
B 1402 heaven blue 1 (1, 1, 1)
C 1406 spring green 1 (1, 1, 1)
D 1411 sun yellow 1 (1, 1, 1)
E 1410 orange 1 (1, 1, 1)
F 1408 light red 1 (1, 1, 1)
G 1412 pink heather 1 (1, 1, 1)
H 1404 glacier blue 1 (1, 1, 1)
I 1413 lilac 1 (1, 1, 1)

4.5mm (US 7) circular needles 40 and 60–80cm (16 and 24–30in), 3.5mm (US 4) circular needle 40 and 80cm, 3.5mm and 4.5mm (US 4 and 7) double pointed needles, markers

GAUGE
10 x 10cm (4 x 4in) = 18 sts and 24 rows in st st using 4.5mm (US 7) needles.

NOTE
Body and sleeves are worked in the round from lower edge to underarms, then joined to work yoke in the round. Each round of the body begins on the left side of the sweater, but the yoke rounds begin where the back of the sweater meets the left sleeve.

Next rnd: dec evenly spaced 8 sts => 152 (168, 184, 200) sts. Knit 6 rnds. Dec 2 sts on either side of body => 148 (164, 180, 196) sts. Work until body measures 58 (60, 62, 64) cm from CO edge.

Long: Knit 12cm. Dec evenly spaced on rnd 16 sts => 192 (208, 224, 240) sts. Knit 5 (6, 7, 8) cm. Place marker on either side of body and dec on each side of marker Sl1, k1, psso, k2tog (2 sts), then in every í 13th (13th, 14th, 14th) rnd, total 8 times => 160 (176, 192, 208) sts. Knit 6 rnds.

Next rnd: dec evenly spaced 8 sts => 152 (168, 184, 200) sts. Knit 6 rnds. Dec 2 sts on either side of body => 148 (164, 180, 196) sts. Work until body measures 68 (70, 72, 74) cm from CO edge. Do not work 5 (6, 6, 7) last sts of body. Set aside and work sleeves.

BODY

CO 208 (224, 240, 256) sts with A using 3.5mm circular needle. Work garter st back and forth for 5 rows (making 3 ridges). Change to 4.5mm circular needle, join in the rnd and work in st st.

Short: Work from **Chart 1**. When complete cont with A and knit 1 rnd. Next rnd: dec evenly spaced 16 sts => 192 (208, 224, 240) sts. Work 5 (6, 7, 8) cm. Place marker on either side of body. Dec 2 sts on each side of marker: Sl1, k1, psso, k2tog, then in every 12th rnd, total 8 times => 160 (176, 192, 208) sts. Knit 5 rnds.

SLEEVES

CO 40 (48, 48, 48) sts with A using 3.5mm dpns. Work garter st back and forth for 5 rows (making 3 ridges). Change to 4.5mm dpns and join in the rnd. Work in st st from **Chart 1**. When complete cont with A and inc 1 st after first st and 1 st before last st of rnd, then in every 9th (12th, 11th, 10th) rnd total 9 (7, 8, 9) times up sleeve => 58 (62, 64, 66) sts. Cont without further shaping until sleeve measures 44 (46, 48, 49) cm from CO edge. Place 10 (12, 13, 14) sts underarm on st holder => 48 (50, 51, 52) sts. Work second sleeve.

Chart 1 – body and sleeves

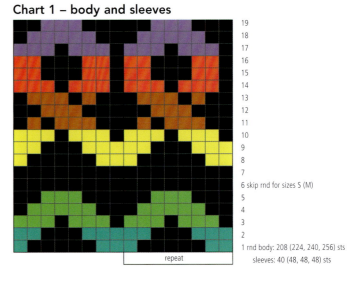

6 skip rnd for sizes S (M)

1 rnd body: 208 (224, 240, 256) sts
sleeves: 40 (48, 48, 48) sts

repeat

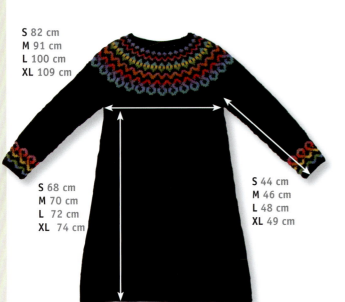

S 82 cm
M 91 cm
L 100 cm
XL 109 cm

S 68 cm
M 70 cm
L 72 cm
XL 74 cm

S 44 cm
M 46 cm
L 48 cm
XL 49 cm

NOTE: See sizes on page 125 for measurements in inches

YOKE

Join body and sleeves as follows: With A using 4.5mm circular needle, place the last 5 (6, 6, 7) sts and the first 5 (6, 7, 7) sts of body on st holder for underarm. Knit 48 (50, 51, 52) sts of first sleeve. Knit 64 (70, 77, 84) sts for front, place next 10 (12, 13, 14) sts of body on st holder for underarm. Knit 48 (50, 51, 52) sts of second sleeve. Knit 64 (70, 77, 84) sts for back => 224 (240, 256, 272) sts. Work patt and dec's from **Chart 2** as indicated. Change to shorter circular needle when necessary. When chart is complete => 84 (90, 96, 102) sts. Short rows at back: Cont with A. Place marker at beg of rnd. When turning, always wrap yarn around the next st that is not knitted to prevent hole.

Row 1: Work 24 (27, 30, 33) sts back, turn.
Row 2: Knit 27 (3, 33, 36) sts, turn.
Row 3: Work 30 (33, 36, 39) sts back, turn.
Row 4: Knit to beg of rnd.

NECKBAND

Change to 3.5mm needle. With A, knit 1 rnd and dec evenly spaced 10 (12, 14, 16) sts => 74 (78, 82, 86) sts. Purl 1 rnd. Knit 1 rnd. BO purlwise.

FINISHING

Graft underarm sts tog and sew garter st ridges at edges together. Weave in loose ends. Rinse dress by hand in lukewarm water and lay flat to dry.

Key – Color / Black and white

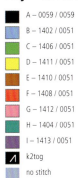

A – 0059 / 0059
B – 1402 / 0051
C – 1406 / 0051
D – 1411 / 0051
E – 1410 / 0051
F – 1408 / 0051
G – 1412 / 0051
H – 1404 / 0051
I – 1413 / 0051
k2tog
no stitch

Chart 2 – yoke

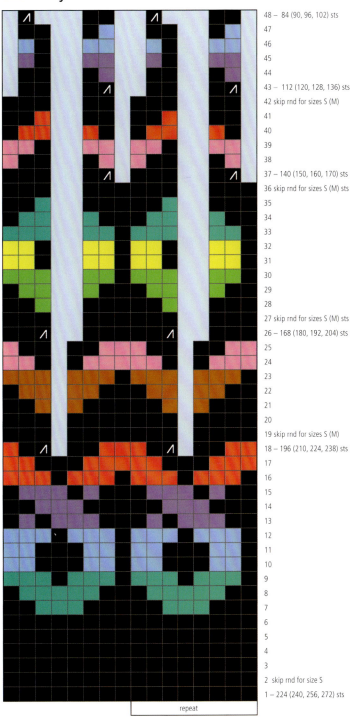

klukka

This pattern is inspired by vintage Icelandic knitted slips that young ladies would wear under their dresses for warmth. The lace edging at the hem adds an extra touch of femininity.

SIZES S (M, L, XL)
Chest: 80/31½" (84/33", 88/34¾", 93/36½")
Width (lower edge): 91/35¾", (93/36½", 96/37¾", 98/38½")
Length: 142/56" (146/54½", 151/60", 155/61")

MATERIALS Létt-Lopi 50g (1.7oz) balls, 100m (109yd)
A 0056 gray 7 (7, 8, 9)
B 0051 white 2 (2, 2, 2)
C 0059 black 1 (1, 1, 1)
D 1406 spring green 1 (1, 1, 1)
E 1408 light red 1 (1, 1, 1)

4.5mm (US 7) circular needles 60 and 80–100cm (24 and 30–40in), 3.5mm (US 4) circular needle 60cm, 3.5mm (US E/4) crochet hook, markers

GAUGE
10 x 10cm (4 x 4in) = 18 sts and 24 rows in st st on 4.5mm (US 7) needles.

NOTE
The dress is worked in the round to armholes, then back and front are worked separately. Crochet around neck and armholes.

DRESS

CO very loosely with B using 4.5mm circular needle => 258 (264, 276, 282) sts. Join in the rnd and work large eyelet rib:

Rnd 1: *p2, k4*, rep from *to* to end.
Rnd 2: *p2, k2tog, yo 2 times, Sl1, k1, psso*, rep from *to* to end.
Rnd 3: *p2, k1, knit into 1st yo, purl into 2nd yo, k1*, rep from *to* to end.
Rnd 4: *p2, k4*, rep from *to* to end.
Rep rnd 1-4, 4 (4, 5, 5) times (vertical row of 5 (5, 6, 6) holes).

Knit 1 rnd and dec evenly spaced 2 (0, 4, 2) sts => 256 (264, 272, 280) sts.

Work in st st patt from chart.

When patt is complete, change to A. Divide the piece into 8 equal parts: 32 (33, 34, 35) sts and place marker after each.

Next rnd: knit and dec 1 st at each marker, then 2 sts (Sl1, k1, psso, k2tog) on each side of marker every 10th rnd, 8 times up to waist => 120 (128, 136, 144) sts. Work until piece measures 49 (50, 52, 53) cm. (Work more/less rnds between dec's if you like the dress longer/shorter).

Change to 3.5mm circular needle and work *k1, p1* rib for 10cm.

Change back to 4.5mm circular needle and work in st st.

Increases:
1: Knit 14 (15, 16, 17) sts, M1R, k1, place marker, k1, M1L, knit 28 (30, 32, 34) sts.
2: M1R, k1, place marker, k1, M1L, k28 (30, 32, 34) sts.
3: M1R, k1, place marker, k1, M1L, k28 (30, 32, 34) sts.
4: M1R, k1, place marker, k1, M1L, k14 (15, 16, 17) sts.
Knit 6 rnds, rep inc at each marker as before, then work another 6 rnds and inc as before => 144 (152, 160, 168) sts. Work until body measures 13 (14), 14, 15) cm from waist rib to armhole.

Do not work last 6 (7, 7, 8) sts of last rnd. BO 12 (14, 14, 16) sts, k 60 (62, 66, 68) sts (front), BO 12 (14, 14, 16) sts, k 60 (62, 66, 68) sts (back). Now work back and forth.

Armhole shaping back: Dec 1 st every other row 5 times => 50 (52, 56, 58) sts. Work until armhole measures 17 (17, 18, 18) cm.

Neck shaping RS: Knit 15 (16, 17, 18) sts, BO center 20 (20, 22, 22) sts, knit to end. Work both sides, dec 1 st at each neck edge every other row 2 times => 13 (14, 15, 16) sts. Work 1 row, BO.

Armhole shaping front: 60 (62, 66, 68) sts. Dec 1 st every other row 5 times => 50 (52, 56, 58) sts. Work until armhole measures 6cm.

Chart

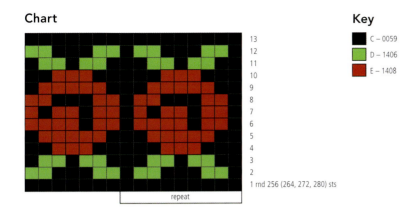

1 rnd 256 (264, 272, 280) sts

Key

- ■ C – 0059
- ■ D – 1406
- ■ E – 1408

NOTE: See sizes on page 129 for measurements in inches

S 80 cm
M 84 cm
L 88 cm
XL 93 cm

S 91 cm
M 93 cm
L 96 cm
XL 98 cm

Neck shaping RS: Knit 15 (16, 17, 18) sts, BO center 20 (20, 22, 22) sts, work to end. Work both sides, dec 1 st every other row at each neck edge 2 times => 13 (14, 15, 16) sts. Work without further shaping 13 (13, 14, 14) cm. Keep sts on needle.

FINISHING

Graft shoulders tog from RS.

Armhole and neck: With A and 3.5mm crochet hook, sc 2 rnds around neck and armholes. Weave in loose ends.

Rinse dress by hand in lukewarm water and lay flat to dry.

kría

A lovely matching set that incorporates a simple, traditional Icelandic color pattern. The hat is a perfect fit for small heads and can be knitted in red at Christmas for a cute, personalized version of a Santa hat.

SIZES – Cardigan 1 (1–2, 2–3, 3–4) years
Chest: 55/21¾" (59/23¼", 64/25", 68/26¾")
Width lower edge: 58/22¾" (62/24½", 67/26½", 71/28")
Length to armhole: 18/7" (20/7¾", 22/8¾", 24/9½")
Sleeve length: 20/7¾" (22/8¾", 24/9½", 26/10¼")
SIZES – Hat – 2–4 years

MATERIALS
Cardigan Létt-Lopi 50g (1.7oz) balls, 100m (109yd)
A 1412 pink 3 (3, 4, 4)
B 0005 black heather 1 (1, 1, 1)
C 0051 white 1 (1, 1, 1)

4.5mm and 3.5mm (US 7 and 4) circular needles 40 and 60cm (16 and 24in), 3.5mm and 4.5mm (US 4 and 7) double pointed needles, zipper, markers

Hat Létt-Lopi 50g (1.07oz) balls, 100m (109yd)
A 1412 pink 1
B 0005 black heather 1
C 0051 white 1

3.5mm and 4.5mm (US 4 and 7) circular needles 40cm (16in), 4.5mm (US 7) double pointed needles

GAUGE for cardigan and hat
10 x 10cm (4 x 4in) = 18 sts and 24 rows in st st on 4.5mm (US 7) needles.

NOTE
Body and sleeves are worked in the round from lower edge to underarms, then joined to work yoke in the round. Round begins and ends with a purl st at front of body. The front is cut open. The hat is worked in the round, first with circular needles then double pointed needles. Moss stitch: See page 250.

BODY

CO 105 (113, 121, 129) sts with A using 3.5mm circular needle. Work back and forth in moss st for 4 rows. Change to 4.5mm circular needle, CO 2 sts (P first and last st of rnd) and join in the rnd => 107 (115, 123, 131) sts. Work in st st patt from **Chart 1**. When patt is complete cont with A and place marker on either side of body. Work 10cm from CO edge, dec 2 sts on each side of marker: ssk , k2tog (see page 259). Dec again 15 (16, 17, 18) cm from edge, total 8 sts => 99 (107, 115, 123) sts. Work until body measures 18 (20, 22, 24) cm from CO edge. Set aside and work sleeves.

SLEEVES

CO 28 (28, 32, 32) sts with A using 3.5mm dpns. Join in the rnd and work in moss st 4 rnds. Change to 4.5mm dpns and work in st st patt from **Chart 1**. When patt is complete cont with A and inc 4 sts evenly spaced on rnd. Then inc 1 st after first st and 1 st before last st of rnd in every 6th (5th, 7th, 7th) rnd, 5 (6, 5, 6) times up sleeve => 42 (44, 46, 48) sts. Cont without further shaping until sleeve measures 20 (22, 24, 26) cm from CO edge. Place 5 (6, 7, 8) sts underarm on st holder => 37 (38, 39, 40) sts.
Work second sleeve.

YOKE

Join body and sleeves as follows: With A using 4.5mm circular needle, work right front (beg with purl st) 22 (24, 25, 27) sts, place next 5 (6, 7, 8) sts of body on st holder for underarm. Knit 37 (38, 39, 40) sts of first sleeve. Knit 45 (47, 51, 53) sts of back, place next 5 (6, 7, 8) sts of body on st holder for underarm. Knit 37 (38, 39, 40) sts of second sleeve. Work left front 22 (24, 25, 27) sts, (end with purl st) => 163 (171, 179, 187) sts. Work patt and dec's from Chart 2 as indicated. Change to shorter needle when necessary. When chart is complete => 64 (67, 70, 73) sts.

NECKBAND

Change to 3.5mm needle. With A BO purl st, knit 1 rnd and dec evenly spaced 7 (8, 9, 10) sts, BO end purl st => 55 (57, 59, 61) sts. Now work back and forth in moss st for 4 rows. Next row WS: knit 1 row. Next row RS: Work in st st for 3 rows. BO loosely.

FINISHING

Graft underarm sts tog. Weave in loose ends but pull the ends by the purl st chain to RS. Sew by machine using straight small stitches across the ends as you sew twice through each chain of purl sts up body front. Rinse cardigan by hand in lukewarm water and lay flat to dry.
Zipper: See page 257.

NOTE: See sizes on page 133 for measurements in inches

1 55 cm
1-2 59 cm
2-3 64 cm
3-4 68 cm

1 20 cm
1-2 22 cm
2-3 24 cm
3-4 26 cm

1 18 cm
1-2 20 cm
2-3 22 cm
3-4 24 cm

Chart 1 – body and sleeves

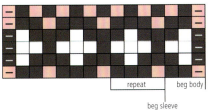

Key

- A – 1412
- B – 0005
- C – 0051
- purl
- k2tog
- ssk
- no stitch

Chart – hat

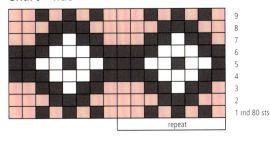

Chart 2 – yoke

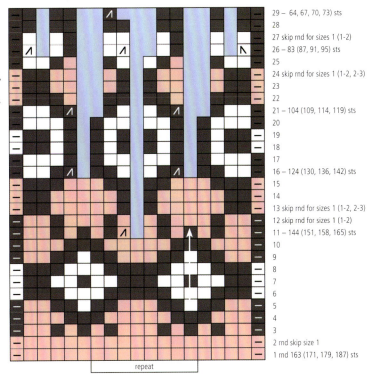

HAT

CO 80 sts with B using 3.5mm circular needle. Join in the rnd and work *k1, p1* rib for 20 rnds. Change to 4.5mm circular needle and knit 2 rnds. Work in st st patt from chart for 9 rnds. Cont with A for 10 rnds.

Shape top:

1st dec rnd: *k8, k2tog*, rep around.

Knit 5 rnds.

2nd dec rnd: *k7, k2tog*, rep around.

Knit 5 rnds.

3rd dec rnd: *k6, k2tog*, rep around.

Knit 5 rnds.

4th dec rnd: *k5, k2tog*, rep around.

Knit 5 rnds.

5th dec rnd: *k4, k2tog*, rep around.

Knit 5 rnds.

6th dec rnd: *k3, k2tog*, rep around.

Knit 5 rnds.

7th dec rnd: *k2, k2tog*, rep around.

Knit 5 rnds.

8th dec rnd: *k1, k2tog*, rep around.

Knit 5 rnds.

9th dec rnd: *k2tog *, rep around.

Break yarn and pull through rem sts.

FINISHING

Weave in loose ends. Rinse by hand in lukewarm water, fold rib in half and lay flat to dry.

Pom-pom: Make round templates approx 4cm (1¾in) in diameter with a 1.5cm (¾in) hole in the middle. See further information on making pompoms, page 258. Make one pom-pom with C. Roll it between your hand to fatten it a bit and fasten to top of hat.

kross

This simple sweater, knitted at a loose gauge, is decorated with a crossed-stitch pattern called an Indian cross.

SIZES XS/S, (M, L, XL)
Chest: 80/31½" (88/34¾" 96/37¾", 104/41")
Length to armhole: 38/15" (40/15¾", 41/16", 42/16½")
Sleeve length: 44/17¼" (45/17¾", 46/18", 47/18½")

MATERIALS Létt-Lopi 50g (1.7oz) balls, 100m (109yd)
A 0052 black sheep heather 1 (1, 1, 1)
B 0867 chocolate heather 1 (1, 1, 1)
C 1420 murky 1 (1, 1, 1)
D 1419 barley 1 (1, 1, 1)
E 1418 straw 6 (6, 7, 7)

6.5mm (US 10.5) circular needles 40 and 80cm (16 and 30in), 5.5mm (US 9) circular needle 80cm, 4.5mm (US 7) circular needle 40cm, 5.5mm and 6.5mm (US 9 and 10.5) double pointed needles

GAUGE
10 x 10cm (4 x 4in) = 15 sts and 20 rows in st st on 6.5mm (US 10.5) needles.

NOTE
Body and sleeves are worked in the round from lower edge to underarms, then joined to work yoke in the round. Each round of the body begins on the left side of the sweater, but the yoke rounds begin where the back of the sweater meets the left sleeve.

BODY

CO loosely 120 (132, 144, 156) sts with A using 5.5mm circular needle. Join in the rnd and work *k1, p1* rib for 2cm. Change to 6.5mm circular needle and knit 2 rnds.

Cross:

**Change to B.

1. *yo twice, k1*, rep from *to* to end of rnd.

2. *Slip the knitted stitch to right needle and drop the yo's*, do not knit the st. This creates a loopy elongated stitch. Rep from *to* to end of rnd.

Change to C and work crosses, each cross is 6 sts:

3. With right needle pull together sts number 1, 2, 3, over sts 4, 5, 6. Arrange sts and knit all 6 stitches in the new order of 4, 5, 6 then 1, 2, 3. Rep to end of rnd. Knit total 4 rnds with C.

Change to D and rep part 1.-2.

Change to E and rep part 3.

Cont with E until body measures 38 (40, 41, 42) cm from CO edge.

SLEEVES

CO loosely 36 (36, 42, 42) sts with A using 5.5mm dpns. Join in the rnd and work *k1, p1* rib for 2cm. Change to 6.5mm dpns and knit 2 rnds. Now work crosses: Rep from **to** (see body) and inc 1 st in in last rnd. Now inc 1 st after first st and 1 st before last st of rnd, then in every 13th (9th, 14th, 12th) rnd total 5 (7, 5, 6) times up sleeve => 47 (51, 53, 55) sts. Cont with E and inc as described until sleeve measures 44 (45, 46, 47) cm from CO edge.

Place 7 (9) 10 (11) sts underarm on st holder => 40 (42, 43, 44) sts.

Work second sleeve.

NOTE: See sizes on page 137 for measurements in inches

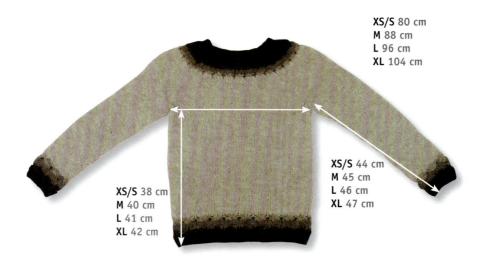

XS/S 80 cm
M 88 cm
L 96 cm
XL 104 cm

XS/S 38 cm
M 40 cm
L 41 cm
XL 42 cm

XS/S 44 cm
M 45 cm
L 46 cm
XL 47 cm

YOKE

Join body and sleeves as follows: with E, using 6.5mm circular needle, place the last 4 (5, 5, 6) sts and the first 3 (4, 5, 5) sts of body on st holder for underarm. Knit 40 (42, 43, 44) sts of first sleeve. Knit 53 (57, 62, 67) sts for front, place next 7 (9, 10, 11) sts of body on st holder for underarm. Knit 40 (42, 43, 44) sts of second sleeve. Knit 53 (57, 62, 67) sts for back => 186 (198, 210, 222) sts. Work patt and dec's from chart as indicated. Change to shorter circular needle when necessary. Change to E.

1. *yo once, k1*, rep from *to* to end of rnd.
2. *Slip the knitted stitch to right needle and drop the yo*, do not knit the st, rep from *to* to end of rnd. Change to C and work crosses, each cross is 4 sts:
3. With right needle pull together sts number 1, 2, over sts 3, 4. Arrange sts and knit all 4 stitches in the new order of 3, 4, then 1, 2. Rep to end of rnd.

Work total 3 rnds with C.
Change to B and rep small cross part 1.-2.
Change to A and rep small cross part 3.
Cont working dec from chart.
When chart is complete => 62 (66, 70, 74) sts.

NECKBAND

Change to 4.5 needle and cont with A. Work *k1, p1* rib for 2cm. BO in rib.

FINISHING

Graft underarm sts tog and weave in loose ends. Rinse sweater by hand in lukewarm water and lay flat to dry.

Chart

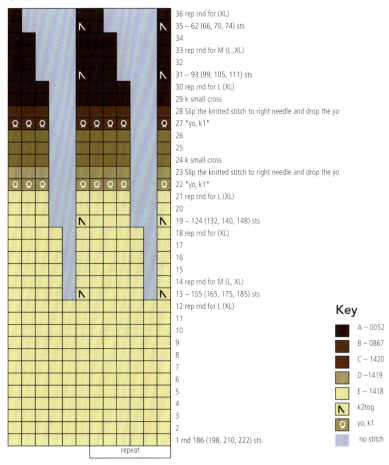

36 rep rnd for (XL)
35 – 62 (66, 70, 74) sts
34
33 rep rnd for M (L, XL)
32
31 – 93 (99, 105, 111) sts
30 rep rnd for L (XL)
29 k small cross
28 Slip the knitted stitch to right needle and drop the yo
27 *yo, k1*
26
25
24 k small cross
23 Slip the knitted stitch to right needle and drop the yo
22 *yo, k1*
21 rep rnd for L (XL)
20
19 – 124 (132, 140, 148) sts
18 rep rnd for (XL)
17
16
15
14 rep rnd for M (L, XL)
13 – 155 (165, 175, 185) sts
12 rep rnd for L (XL)
11
10
9
8
7
6
5
4
3
2
1 rnd 186 (198, 210, 222) sts

repeat

Key

- A – 0052
- B – 0867
- C – 1420
- D – 1419
- E – 1418
- k2tog
- yo, k1
- no stitch

lamb and bjalla

This balaclava will keep the ears and neck warm in the cold winter months. The mittens have an extra long cuff to prevent cold winds from reaching little hands.

LAMB – balaclava

CO 44 (46, 48) sts loosely with A on 5mm needles. Knit in a brioche stitch back and forth: See Note.
Knit 20 (22, 24) rows in all. Change to 4mm needles and join in the rnd. Knit ribbing: *k1, p1* (matching the position of the brioche stitches), 12 (12, 14) rnds.
Change to 5mm and st st:
Row 1: Inc 6 st evenly over the 1st 17 (18, 19) sts, BO 10 st for the face and inc 6 sts evenly over the last 17 (18, 19) sts => 46 (48, 50) st. The join is in the back.
Row 2: Place a marker at each side of the centre 12 sts in the back. Inc 1 sts to the left of the 1st marker and 1 st to the right of the second marker every other row, 4 times => 54 (56, 58) st (the number of stitches between the markers increases). After 6 rows from the ribbing

change to B. Knit 11 (12, 13) cm from the BO for the face opening.

Row 3: CO 10 sts over the face opening and join in the rnd (the join is still in the back). Knit 5 (6, 7) rnds with B. Change to C and knit 7 (7, 8) rnds.

Next rnd: Change to 4mm needles 4 and dec 8 (10, 12) sts evenly over the rnd. Knit in rib *k1,p1*, for 6 rnds.

Next rnd: *k2tog* rep. to the end of the rnd. Break yarn and thread the end though the rem sts. Weave in ends. Crochet a rnd of DC and color A around the face opening, in every other row at the sides and in every st at the top and bottom. Sew together the brioche stitch on the RS and weave in ends.

BJALLA – mittens

Right mitten

CO 32 (34, 36) sts with A on 4mm needles. Knit back and forth.

Row 1: *k1, yo, sl1 purlwise*, rep *from* to the end of row. Turn.

Row 2: *k1tog with the yo of the previous row, yo, sl1 (the knit st from the previous row) *, from *to* , to the end of the row. Turn.

Knit 20 rows. Change to 4mm needles and join in the rnd. Dec 8 (6, 6) sts evenly in the 1st rnd => 24 (28, 30) sts. Divide the sts evenly on 4 needles and knit 4 rows ribbing *k1, p1*. Change to 4mm needles and B. Knit 7 (9, 11) rows st st.

Place thumb: k1, knit next 4 (4, 5) sts on waste yarn, place these stitches back on the left needle and knit them again, continue to end of rnd. Knit 8 (10, 12) rnds. Change to C and knit 5 (6, 7) rnds.

Dec 2 sts every 2 rnds:

Needles 1 and 3: Sl1, k1, psso, knit to end.

Needles 2 and 4: Knit until 2 sts are left, k2tog.

Then dec every rnd until 4 sts are left. Break yarn and thread through these 4 sts.

Thumb: Pull out the waste yarn and pick up 9 (10, 12) sts. Knit 8 (10, 12) rnds.

k1, k2tog rep until 4 sts are left. Break yarn and thread through these 4 sts.

SIZES Lamb – Balaclava 2 (4, 6) years

MATERIAL

Álafoss Lopi 100g (3.5oz) balls, 100m (109yd)
A 9987 dark olive 1 (1, 1)
B 9972 ecru heather 1 (1, 1)
C 1230 green moss 1 (1, 1)

4mm and 5mm (US 6 and 8) circular needles,
4mm (US 6) double pointed needles

GAUGE

10 x 10cm (4 x 4in) = 14 sts and 22 rows in st st on 5mm (US 8) needles.

SIZES Bjalla – Mittens 2 (4, 6) years

MATERIAL

Létt-Lopi 50g (1.7oz) balls, 100m (109yd)
A 1407 pine green heather 1 (1, 1
B 1418 straw 1 (1, 1)
C 1417 frostbite 1 (1, 1)

3.5mm and 4mm (US 4 and 6) double pointed needles.

NOTE

Brioche stitch. See page 250.

Left mitten

Knit like the right mitten except the thumb is on the left side of the palm: Knit until 5 (5, 6) sts are left on needle 2, knit 4 (4, 5) sts on waste yarn.

FINISHING

Sew the brioche stitch tog on RS. Weave in all ends. Wash and block the mittens.

land

A particularly feminine sweater jacket knitted using two strands of unspun Icelandic wool. The colors interpret the Icelandic mountains.

SIZES XS (S, M, L, XL)
Chest: 89/35" (95/37½", 100/39½", 107/42", 112/44")
Width at lower edge: 112/44" (118/46½", 123/48½", 129/50¾", 135/53")
Length to armhole: 60/23¾" (62/24½", 64/25", 66/26", 68/26¾")
Sleeve length: 45/17¾" (46/18", 47/18½", 48/18¾", 49/19¼")

MATERIALS Plötulopi approx 100g (3.5oz) plates, 300m (328yd)
A 0059 black 2 (2, 2, 2, 2)
B 0709 midnight blue 1 (1, 1, 1, 1)
C 0118 navy 1 (1, 1, 1, 1)
D 1432 winter blue heather 1 (1, 1, 1, 1)
E 1052 denim heather 1 (1, 1, 1, 1)
F 1053 faded denim heather 1 (1, 1, 1, 1)
G 0001 white 2 (2, 2, 2, 2)

5.5mm (US 9) circular needles 40 and 80cm (16 and 30in), 4.5mm (US 7) circular needle 80cm, 4.5mm and 5.5mm (US 7 and 9) double pointed needles, 5 hooks and bars or clasps, thin ribbon 2.5cm (1in) wide and 170 (175, 180, 185, 190)cm (67, 69, 71, 73, 75in) long, markers

GAUGE
2-ply Plötulopi: 10 x 10cm (4 x 4in) = 14 sts and 19 rows in st st on 5.5mm (US 9) needles.

NOTE
Jacket is knitted in 2 strands of plötulopi. Body and sleeves are worked in the round from lower edge to underarms, then joined to work yoke in the round. Round begins and ends with a purl st at front of body. The front is cut open. See page 251.
Knit from the plates or carefully wind two strands of wool together for each color. If you like the jacket to have zip or crochet buttonband reduce 6 sts from body front.

BODY

CO 162 (170, 178, 186, 194) sts with **A+A** using 4.5mm circular needle. Work back and forth in st st 6 rows. RS: Purl 1 row. Work 6 rows in st st. Change to 5.5mm circular needle. CO 2 sts (p first and last st of rnd) and join in the rnd => 164 (172, 180, 188, 196) sts.

Color changes and dec:

1: Cont in st st with A+A work 11cm from purl row.

2: Change to A+B, work 10 (11, 11, 12, 12) cm.

1. Dec: Dec 8 sts as foll and place marker at each dec:

work 15 (15, 16, 16, 17) sts,

*1: Sl1, k1, psso, work 24 (26, 27, 29, 30) sts

2: k2tog

3: Sl1, k1, psso, work 24 (26, 27, 29, 30) sts

4: k2tog* work 22 (22, 24, 24, 26) sts (back)

rep from *to*, work 15 (15, 16, 16, 17) sts.

3: Change to B+C, work 10 (11, 11, 11, 12) cm.

2. Dec: Dec 8 sts as foll:

work 15 (15, 16, 16, 17) sts,

*1: Sl1, k1, psso, work 22 (24, 25, 27, 28) sts

2: k2tog

3: Sl1, k1, psso, work 22 (24, 25, 27, 28) sts

4: k2tog* work 22 (22, 24, 24, 26) sts (back)

rep from *to*, work 15 (15, 16, 16, 17) sts.

4: Change to C+D, work 10 (10, 11, 11, 12) cm.

3. Dec: Dec 8 sts as foll:

work 15 (15, 16, 16, 17) sts,

*1: Sl1, k1, psso, work 20 (22, 23, 25, 26) sts

2: k2tog

3: Sl1, k1, psso, work 20 (22, 23, 25, 26) sts

4: k2tog* work 22 (22, 24, 24, 26) sts (back)

rep from *to*, work 15 (15, 16, 16, 17) sts.

5: Change to D+E, work 10 (10, 11, 11, 11) cm.

4. Dec: Dec 8 sts as foll:

work 15 (15, 16, 16, 17) sts,

*1: Sl1, k1, psso, work 18 (20, 21, 23, 24) sts

2: k2tog

3: Sl1, k1, psso, work 18 (20, 21, 23, 24) sts

4: k2tog* work 22 (22, 24, 24, 26) sts (back) rep from *to*, work 15 (15, 16, 16, 17) sts => 132 (140, 148, 156, 164) sts.

6: Change to E+F, work to armhole until body measures 60 (62, 64, 66, 68) cm from purl row.

Do not break yarn, set aside and work sleeves.

SLEEVES

CO 34 (34, 36, 38, 40) sts with **A+A** using 4.5mm dpns. Join in the rnd and knit 6 rnds. Purl 1 rnd. Knit 6 rnds. Change to 5.5mm needles and cont in st st. Inc 1 st after first st and 1 st before last st of rnd every 12th (12th, 12th, 13th, 13th) rnd (from purl rnd) 6 times up sleeve => 46 (46, 48, 50, 52) sts. Change colors at same time.

Color changes:

1: Cont with **A+A**, work 7 (7, 7, 8, 8) cm from purl rnd.

2: Change to **A+B**, work 8cm.

3: Change to **B+C**, work 8cm.

4: Change to **C+D**, work 8cm.

5: Change to **D+E**, work 7 (8, 8, 8, 9) cm.

6: Change to **E+F**, and work until sleeve measures 45 (46, 47, 48, 49) cm from purl rnd. Place 7 (7, 8, 9, 10) sts underarm on st holder => 39 (39, 40, 41, 42) sts. Work second sleeve.

YOKE

Join body and sleeves as follows: With **E+F** and 5.5mm circular needle, work right front (beg p1) 33 (35, 36, 37, 39) sts, place next 7 (7, 8, 9, 10) sts of body on st holder for underarm. Knit 39 (39, 40, 41, 42) sts of first sleeve. Knit 52 (56, 60, 64, 66) sts of back, place next 7 (7, 8, 9, 10) sts of body on st holder for underarm. Knit 39 (39, 40, 41, 42) sts of second sleeve. Work left front 33 (35, 36, 37, 39) sts (end p1) => 196 (204, 212, 220, 228) sts. Work dec's and color changes from chart as indicated. Change to shorter circular needle when necessary. When chart is complete => 81 (84, 87, 90, 93) sts.

COLLAR

Change to 4.5mm needles and cont with **G+G**. BO first

purl st, knit 1 rnd and dec evenly spaced 16 (17, 18, 19, 22) sts, BO end purl st => 63 (65, 67, 69, 69) sts. Work back and forth: *k1, p1* rib for 3cm. Inc evenly spaced 14 sts => 77 (79, 81, 83, 83) sts. Work until rib measures 20cm. BO in rib.

FINISHING

Graft underarm sts tog. Fold hem on body and sleeves to inside at purl row and stitch in place. Weave in loose ends but pull the ends by the purl st chain to RS. Sew by machine using straight small stitches across the ends as you sew twice through each chain of purl sts up body front. Use matching dark thread for lower part of body and lighter thread for upper part. Rinse jacket by hand in lukewarm water and lay flat to dry. Cut between sewn rows at front.

Sew thin woven ribbon over the machine stitch close to knit sts up body front. Fold to inside and stitch in place. Sew 5 hooks and bars or clasps to front (overlapping 5 sts).

Key

- E+F 1052+1053
- F+G 1053+0001
- G+G 0001
- ∕ k2tog
- ⟍ ssk
- − purl
- no stitch

Chart – yoke

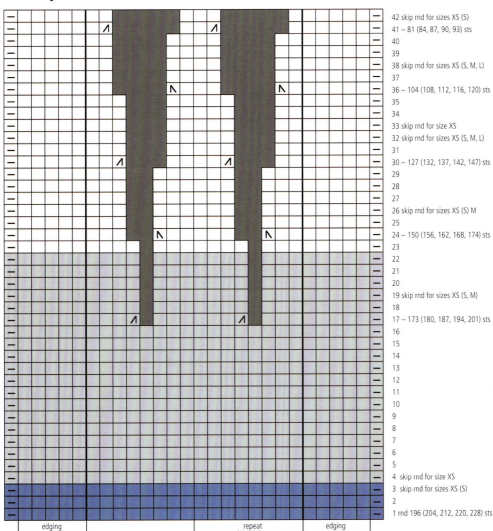

lappi

Dogs, mountains, birds and sky decorate this colorful children's sweater. It is knitted in the round with a zipper for closure.

SIZES 1-2 (2-3, 3-4, 4, 6, 8) years
Chest: 59/23¼" (64/25", 68/26¾", 72/28¼", 77/30¼", 81/31¾")
Length to armhole: 20/7¾" (22/8¾", 24/9½", 26/10¼", 28/11", 30/11¾")
Sleeve length: 22/8¾", (24/9½", 26/10¼", 28/11", 30/11¾", 32/12½")

MATERIAL Létt-Lopi 50g (1.7oz) balls, 100m (109yd)
Green sweater
A 1407 pine green 3 (4, 4, 5, 5, 5)
B 1406 spring green 1 (1, 1, 1, 1, 1)
C 1401 hazel 1 (1, 1, 1, 1, 1)
D 0051 white 1 (1, 1, 1, 1, 1)
E 1403 lapis blue 1 (1, 1, 1, 1, 1)
F 1402 heaven blue 1 (1, 1, 1, 1, 1)
G 1404 glacier blue 1 (1, 1, 1, 1, 1)

Red sweater
A 9434 crimson red 3 (4, 4, 5, 5, 5)
B 1406 spring green 1 (1, 1, 1, 1, 1)
C 0059 black 1 (1, 1, 1, 1, 1)
D 0051 white 1 (1, 1, 1, 1, 1)
E 1403 lapis blue 1 (1, 1, 1, 1, 1)
F 1402 heaven blue 1 (1, 1, 1, 1, 1)
G 1404 glacier blue 1 (1, 1, 1, 1, 1)
3.5mm and 4.5mm (US 4 and 7) circular needles 60-70cm (24–28in), 3.5mm and 4.5mm (US 4 and 7) double pointed needles, zipper 30 (35, 40, 40, 45, 45) cm (12, 14, 16, 16, 18, 18in)

GAUGE
10 x 10cm (4 x 4in) = 18 sts and 24 rows in st st using 4.5mm (US 7) needles.

NOTE
Body and sleeves are worked in the round from lower edge to underarms, then joined to work yoke in the round. Round begins and ends with a purl st at front of body. The front is cut open.

BODY

CO 107 (115, 123, 131, 139, 147) sts with A using 3.5mm circular needle. purl first and last st of rnd (purl sts are worked up body front). Work back and forth 4 rnds st st (RS), work 1 rnd page Join in the rnd and work 5 rnds st st. Change to 4.5mm circular needle and work st st until body measures 20 (22, 24, 26, 28, 30) cm from purl rnd. Set aside and work sleeves. Do not break yarn.

SLEEVES

CO 30 (30, 32, 32, 34, 34) sts with A using 3.5mm dpn. Join in the rnd and work 4 rnds st st (RS). Work 1 rnd page Work 5 rnds st st. Change to 4.5mm dpn and inc 2 sts (1 st after first st and 1 st before last st of rnd) in every 7th rnd, a total of 6 (6, 6, 7, 7, 8) times => 42 (42, 44, 46, 48, 50) sts. Continue without further shaping until work measures 22 (24, 26, 28, 30, 32) cm from purl rnd. Place 5 (5, 6, 7, 8, 9) sts underarm on st holder => 37 (37, 38, 39, 40, 41) sts. Work second sleeve.

YOKE

Join body and sleeves as follows: With A and 4.5mm circular needle, knit 25 (27, 28, 30, 31, 33) sts across right front. Place next 5 (5, 6, 7, 8, 9) sts of body on st holder. Knit 37 (37, 38, 39, 40, 41) sts across first sleeve. Knit 47 (51, 55, 57, 61, 63) sts across back, place next 5 (5, 6, 7, 8, 9) sts of body on st holder. Knit 37 (37, 38, 39, 40, 41) sts across second sleeve. Knit 25 (27, 28, 30, 31, 33) sts (left front) => 171 (179, 187, 195, 203, 211) sts. Work pattern from **Chart 1** and dec as shown (do not dec in 4 sts at front, p2 and k1 at each side). Change to shorter needles when rnd gets smaller. When pattern is complete there are => 67 (70, 73, 76, 79, 82) sts left.

NECKBAND

Change to 3.5mm dpn and A work 1 rnd st st, dec 12 (13, 14, 15, 16, 17) sts evenly over rnd => 55 (57, 59, 61, 63, 65) sts. Work pattern from **Chart 2**. Now work back and forth. Knit 1 rnd from WS (P from RS), then 5 rnds st st (from RS). BO loosely.

FINISHING

Weave in any loose ends and graft underarm st tog. Using a machine, sew two rows of small straight stitches into each purl stitch up body front. Cut up between each pair of sewn rows. Rinse sweater and lay flat to dry. Sew zipper by hand under front edge twice: first from RS where edge is folded, then slip stitch edge of zipper from WS. Fold neckband in half to WS and slip stitch in place, hiding zipper end in collar. Fold borders on body and sleeves along purl row to WS and slip stitch in position.

Chart 1 – yoke

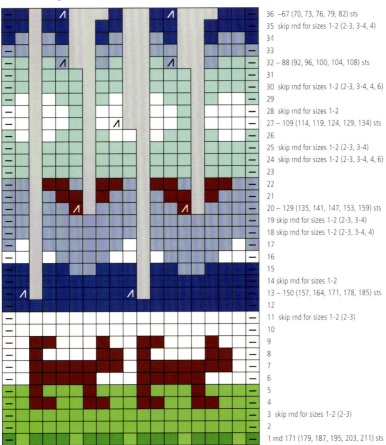

36 —67 (70, 73, 76, 79, 82) sts
35 skip rnd for sizes 1-2 (2-3, 3-4, 4)
34
33
32 — 88 (92, 96, 100, 104, 108) sts
31
30 skip rnd for sizes 1-2 (2-3, 3-4, 4, 6)
29
28 skip rnd for sizes 1-2
27 — 109 (114, 119, 124, 129, 134) sts
26
25 skip rnd for sizes 1-2 (2-3, 3-4)
24 skip rnd for sizes 1-2 (2-3, 3-4, 4, 6)
23
22
21
20 — 129 (135, 141, 147, 153, 159) sts
19 skip rnd for sizes 1-2 (2-3, 3-4)
18 skip rnd for sizes 1-2 (2-3, 3-4, 4)
17
16
15
14 skip rnd for sizes 1-2
13 — 150 (157, 164, 171, 178, 185) sts
12
11 skip rnd for sizes 1-2 (2-3)
10
9
8
7
6
5
4
3 skip rnd for sizes 1-2 (2-3)
2
1 rnd 171 (179, 187, 195, 203, 211) sts

repeat

Chart 2 – collar

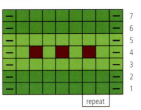

7
6
5
4
3
2
1

repeat

Key Green / Red

A – 1407 / 9434
B – 1406
C – 1401 / 0059
D – 0051
E – 1403
F – 1402
G – 1404
— purl
⟋ k2tog
no stitch

1-2 59 cm
2-3 64 cm
3-4 68 cm
4 72 cm
6 77 cm
8 81 cm

1-2 20 cm
2-3 22 cm
3-4 24 cm
4 26 cm
6 28 cm
8 30 cm

1-2 22 cm
2-3 24 cm
3-4 26 cm
4 28 cm
6 30 cm
8 32 cm

NOTE: See sizes on page 147 for measurements in inches

leggur

Fitted leg warmers that are well suited to either a mountain hike or a winter's walk in the city.

LEG WARMERS

CO 56 (60) sts with A using four or three 3.5mm dpns. Join in the rnd and work *k1tbl, p1* rib for 5cm. Change to 4.5mm dpns and work either:

Roses: Work in st st patt from chart. When patt is complete cont with A for 5 (6) cm.

Stripe: With B, knit 10 (11) cm.

Next rnd dec: k2tog , knit to last 2 sts, Sl1, k1, psso. Rep dec every 6th rnd 6 times => 44 (48) sts. Cont without further shaping until piece measures 32 (34) cm from CO edge, or as long as needed. Place marker center front.

Next rnd inc: *knit to 1 st before marker, M1R, k2 sts, M1L (see page 259) , knit to end. Knit 4 rnds*. Rep from *to* ones. Rep inc ones more => 50 (54) sts. Work 3 rnds *k1tbl, p1* rib. BO in rib.

Work second leg warmer to match.

FINISHING

Weave in loose ends. Rinse by hand in lukewarm water and lay flat to dry.

SIZES S/M (L/XL)

MATERIALS

Létt-Lopi 50g (1.7oz) balls, 100m (109yd)

Roses
A 1401 hazel heather 3 (3)
B 0059 black 1 (1)
C 9421 celery green heather 1 (1)
D 9418 stone blue heather 1 (1)

Stripe
A 1410 orange 1 (1)
B 1405 bottle green heather 2 (3)

3.5mm and 4.5mm (US 4 and 7) double pointed needles

GAUGE

10 x 10cm (4 x 4in) = 18 sts and 24 rows in st st on 4.5mm (US 7) needles.

NOTE

The leg warmers are worked in the round. Each round begins at back of the leg.

Chart

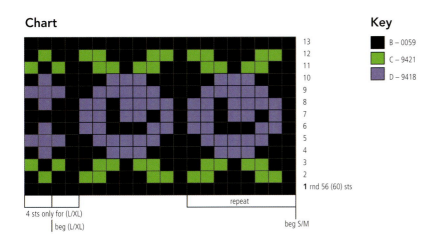

Key

- ■ B – 0059
- ■ C – 9421
- ■ D – 9418

leistar

These colorful socks come in handy during both the cold winter months and on summer camping trips.

SOCKS

Ribbing: Using A and 5mm dpn, CO 28 (32, 36) sts. Divide sts evenly between 4 needles and join in the rnd. Work 2x2 ribbing *k2, p2*, rep from * to *. Work 8 (8, 10) rnds using A, 6 (8, 8) rnds using B+C, 10 (10, 12) using C+D and 4 (6, 6) rnds using A. Switch to 6mm dpn and knit 7 (8, 9) rnds in st st.

Heel flap: Knit the sts from the first and second needles onto one needle. Work these sts back and forth in st st (k on the RS, purl on the WS), while leaving the instep sts to be worked later. Knit 14 (16, 18) rows, always slipping the first st in every row (so that they are easier to pick up later on).

Turn heel: Keep working back and forth on two needles. The heel is turned and shaped by dec sts on the edges of the heel flap. Place a marker in the middle of the heel flap.
Row 1: Start with a WS row. Purl until 2 (2, 2) sts past marker, p2tog and turn.
Row 2: Sl1, k4 (4, 4) (2 sts past marker), sl1, k1, psso. Turn.
Repeat these 2 rows until 6 (6, 6) sts remain on the needle. End with a RS row.

Pick up and ktbl 7 (8, 9) sts along the side of the heel flap, knit the instep sts, pick up and ktbl 7 (8, 9) sts along the other side of the heel flap, knit to marker (each rnd now starts at the sole of the foot). Divide the heel sts evenly between 2 needles, 10 (11, 12) sts on each needle.
Instep shaping: needle 1: knit until 2 sts remain, k2tog. Knit needles 2 and 3. Needle 4: sl1, k1, psso, knit to end of rnd.
Knit 1 rnd. Repeat the dec rnd, followed by a knit rnd, until each needle has the same number of sts, 7 (8, 9) sts.

SIZES children (women, men)
Shoe size: 30–34 /US 12–2.5 (35–39/US 3.5–7 , 42–44/US 8.5–10.5)

MATERIALS Álafoss Lopi 100g (3.5oz) balls, 100m (109yd)
A 9961 cypress green heather 1 (2, 2)
Létt-Lopi 50g (1.7oz) balls, 100m (109yd)
B 1410 orange 1 (1, 1)
C 9427 reust heather 1 (1, 1)
D 1416 moss green 1 (1, 1)

5mm (US 8) and 6mm (US 10) double pointed needles

GAUGE
Álafoss Lopi: 10 x 10 cm (4 x 4in) = 13 sts and 19 rows in st st on 6mm (US 10) needles.

NOTE
Socks are knitted with Létt-Lopi held double and a single strand of Álafoss Lopi.

Foot: knit 28 (32, 36) rnds (counting from the heel flap), or knit until sock covers little toe. Work a 5- (6-, 8-) row stripe, using C+D, and place anywhere on the foot (the socks don't have to match).

Toe decreases:
Needle 1: knit until 3 sts remain, k2tog, k1.
Needle 2: k1, sl1, k1, psso, k to end of needle.
Needle 3: same as needle 1.
Needle 4: same as needle 2.
Knit 3 rnds after the first dec rnd, knit 2 rnds after the next decrnd and knit 1 rnd after the 3rd dec rnd. Then dec every rnd until 8 sts remain. Break the yarn and pull it through the rem sts.

FINISHING
Weave in ends. Gently block the socks into shape.

ljúfa

Icelandic wool can be used for garments other than the traditional patterned sweaters. This tunic is a flattering A-line shape with flared sleeves.

SIZES XS (S, M, L, XL)
Chest : 84/33" (92/36¼", 100/39½", 109/43, 119/46¾")
Length to armhole: 50/19¾" (52/20½", 54/21½", 56/22", 58/22¾")
Sleeve length: 44/17¼" (46/18", 48/18¾", 49/19¼", 51/20")cm

MATERIALS Létt-Lopi 50g (1.7oz) balls, 100m (109yd)
A 1418 woodchip 6 (6, 7, 7, 7)
B 1401 hazel heather 2 (2, 2, 3, 3)

5.5mm (US 9) circular needles 40 and 80cm (16 and 30in)
5.5mm (US 9) double pointed needles

GAUGE
10 x 10cm (4 x 4in) = 15 sts and 20 rows in st st on 5.5mm (US 9) needles.

NOTE
The sleeves are knit in the round up to the armholes but the sleeve caps are knit back and forth. The sweater has slits on each side and so the front and back pieces are worked separately to begin with, then joined on a circular needle for knitting in the round. At the armholes, the body is again split into front and back pieces that are worked separately up to the shoulders. The sleeves are sewn in afterwards. The sweater has an A-line cut; it's wider at the hips than at the chest.

BODY

Using B and the 5.5mm circular needle, CO 67 (73, 81, 87, 94) sts. Work 3 rows garter stitch (1 garter ridge plus CO edge). Next row: Begin working st st (knit on the RS, purl on the WS). Work 6 rows using B, 1 row using A, 5 rows using B, 3 rows using A, 4 rows using B and 6 rows using A. Set the front piece aside and work the back piece in the same manner. Join the front and back pieces on a circular needle. Using B, knit together the first and last sts of the two pieces (k2tog above the slits) => 132 (144, 160, 172, 186) sts. Knit 1 more rnd using B, then 9 rnds using A, 1 rnd using B, 11 rnds using A and 1 rnd using B. At the same time dec 2 sts on each side (1 st before and 1 st after the center side sts). The first dec is placed 14cm from the CO edge (for all sizes) and then as follows: XS dec at 26 and 38cm, S dec at 27 and 40cm (3 dec rnds for sizes XS and S). For other sizes: M dec at 24, 34 and 44cm, L dec at 24, 34 and 45cm, XL dec at 25, 36 and 47cm (4 dec rnds for sizes M, L and XL) => 126 (138, 152, 164, 178) sts. Knit until body measures 50 (52, 54, 56, 58) cm from CO edge.

Divide the body into front and back pieces; each piece has 63 (69, 76, 82, 89) sts.

Front piece: BO 3 (3, 4, 4, 5) at the beg of the next two rows and then 1 st at the beg of each row 3 (4, 4, 4, 4) times => 51 (55, 60, 66, 71) sts. Work st st until piece measures 7cm from beg of armhole (all sizes). Neckline: On a right-side row, k 9 (10, 12, 12, 13) sts, place next 33 (35, 36, 42, 45) sts on a stitch holder or scrap yarn and knit the last 9 (10, 12, 12, 13) sts. Work each shoulder separately in st st until piece measures 16 (17, 18, 19, 20) cm from beg of armhole. Place shoulder sts on a stitch holder or scrap yarn.

Back piece: Work armhole decs as for the front piece. Work st st until piece measures 11 (12, 13, 14, 15) cm from beg of armhole. Next right-side row: k 9 (10, 12, 12, 13) sts, place next 33 (35, 36, 42, 45) sts on a stitch holder or scrap yarn and knit the last 9 (10, 12, 12, 13) sts. Work each shoulder separately until piece measures 16 (17, 18, 19, 20) cm from bottom of armhole. BO shoulder sts. Set the body aside and knit sleeves.

SLEEVES

Using B and 5.5mm dpn, CO 52 (56, 58, 62, 66) sts. Work 3 rows garter st (1 garter ridge plus CO edge). Join for knitting in the rnd and knit 3 rnds using B, 1 rnd using A, 4 rnds using B, 2 rnds using A, 3 rnds using B, 7 rnds using A and finally 1 rnd using B. At the same time dec by 2 sts (at the beg and end of rnds) 5, 10 and 15cm from the CO edge (all sizes) => 46 (50, 52, 56, 60) sts. Knit using A until sleeve measures 44 (46, 48, 49, 51) cm from CO edge. Begin working st st back and forth in st st. BO 3 (3, 4, 4, 4) sts at the beg of the next 2 rows. BO at the beg of each row (both sides) as follows: 1 x 2 sts (all sizes), 6 (7, 8, 9, 9) x 1 st, 2 x 2 sts, 3

(3, 3, 3, 4) x 1 st => 10 (12, 10, 12, 14) sts. BO the rem sts and make the other sleeve.

NECKLINE EDGING

Graft the shoulder stitches (the live stitches from the front piece and the cast-off stitches from the back piece). Pick up sts for neckline edging as follows: Using A, begin at the left shoulder seam and pick up 1 st for every other st down to the front neckline. Pick up 1 st in the corner between the side and front of the neckline and then knit the 35 (35, 37, 43, 46) sts held on a stitch holder or scrap yarn. Mirror this process for the other side of the neckline (don't forget to pick up the corner sts), knit the 35 (35, 37, 43, 46) held for the back neckline and then pick up sts up to the left shoulder seam. Next row: Using B, ktbl along the sides of the neckline (to prevent holes from forming) until 1 st before the corner st. Dec: *Slip 2 sts knitwise, k1 and pass the slipped sts over. Knit (do not ktbl) until 1 st before the next corner*. Repeat from * to * 3 times (once in every corner). Knit to end of rnd. Dec in every other rnd up to the garter st edge. Work the color pattern like this (following the first rnd using B): 3 rnds using A, 1 rnd using B, 1 rnd using A and 2 (2, 3, 3, 3) rnds using B. Purl 1 rnd, knit 1 rnd and then work a purled cast-off.

FINISHING

Sew the sleeves into the armholes from the WS using back stitch. Turn the sweater inside out and pin the sleeve cap into the armholes, starting with the top and the bottom and ending with the sides of the cap. Sew the pieces' edge sts together using back stitch. Weave in loose ends. Gently block the sweater into shape.

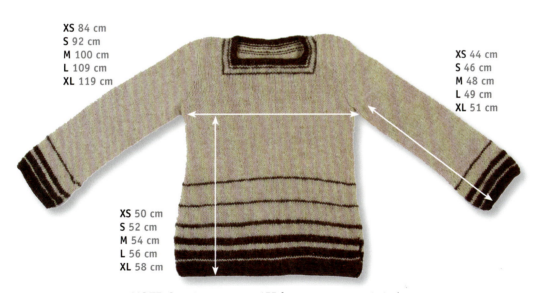

NOTE: See sizes on page 155 for measurements in inches

mark

A delicate beret inspired by the laws of mathematics. Who says science can't be romantic?

SIZE M/L

MATERIALS Einband 50g (1.7oz) balls, 225m (245yd)
A 0151 black heather 1
B 9076 tawny 1
C 0851 white 1
D 9102 dark gray 1

3mm (US 2) circular needles 40 and 60cm (16 and 24in)
3mm (US 2) double pointed needles

NOTE
The beret is worked in the round from the center outward.

2nd inc: *k1, yo* rep from *to* to end of rnd => 36 sts. Knit 6 rnds.

3rd inc: *k1, yo* rep from *to* to end of rnd => 72 sts. Change to B and work patt 1, total 12 rnds.

4th inc: *k1, yo* rep from *to* to end of rnd => 144 sts.

Change to C and work patt 2, total 24 rnds.

5th Inc: *k1, yo* rep from *to* to end of rnd => 288 sts.

Change to D and work patt 3, total 17 rnds. Now chart is complete.

1st decrease: k2tog to end of rnd => 144 sts. Change to A and knit 1 rnd.

2nd dec: *k1, k2tog* rep from *to* to end of rnd => 96 sts.

Work *k1, p1* rib for 6cm.

BO loosely in rib.

FINISHING

Weave in loose ends. Rinse by hand in lukewarm water, squeeze out excess water with towel and lay flat to dry.

BERET

With A and 3mm dpns CO 9 sts using circle CO: Hold the tail in your right hand and lay the yarn in a circle, make a loop by pulling the yarn through the circle with the needle in you right hand. Hold the circle open with your left hand, ring and little finger. CO by bringing needle over and under the yarn that holds the circle, forming yarn over on the needle. Now place 3 sts on each needle and pull the tail to close the circle. Knit 1 rnd, knitting into the back of the loops (every other st) made with the yarn over to keep the stitch orientation correct.

1st increase: *k1, yo* rep from *to* to end of rnd => 18 sts.

Knit 3 rnds.

Chart shows every round

288 sts **patt 3** color D
5th inc

144 sts **patt 2** color C
4th increase

72 sts **patt 1** color B

repeat

Key

☐ knit
O yo
／ k2tog
＼ ssk
V lifted stitch
− purl
▪ no stitch

miðja

This beautiful dress, knitted with lace-weight wool, came from the designer's wish for a lace dress worthy of special occasions. The darkest part of the dress shows off the wavy lace pattern while accentuating the waist.

SIZES after blocking S (M, L/XL)
Chest (knit stretches): 77/30¼" (86/33¾", 96/37¾")cm
Width (lower edge): 120/47¼" (135/53", 150/59")cm
Length to armhole: 78/30¾" (81/31¾", 85/33½")cm
Sleeve length (long): 40/15¾" (42/16½", 44/17¼")cm

MATERIALS
Einband 50g (1.7oz) balls, 225m (245yd)

White-gray
A 0851 white 4 (5, 6)
Long sleeves: 5 (6, 7)
B 1026 ash heather 1 (1, 1)
C 1027 light gray 1 (1, 1)
D 9102 gray 1 (1, 1)

Sand-black
A 9075 sandstorm 4 (5, 6)
Long sleeves: 5 (6, 7)
B 0867 chocolate 1 (1, 1)
C 0052 black sheep 1 (1, 1)
D 0059 black 1 (1, 1)

4mm (US 6) circular needles 60 and 80cm (24 and 30in), 5mm (US 8) circular needle 80cm, 3mm (US 2) circular needle 40cm (16in), 4mm (US 6) and 5mm (US 8) double pointed needles

BLOCKED GAUGE
1 pat rep at chest: 9.5cm x 2.3cm = 24 sts and 6 rnds.
1 pat rep at lower edge: 15cm x 2.3cm = 39 sts and 6 rnds.

NOTE
Body and sleeves are worked in the round, then joined and yoke is worked in the round. Size S and (L/XL): Round begins at left side of body but on yoke, round begins at joining of body and sleeve on left side of back. Size (M): Round begins at center back.

Key

	knit
O	yo
/	k2tog
	ktbl
—	purl
V	lifted stitch
⌐ ¬	pattern repeat

DRESS

With A using 5mm needle CO very loosely 312 (351) (390) sts. Change to 4mm needle and Knit 1 row from WS, forming 1 ridge. Join in the rnd and place marker. Knit 5 rnds.

1st patt 39 sts:

Lace rnd: k2tog 7 times => 7 sts. *yo , k1, 13 times => 26 L. k2tog 13 times => 13 sts*. Rep from *to*, to last 12 sts: k2tog 6 times.

Knit 5 rnds, work 1 lace rnd total 7 (7) (8) times.

Dec: pattern consists of 6 rnds, dec are made in 2nd rnd. 3 sts are dec in every rep.
Knit 1 rnd.

1st Dec rnd: k2tog, K5, *k2tog, k22, k2tog, K6, k2tog, K5*. Rep from *to*, K6 last sts => 288 (324) (360) sts. Knit 3 rnds.

2nd patt 36 sts:

Lace rnd: k2tog 6 times => 6 sts. *yo , k1, 12 times => 24 sts. k2tog 12 times => 12 sts*. Rep from *to*, to last 12 sts: k2tog 6 times.

Knit 5 rnds, work 1 lace rnd, total 4 (5) (5) times. Knit 1 rnd.

2nd Dec rnd: k2tog, K5, *k2tog, k20, k2tog, K5, k2tog, K5*. Rep from *to*, K5 last sts, => 264 (297) (330) sts. Knit 3 rnds.

3rd patt 33 sts:

Lace rnd: k2tog 6 times => 6 sts. *yo , k1, 11 times => 22 sts. k2tog 11 times => 11 sts*.
Rep from *to* to last 10 sts: k2tog 5 times.
Knit 5 rnds, work 1 lace rnd, total 3 times.

Knit 1 rnd.

3rd Dec rnd: k2tog, K4, *k2tog, k18, k2tog, K5, k2tog, K4*. Rep from *to*, K5 last sts => 240 (270) (300) sts. Knit 3 rnds.

4th patt 30 sts:

Lace rnd: k2tog 5 times => 5 sts. *yo , k1, 10 times => 20 sts. k2tog 10 times => 10 sts*.
Rep from *to* to last 10 sts: k2tog 5 times.
Knit 5 rnds, work 1 lace rnd, total 2 times.

Knit 1 rnd.

4th Dec rnd: k2tog, K4, *k2tog, k16, k2tog, K4, k2tog, K4*. Rep from *to* K4 last sts => 216 (243) (270) sts. Knit 3 rnds.

5th patt 27 sts:

Lace rnd: k2tog 5 times => 5 sts. *yo , k1, 9 times => 18 sts. k2tog 9 times => 9 sts*. Rep from *to* to last 8 sts: k2tog 4 times.

Knit 5 rnds, **change to B and work lace rnd.**

Knit 1 rnd.

5th Dec rnd: k2tog, k3, *k2tog, k14, k2tog, K4, k2tog, k3*. Rep from *to* K4 last sts => 192 (216) (240) sts. Knit 3 rnds.

Chart – body

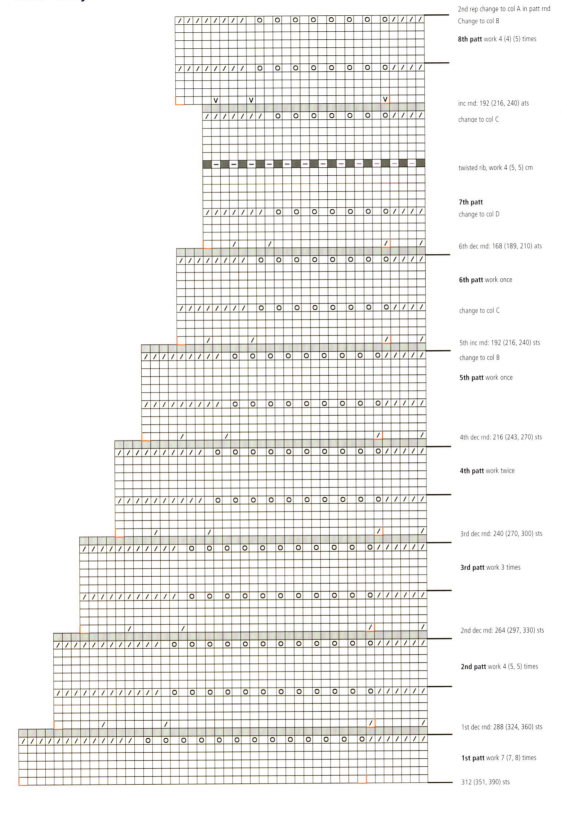

6th patt 24 sts:
Lace rnd: Change to C. k2tog 4 times => 4 sts. *yo , k1, 8 times => 16 sts. k2tog 8 times => 8 sts*. Rep from *to* to last 8 sts: k2tog 4 times.
Work: knit 5 rnds, work 1 lace rnd.

K 1 rnd.
6th dec rnd: k2tog, K3, *K2tog, k12, k2tog, K3, K2tog, K3*. Rep from *to* K3 last sts => 168 (189) (210) sts.
Knit 3 rnds.

7th patt 21 sts:
Lace rnd: change to D. k2tog 4 times => 4 sts. *yo , k1, 7 times => 14 sts. k2tog 7 times => 7 sts*.
Rep from *to*, to last 6 sts: k2tog 3 times.
Knit 5 rnds.

Waist: Work twisted rib: *k1tbl, p1*, 4 (5) (5) cm long.

Knit 5 rnds.
Lace rnd: Change to C. k2tog 4 times => 4 sts. *yo , k1, 7 times => 14 sts. k2tog 7 times => 7 sts*.
Rep from *to*, to last 6 sts: k2tog 3 times.

Knit 1 rnd.
Inc rnd: k4, *M1 with lifted inc, k14, M1 lifted inc, K3, M1 lifted inc, K4*.
Rep from *to*, k3 last sts and M1 lifted inc => 192 (216) (240) sts.
Knit 3 rnds.

8th patt 24 sts:
Lace rnd: k2tog 4 times => 4 sts. *yo , k1, 8 times => 16 sts. k2tog 8 times => 8 sts*. Rep from *to*, to last 8 sts: k2tog 4 times.
Knit 5 rnds, **change to B and work lace rnd.**
Knit 5 rnds, **change to A and work lace rnd.**
Knit 5 rnds, work 1 lace rnd, total 2 (2) (3) times.
Knit 2 rnds.
S and (L): Do not work last 12 sts of last rnd.
Set aside and work sleeves.

SLEEVES
With A using 5mm needles CO very loosely 72 (72) (96) sts. Change to 4mm needle and knit 1 row from WS, forming 1 ridge. Join in the rnd and place marker.
Knit 5 rnds.

8th patt 24 sts:
Lace rnd: k2tog 4 times => 4 sts. *yo , k1, 8 times => 16 sts. k2tog 8 times => 8 sts*. Rep from *to*, to last 8 sts: k2tog 4 times.
Short sleeve: *Knit 5 rnds, work 1 lace rnd*, 4 (5) (5) times.
Long sleeve: *5 rnds, work 1 lace rnd*, 17 (18) (19) times.
Knit 2 rnds.
S and (L): Place 24 (24) sts underarm on st holder => 48 (72) sts.
(M): Left sleeve: Place 18 first and 6 last sts on st holder,
Right sleeve: Place 6 first and 18 last sts on st holder => (48) sts.
Work second sleeve.

Join body and sleeves as follows: Place last 12 sts and first 12 sts of body on st holder for underarm. With A using 4mm circular needle, knit 48 (72) sts of first sleeve. Knit 72 (96) sts for front, place next 24 (24) sts of body on st holder for underarm. Knit 48 (72) sts of second sleeve. Knit 72 (96) sts for back => 240 (336) sts on needle.

Knit 2 rnds.
8th patt 24 sts:
Lace rnd: *yo , k1* 4 times => 8 sts.
k2tog 8 times => 8 sts. yo , k1, 8 times => 16 sts.
Rep from *to*, to last 4 sts: yo , k1, 4 times.
Knit 5 rnds, work 1 lace rnd.

Knit 1 rnd.
1st dec rnd: k6, k2tog, *K3, k2tog, k3, k2tog, k12, k2tog*.
Rep from *to*, to last 8 sts: k2tog, K6 => 210 (294) sts.

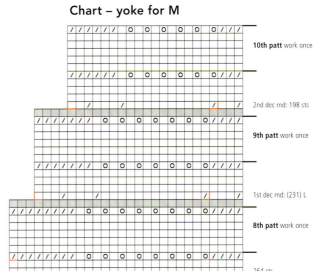

Chart – yoke for S and (L/XL)

- 3rd dec rnd (L/XL) (210) sts
- 10th patt work once
- 2nd dec: 180 (252) sts
- 9th patt work once
- 1st dec rnd: 210 (294) sts
- 8th patt work once
- 240 (336) sts

Chart – yoke for M

- 10th patt work once
- 2nd dec rnd: 198 sts
- 9th patt work once
- 1st dec rnd: (231) L
- 8th patt work once
- 264 sts

Knit 3 rnds.
9th patt 21 sts:
Lace rnd: *k1, yo * 3 times, k1=> 7 sts.
k2tog 7 times => 7 sts. yo , k1, 7 times => 14 sts.
Rep from *to*, to last 3 sts: yo , k1, 3 times, yo => 7 sts.
Knit 5 rnds, work 1 lace rnd.

Knit 1 rnd.
2nd dec rnd: K5, k2tog,
K3, k2tog, k2, k2tog, k10, k2tog.
Rep from *to*, to last 7 sts: k2tog, K5 => 180 (252) sts.
Knit 3 rnds.
10th patt 18 sts:
Lace rnd: *yo , k1* 3 times => 6 sts.
k2tog 6 times => 6 sts. yo , k1, 6 times => 12 sts.
Rep from *to*, to last 3 sts: yo , k1, 3 times => 6 sts.
Knit 5 rnds, work 1 lace rnd.
Size (L/XL) only:
Knit 1 rnd.
3rd dec rnd: k4, k2tog,
K2, k2tog, k2, k2tog, K8, k2tog.

Rep from *to*, to last 6 sts: k2tog, K4 => (210) sts.
Knit 3 rnds.
11th patt 15 sts:
Lace rnd: *k1, yo* 2 times, k1=> 5 sts.
k2tog 5 times => 5 sts. yo , k1, 5 times => 10 sts. Rep from *to*, to last 2 sts: yo , k1, 2 times, yo => 5 sts.

Join body and sleeves as follows: With A using 4mm circular needle, Knit (42) sts for back, place (24) sts of body on st holder for underarm. Knit (48) sts of first sleeve. Knit (84) sts for front, place next (24) sts of body on st holder for underarm. Knit (48) sts of second sleeve. Knit (42) sts for back => (264) sts on needle.
Knit 2 rnds.

8th patt 24 sts:
Lace rnd: k2tog 4 times => 4 sts. *yo , k1, 8 times => 16 sts. k2tog 8 times => 8 sts*. Rep from *to*, to last 8 sts: k2tog 4 times.
Knit 5 rnds, work 1 lace rnd, total 1- 2 times depending on bust size.

Knit 1 rnd.

1st Dec rnd: k2tog, k3, *k2tog, k12, k2tog, k3, k2tog, k3*. Rep from *to* k3 last sts => (231) sts.

Knit 3 rnds.

9th patt 21 sts:

Lace rnd: k2tog 4 times => 4 sts. *yo , k1, 7 times => 14 sts. k2tog 7 times => 7 sts*.

Rep from *to*, to last 6 sts: k2tog 3 times.

Knit 5 rnds, work 1 lace rnd.

NOTE: See sizes on page 163 for measurements in inches

S 77 cm
M 86 cm
L/XL 96 cm

S 120 cm
M 135 cm
L/XL 150 cm

S 78 cm
M 81 cm
L/XL 85 cm

Knit 1 rnd.

2nd Dec rnd: k2tog, k2, *k2tog, k10, k2tog, k3, k2tog, k2*. Rep from *to* k3 last sts => (198) sts.

Knit 3 rnds.

10th patt 18 sts:

Lace rnd: k2tog 3 times => 3 sts. *yo , k1, 6 times => 12 sts. k2tog 6 times => 6 sts*.

Rep from *to*, to last 6 sts: k2tog 3 times.

Knit 5 rnds, work 1 lace rnd.

All sizes:

Knit 3 rnds.

Next rnd: *K2tog, k1* => 120 (132) (140) sts.

Knit 2 rnds.

Next rnd: knit and dec evenly spaced 20 (24) (24) sts => 100 (108) (116) sts.

Neckline: Change to 3mm needle. Work twisted rib: *k1tbl, p1*, 2cm long. BO in rib.

FINISHING
Graft underarm sts carefully together and weave in loose ends. Rinse dress by hand in lukewarm water and squeeze excess water out with towel. Lay flat to dry, stretched in right shape and measurements.

nost

The classic rose pattern reworked with a modern twist. This raglan pullover is knitted using two highly contrasting colors for maximum visual impact.

SIZES S (M, L, XL)
Chest: 87/34¼" (93/36½", 100/39½", 107/42")
Length to armhole: 38/15" (39/15½", 42/16½", 43/17")
Sleeve length: 46/18" (47/18½", 51/20", 52/20½")

MATERIALS Létt-Lopi 50g (1.7oz) balls, 100m (109yd)
A 0054 ash 6 (6, 7, 8)
B 0005 black heather 5 (5, 6, 7)

4.5mm (US 7) circular needles 40 and 80cm (16 and 30in), 3.5mm (US 4) circular needle 80cm, 3.5mm and 4.5mm (US 4 and 7) double pointed needles, markers

GAUGE
10 x 10cm (4 x 4in) = 18 sts and 24 rows in st st on 4.5mm (US 7) needles.

NOTE
Body and sleeves are worked in the round from lower edge to underarms, then joined to work yoke in the round. Each round of the body begins on the left side of the sweater, but the yoke rounds begin where the back of the sweater meets the left sleeve. When knitting the eight-petal rose the continental way, always carry the rose color across the top (over left index finger) with two colors to make it dominant. See instructions for knitting on page 251.

BODY

CO 156 (168, 180, 192) sts with A using 3.5mm circular needle. Join in the rnd and work *k2, p2* rib for 7 (8, 7, 8) cm. Change to 4.5mm circular needle and work in st st patt from **chart**. Rep patt and work 75 (75) 83 (83) rnds (= 2 (2, 3, 3) rnds in solid-color after last rnd of eight-petal rose) and body measures 38 (39, 42, 43) cm from CO edge. Do not work last 4 (5, 5, 6) sts of last rnd. Set aside and work sleeves.

SLEEVES

CO 40 (40, 44, 44) sts with A using 3.5mm dpns. Join in the rnd and work *k2, p2* rib for 7 (8, 7, 8) cm. Change to 4.5mm needles and work in st st. Inc evenly spaced 4 (6, 4, 6) sts => 44 (46, 48, 50) sts, work patt from chart. Inc 1 st after first st and 1 st before last st of rnd in 8th (7th) 8th (7th) rnd up sleeve, total 10 (11, 12, 13) times => 64 (68, 72, 76) sts. Cont without further shaping 94 (94, 104, 104) rnd (= 2 (2, 3, 3) rnds in solid-color after last rnd of eight-petal rose), and sleeve measures 46 (47, 51, 52) cm from CO edge. Place 8 (10, 10, 12) sts underarm on st holder => 56 (58, 62, 64) sts. Work second sleeve.

YOKE

Join body and sleeves as follows: With A using 4.5mm circular needle, place 4 (5, 5, 6) last sts and 4 (5, 5, 6) first sts of body on st holder for underarm. Knit 56 (58, 62, 64) sts of first sleeve, place marker. Knit 70 (74, 80, 84) sts for front, place marker, place next 8 (10, 10, 12) sts of body on st holder for underarm. Knit 56 (58, 62, 64) sts of second sleeve, place marker. Knit 70 (74, 80, 84) sts for back, place marker => 252 (264, 284, 296) sts and 4 markers on joining of body and sleeves.

Raglan shaping: k2tog, *work patt as set: knit 2 sts before and 2 sts after marker with background-color in each patt. Work to last 2 sts before marker, Sl1, k1, psso, k2tog* rep from *to* end Sl1, k1, psso => 8 dec. Cont to work patt and dec every other rnd total 21 (22, 23, 24) times => 84 (88, 100, 104) sts.

Short rows at back: Place marker at center front and cont with B.

1. K to within 9 (10, 12, 13) sts of center front (=CF) turn, when turning always wrap next st to prevent hole.
2. Work back within same sts from CF in RS, turn.
3. Dec at joining of sleeves and back as before, turn within 10 (11, 13, 14) sts from CF.
4. Work back within same sts from CF, turn.
5. Dec at joining of sleeves and back, turn within 11 (12, 14, 15) sts from CF.
6. Work back within same sts from CF, turn.
7. Work to beg of rnd; joining of back and sleeve on left side of back => total 23 (24, 25, 26) dec. Now there are => 68 (72, 84, 88) sts left on needle.

NOTE: See sizes on page 171 for measurements in inches

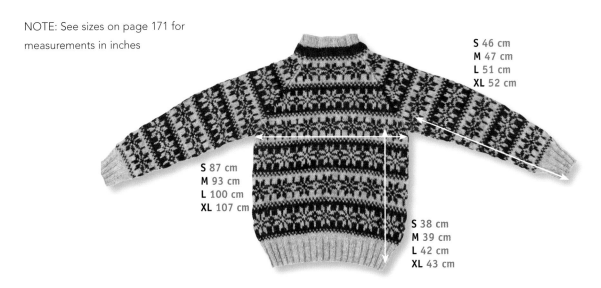

S 46 cm
M 47 cm
L 51 cm
XL 52 cm

S 87 cm
M 93 cm
L 100 cm
XL 107 cm

S 38 cm
M 39 cm
L 42 cm
XL 43 cm

NECKBAND

Change to 3.5mm needle and A, knit 1 rnd and dec evenly spaced 0 (0) 8 (8) sts => 68 (72, 76, 80) sts. Work *k2, p2* rib for 3cm. BO in rib.

FINISHING

Graft underarm sts tog and weave in loose ends. Rinse sweater by hand in lukewarm water and lay flat to dry.

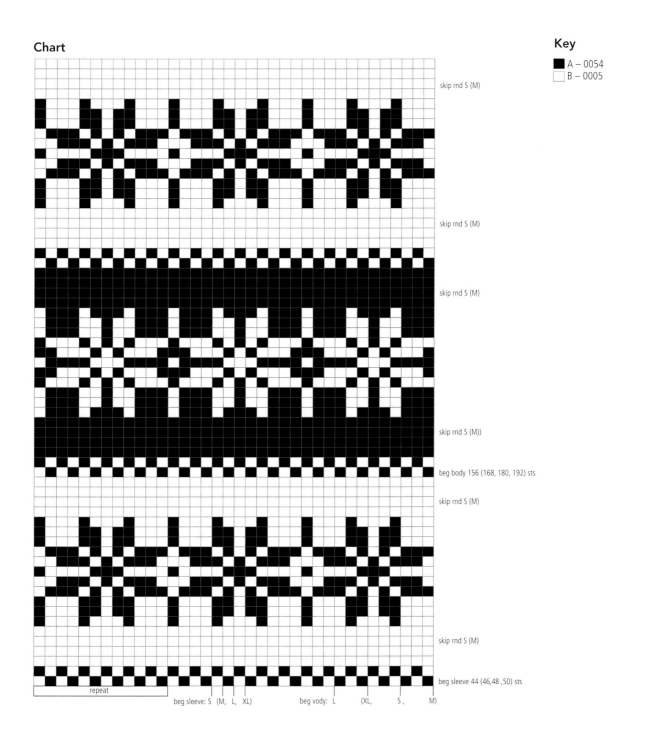

nú

A simple, modern sweater knit using Bulky Lopi. The decreases form a decorative pattern on the yoke.

SIZES S (M, L)
Chest: 95/37½" (100/39½", 110/43¼")
Length to armhole: 56/22" (58/22¾", 60/23¾")
Sleeve length: 46/18" (47/18½", 48/18¾")

MATERIAL Bulky Lopi 100g (3.5oz) skeins, 60m (66yd)
0054 ash heather 7 (7, 8)

12mm (US 17) circular needle 80cm (30in), 10mm (US 15) circular needle 40cm (16in), 12mm (US 17) double pointed needles

GAUGE
10 x 10cm (4 x 4in) = 8 sts and 11 rows in st st on 12mm (US 17) needles.

NOTE
Body and sleeves are worked in the round from lower edge to underarms, then joined to work yoke in the round. Each round of the body begins on the left side of the sweater, but the yoke rounds begin where the back of the sweater meets the left sleeve.
The sweater is loosely knitted and could grow a little longer after rinsing.

BODY

CO 76 (80, 88) sts with 12mm needles. Join in the rnd and work st st until body measures 40 (41, 42) cm from CO edge. Do not work last 3 (3, 3) sts of rnd. Set aside and work sleeves.

SLEEVES

CO 20 (22, 22) sts with 12mm dpn. Join in the rnd and work st st. Inc 1 st at beg of rnd in every 6th rnd, 6 times => 26 (28, 28) sts. Work without further shaping until sleeve measures 46 (47, 48) cm. Place 6 (6, 6) sts underarm on st holder => 20 (22, 22) sts. Work second sleeve.

YOKE

Join body and sleeves using 12mm, 80cm circular needle. Place 3 (3, 3) last sts and 3 (3, 3) first sts on st holder. Knit across first sleeve 20 (22, 22) sts. Knit 32 (34, 38) sts across body (front). Place next 6 (6, 6) sts on st holder. Knit second sleeve 20 (22, 22) sts. Knit 32 (34, 38) sts across body (back) now there are => 104 (112, 120) sts.

Work next 18 (19, 20) rnds as follows (change to dpn when rnd gets smaller):

Work 5 (6, 6) rnds st st.

1st dec: *sl1, k1, psso, k6* rep to end of rnd => 91 (98, 105) sts.

Work 2 (2, 2) rnds st st.

2nd dec: *sl1, k1, psso, k5* rep to end of rnd => 78 (84, 90) sts.

Work 2 (2, 2) rnds st st.

3rd dec: *sl1, k1, psso, k4* rep to end of rnd => 65 (70, 75) sts.

Work 2 (2, 2) rnds st st.

4th dec: *sl1, k1, psso, k3* rep to end of rnd => 52 (56, 60) sts.

Work 2 (2, 2) rnds st st.

5th dec: *sl1, k1, psso, k2* rep to end of rnd => 39 (42, 45) sts.

Work 0 (0, 1 rnds st st.

Dec evenly over rnd 5 (8, 9) sts => 34 (34, 36) sts.

Change to 10mm needle and work 2 rnds st st. In the 2nd rnd inc 12 sts evenly over rnd => 46 (46, 48) sts.

Work 16cm rib: *k1, p1*. BO loosely in rib.

FINISHING

Weave in any loose ends and graft underarm sts tog. Rinse and lay flat to dry.

NOTE: See sizes on page 175 for measurements in inches

S 95 cm
M 100 cm
L 110 cm

S 56 cm
M 58 cm
L 60 cm

S 46 cm
M 47 cm
L 48 cm

óroi

A classic color pattern was taken apart and put back together in an unstructured manner and the unique neckline adds character.

SIZES S (M, L, XL, XXL)
Chest: 92/36¼" (98/38½", 105/41¼", 111/43½", 117/46")
Length to armhole: 41/16" (42/16½", 43/17", 44/17¼", 45/17¾")
Sleeve length:
Men's: 48/18¾" (49/19¼", 50/19¾", 51/20", 52/20½")
Women's: 45/17¾" (46/18", 47/18½", 48/18¾", 49/19¼")

MATERIALS Álafoss Lopi 100g (3.5oz) balls, 100m (109yd)
Brown sweater
A 0005 black heather 2 (3, 3, 3, 3)
B 9976 beige tweed 5 (5, 6, 6, 7)
C 0053 acorn 1 (1, 1, 1, 1)
D 0051 white 1 (1, 1, 1, 1)

Gray sweater
A 0005 black heather 2 (3, 3, 3, 3)
B 9974 light gray tweed 5 (5, 6, 6, 7)
C 0056 light gray 1 (1, 1, 1, 1)
D 0051 white 1 (1, 1, 1, 1)

6mm and 4.5mm (US 10 and 7) circular needles 40 and 80cm (16 and 30in), 4.5mm and 6mm (US 7 and 10) double pointed needles, 6 clasps (15mm) or hooks and bars

GAUGE
10 x 10cm (4 x 4in) = 13 sts and 18 rows in st st on 6mm (US 10) needles.

NOTE
Body and sleeves are worked in the round from lower edge to underarms, then joined to work yoke in the round. Each round of the body begins on the left side of the sweater, but the yoke rounds begin first where the back of the sweater meets the left sleeve, then at front opening.

BODY

CO 114 (122, 130, 138, 146) sts with A using 4.5mm circular needle. Join in the rnd and work *k1, p1* rib for 3cm. Change to 6mm circular needle and work in st st . Inc evenly spaced 6 sts => 120 (128, 136, 144, 152) sts. Work patt from **Chart 1**. Cont with B until body measures 41 (42) 43 (44) 45) cm from CO edge. Do not work last 4 (4) 5 (5) 6) sts of last rnd. Set aside and work sleeves.

SLEEVES

CO 33 (33, 35, 37, 37) sts with A using 4.5mm dpns. Work back and forth *k1, p1* rib for 3cm. Join in the rnd, change to 6mm needles and work in st st . Inc evenly spaced 3 sts => 36 (36, 38, 40, 40) sts. Work patt from **Chart 1** (stitch rep is not complete in all sizes, see page 258). Cont with B and inc 1 st after first st and 1 st before last st of rnd, men's: in 8th (8th, 8th, 9th, 8th) rnd, women's: in 7th (7th, 8th, 8th, 7th) rnd, 8 (8, 8, 8, 9) times up sleeve => 52 (52, 54, 56, 58) sts. Cont without further shaping until sleeve measures men's: 48 (49, 50, 51, 52) cm, women's: 45 (46, 47, 48, 49) cm from CO edge. Place 8 (8, 9, 10, 11) sts underarm on st holder => 44 (44, 45, 46, 47) sts. Work second sleeve.

YOKE

Join body and sleeves as follows: With A using 6mm circular needle, place 4 (4, 5, 5, 6) last sts and 4 (4) 4 (5) 5) first sts of body on st holder for underarm. Knit 44 (44, 45, 46, 47) sts of first sleeve. Knit 52 (56, 59, 62, 65) sts for front, place next 8 (8, 9, 10, 11) sts of body on st holder for underarm. Knit 44 (44, 45, 46, 47) sts of second sleeve. Knit 52 (56, 59, 62, 65) sts for back => 192 (200, 208, 216, 224) sts. Work patt from **Chart 2**. Note: patt beg differently depending on size. Break yarn when **Chart 2** is complete.
Rnd 8: Beg 46 (48, 50, 52, 54) sts from end of last rnd: Place 5 sts on st holder, CO 1 st (first st of rnd), work **Chart 3**, CO 1 st (last st of rnd) purl first and last st up front, join in the rnd => 189 (197, 205, 213, 221) sts. Work patt and dec's from chart as indicated. Change to shorter circular needle when necessary. BO 2 purl sts in last rnd => 72 (75, 78, 81, 84) sts.

FINISHING

Graft underarm sts tog and weave in loose ends. Sew by machine using straight small stitches and matching thread twice through each chain of purl sts up body front. Cut between sewn rows.
Right band: RS: Slip 5 sts from st holder onto 4.5mm needle. With A CO 3 sts for facing (to hide the machine sewing), work back and forth.
WS: purl 3 sts (facing), work 5 sts in *p1, k1* rib.
RS: Work 5 sts in *k1, p1* rib, k 3 sts (facing).
Work band as long as front opening (stretch the band slightly when measuring), BO 3 sts for facing, place 5 rib sts on st holder.
Sew band from RS in place: Sew between rib st and facing st to knit st on yoke. Fold facing, over machine stitch on WS and slip stitch in place.
Left band: CO 10 sts with A using 4.5mm needles. Work back and forth.
RS: knit 3 sts (facing), work 7 sts in *k1, p1* rib.
WS: work 7 sts in *p1, k1* rib, purl 3 sts (facing).
Rep until band reaches neckline and 1.5cm lower than opening. BO 3 sts for facing, place 7 rib sts on st holder. Sew band as before.

COLLAR

With RS facing and A using 4.5mm needle work 5 sts *k1, p1* rib of band as set, knit 1 rnd and dec evenly spaced 13 (14, 5, 16, 19) sts => 59 (61, 63, 65, 65) sts, work 7 sts *k1, p1* rib, of band => 71 (73, 75, 77, 77) sts.
Work *k1, p1* rib for 3cm. Inc evenly spaced 10 sts => 81 (83, 85, 87, 87) sts, work 8cm. BO loosely in rib.

FINAL FINISHING

Rinse sweater by hand in lukewarm water and lay flat to dry. Sew 4 clasps to band and 2 clasps to neckband or 4 hooks and bars to band and one at each wrist rib.

NOTE: See sizes on page 179 for measurements in inches

S 92 cm
M 98 cm
L 105 cm
XL 111 cm
XXL 117 cm

S 48 cm
M 49 cm
L 50 cm
XL 51 cm
XXL 52 cm

S 41 cm
M 42 cm
L 43 cm
XL 44 cm
XXL 45 cm

Chart 1 – body and sleeves

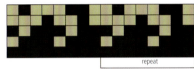

4
3
2
1 – 120 (128, 136, 144, 152) body sts – 36 (36, 38, 40, 40) sleeve sts

repeat

Chart 2 – yoke

5 sts for edging

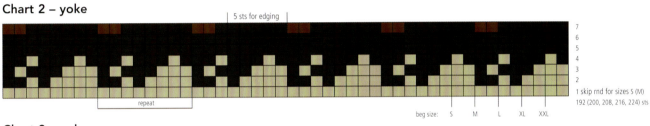

7
6
5
4
3
2
1 skip rnd for sizes S (M)
192 (200, 208, 216, 224) sts

repeat

beg size: S M L XL XXL

Chart 3 – yoke

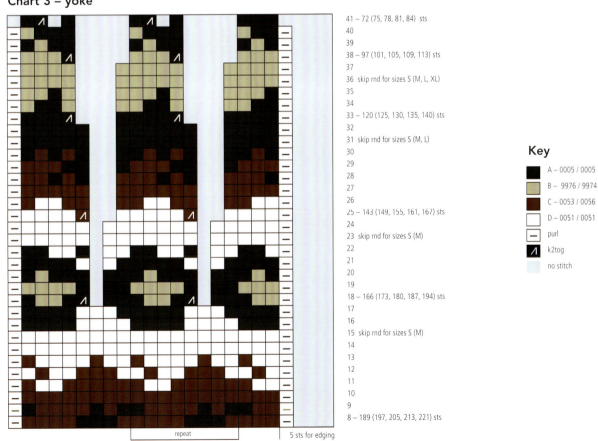

41 – 72 (75, 78, 81, 84) sts
40
39
38 – 97 (101, 105, 109, 113) sts
37
36 skip rnd for sizes S (M, L, XL)
35
34
33 – 120 (125, 130, 135, 140) sts
32
31 skip rnd for sizes S (M, L)
30
29
28
27
26
25 – 143 (149, 155, 161, 167) sts
24
23 skip rnd for sizes S (M)
22
21
20
19
18 – 166 (173, 180, 187, 194) sts
17
16
15 skip rnd for sizes S (M)
14
13
12
11
10
9
8 – 189 (197, 205, 213, 221) sts

repeat   5 sts for edging

Key

A – 0005 / 0005
B – 9976 / 9974
C – 0053 / 0056
D – 0051 / 0051
— purl
⋀ k2tog
no stitch

181

prýði

This cardigan was originally knitted using Álafoss Lopi, but this version is knitted with the more lightweight Létt-Lopi. Beautiful edging details give this cardigan an air of sophistication.

SIZES XS (S, M, L)
Chest: 88/34¾" (93/36½", 97/38", 102/40")
Length to armhole: 58/22¾" (60/23¾", 62/24½", 64/25")
Sleeve length: 45/17¾" (46/18", 48/18¾", 49/19¼")

MATERIALS Létt-Lopi 50g (1.7oz) balls, 100m (109yd)
A 0051 white 9 (9, 10, 10)
B 0052 black sheep heather 3 (3, 3, 3)
C 1418 woodchip 2 (2, 2, 2)
D 1420 shadow 2 (2, 2, 2)

4.5mm (US 7) circular needles 40 and 80cm (16 and 30in), 4.5mm (US 7) double pointed needles, 7 (7, 8, 8) buttons

GAUGE
10 x 10cm (4 x 4in) = 18 sts and 24 rows in st st on 4.5mm (US 7) needles.

NOTE
Body and sleeves are worked in the round from lower edge to underarms, then joined to work yoke in the round. Round begins and ends with a purl st at front of body. The front is cut open.

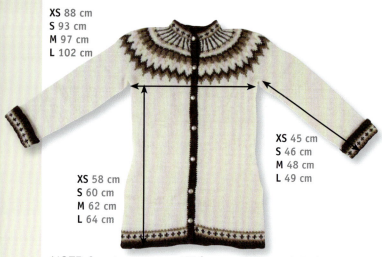

XS 88 cm
S 93 cm
M 97 cm
L 102 cm

XS 45 cm
S 46 cm
M 48 cm
L 49 cm

XS 58 cm
S 60 cm
M 62 cm
L 64 cm

NOTE: See sizes on page 183 for measurements in inches

BODY

Using B and 4.5mm circular needles, CO 163 (171,179, 187) sts. Work garter st back and forth for 6 rows (3 ridges). Join in the rnd and CO 2 sts (these count as the first and last sts in the charts and are always purled) => 165 (173, 181, 189) sts. Work **Chart 1** for Body and then, using A, knit until body measures 21 (22, 24, 24) cm long from CO edge. Place markers so that each cardigan front contains 41 (44, 45, 47) sts and the back contains 83 (87, 91, 95) sts. Dec 2 sts in each side every 10th rnd 5 times (20 sts dec) => 145 (153, 161, 169) sts. Knit 12 rnds. Inc 2 sts in each side every 10th rnd 3 times (12 sts inc) => 157 (165, 173, 181) sts. Knit until body measures 58 (60, 62, 64) cm from CO edge. Set the body aside and make the sleeves.

SLEEVES

Using B and 4.5mm dpn, CO 48 (48, 52, 56) sts. Work garter st for 6 rows (3 ridges). Join in the rnd and work **Chart 1** for sleeves. Using B, knit 1 rnd. Turn the sleeve inside out and knit 1 rnd to form the sleeve's cuff. Now work ribbing: *k1, p1*, rep from * to *, for 11 rnds. Switch to A and k, inc 2 sts (1 st after the first st in the rnd and 1 st before the last st in the rnd) immediately and every 10th rnd after that 6 (7, 7, 6) times => 60 (62, 66, 68) sts. Knit without shaping until sleeve measures 45 (46, 48, 49) cm from the purled row at the bottom of the folded cuff. Place 10 (10, 11, 13) underarm sts on a stitch holder or scrap yarn => 50 (52, 55, 55) sts. Make the other sleeve.

YOKE

Using A and the longer 4.5mm circular needle, join the body and sleeves to work in the rnd. Knit 33 (35, 37, 38) body sts (right front). Place next 11 (11, 12, 13) sts on a stitch holder or scrap yarn. Knit right sleeve 50 (52, 55, 55) sts, knit 69 (73, 75, 79) body sts (back), knit left sleeve 50 (52, 55, 55) sts, knit 33 (35, 37, 38) body sts (left front) => 235 (247, 259, 265) sts. Work **Chart 2**, dec in rnds 1, 22 and 29 according to the chart. In rnd 32, dec 7 (5, 3, 2) sts evenly throughout => 150 (160, 170, 175) sts. Dec according to the chart in rnds 34, 39 and 44. In rnd 47, dec 9 (9, 9, 7) evenly throughout => 57 (61, 65, 69) sts. Switch to a shorter circular needle as the circumference of the yoke becomes smaller.

COLLAR

Work **Chart 3** and then, using B, knit 1 rnd, purl 1 rnd (fold line), knit 8 rnds. BO.

FINISHING

Graft underarm sts. Weave in loose ends, except as follows: pull the loose ends at the front of the sweater out to the RS and lay them down on top of the purl sts. Using a sewing machine and a straight, small stitch, sew 2 lines into each of the purl sts up the front of the sweater, sewing into the loose ends as well along the way. Fold the collar down and stitch it to the WS of the neckline. Cut the front of the sweater.

Buttonband: Using B, work sc along the left edge of the cardigan. Crochet in every other row from the top of the collar to the lower edge. Work 4 rows sc.

Buttonhole band: Using B, work sc along the right edge of the cardigan. Crochet in every other row from the top of the collar to the lower edge. In the next row make 7 (7, 8, 8) buttonholes, evenly spaced. The lowest buttonhole should be placed about 6cm from the CO edge and the highest one in the middle of the collar. Make the buttonholes as follows: chain 1, skip one sc in the row below. In the next row, work 1 sc into the buttonhole. Crochet 2 more rows.

Sew buttons onto the buttonband.

Key

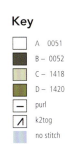

- A 0051
- B – 0052
- C – 1418
- D – 1420
- — purl
- ∕ k2tog
- no stitch

Chart 2 – yoke

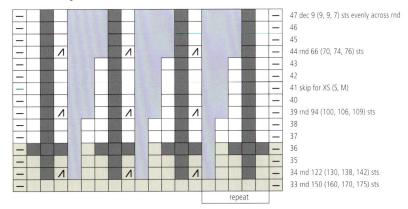

- 47 dec 9 (9, 9, 7) sts evenly across rnd
- 46
- 45
- 44 rnd 66 (70, 74, 76) sts
- 43
- 42
- 41 skip for XS (S, M)
- 40
- 39 rnd 94 (100, 106, 109) sts
- 38
- 37
- 36
- 35
- 34 rnd 122 (130, 138, 142) sts
- 33 rnd 150 (160, 170, 175) sts
- 32 dec 7 (5, 3, 2) L evenly across rnd
- 31
- 30
- 29 rnd 157 (165, 173, 177) sts
- 28
- 27
- 26
- 25
- 24 skip for XS (S, M, L)
- 23
- 22 rnd 196 (206, 216, 221) sts
- 21
- 20
- 19
- 18
- 17
- 16 skip for XS (S)
- 15
- 14
- 13
- 12
- 11
- 10
- 9
- 8
- 7
- 6
- 5
- 4
- 3 skip for XS (S, M, L)
- 2 skip for XS
- 1 rnd 235 (247, 259, 265) sts

Chart 1 – body

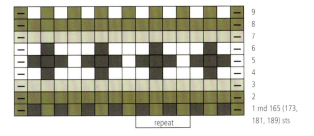

- 9
- 8
- 7
- 6
- 5
- 4
- 3
- 2
- 1 rnd 165 (173, 181, 189) sts

Chart 1 – sleeves

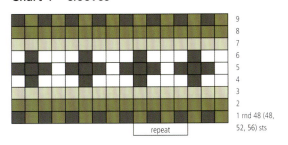

- 9
- 8
- 7
- 6
- 5
- 4
- 3
- 2
- 1 rnd 48 (48, 52, 56) sts

Chart 3 – collar

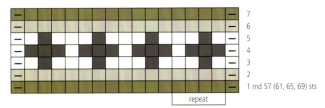

- 7
- 6
- 5
- 4
- 3
- 2
- 1 rnd 57 (61, 65, 69) sts

ranga

Ranga means 'reverse,' so why not celebrate the wrong side? The idea for this garment came as its designer gazed upon a sweater that had been turned inside out.

SIZES S (M, L, XL)
Chest: 89/35" (94/37", 98/38½", 103/40½")
Length to armhole: 36/14" (38/15", 40/15¾", 42/16½")
Sleeve length: 46/18" (47/18½", 48/18¾", 49/19¼")

MATERIALS
Álafoss Lopi 100g (3.5oz) balls, 100m (109yd)
A 0005 black heather 2 (2, 2, 2)
B 0054 ash heather 1 (1, 1, 1)

Létt-Lopi 50g (1.7oz) balls, 100m (109yd)
C 0005 black heather 6 (7, 7, 8)
D 0054 ash heather 2 (2, 3, 3)

6mm (US 10) circular needle 40 and 80cm (16 and 30in), 4.5mm (US 7) circular needles 40, 60–80cm, 4.5 and 6mm (US 7 and 10) double pointed needles, double-ended zipper

GAUGE
10 x 10cm (4 x 4in) = 18 sts and 24 rows of Létt-Lopi in st st on 4.5mm (US 7) needles.

NOTE
Ribbing is worked in Álafoss Lopi but body and sleeves are worked in Létt-Lopi. Body and sleeves are worked in the round from lower edge to underarms, then joined to work yoke in the round. Round begins and ends with a purl st at front of body. The front is cut open.

BODY
CO 150 (158, 162, 170) sts with Álafoss Lopi A using 6mm circular needle. Work back and forth: *p2, k2*, p2 rib for 11 (11, 12, 12) cm. RS: Change to Létt-Lopi C and 4.5mm circular needle, CO 2 sts (p first and last st of rnd) and join in the rnd. Work in st st and inc evenly spaced in first rnd 9 (9, 13, 13) sts => 161 (169, 177, 185) sts. Work until body measures 36 (38, 40, 42) cm.

SLEEVES
CO 32 (32, 36, 36) sts with Álafoss Lopi A using 6mm dpns. Join in the rnd and work *k2, p2* rib for 14cm. Change to Létt-Lopi C and 4.5mm needles. Work in st st and inc evenly spaced in first rnd 28 (32, 32, 36) sts => 60 (64, 68, 72) sts. Work until sleeve measures 46 (47, 48, 49) cm from CO edge. Place 10 (10, 12, 12) sts underarm on st holder => 50 (54, 56, 60) sts. Work second sleeve.

YOKE
Join body and sleeves as follows: With C and 4.5mm circular needle, work right front (beg with purl st) 36 (38, 39, 41) sts, place next 10 (10, 12, 12) sts of body on st holder for underarm. Knit 50 (54, 56, 60) sts of first sleeve. Knit 69 (73, 75, 79) sts of back, place next 10 (10, 12, 12) sts of body on st holder for underarm. Knit 50 (54, 56, 60) sts of second sleeve. Work left front 36 (38, 39, 41) sts (end with purl st) => 241 (257, 265, 281) sts. Work patt and dec's from chart. Change to shorter needle when necessary. When chart is complete => 63 (67, 69, 73) sts, BO 2 purl sts at front => 61 (65, 67, 71) sts.

COLLAR
Change to Álafoss Lopi B and 6mm needle, work rib back and forth: *k2, p2* k2. In first rnd size S: inc 1 st, sizes (M, L, XL): dec (3, 1, 5) sts => 62 (62, 66, 66) sts. Work rib for 8cm. BO in rib.

FINISHING
Graft underarm sts tog and weave in loose ends but pull the ends next to the purl st chain to RS. Sew by machine using straight small stitches twice through each chain of purl sts up body front.
Rinse cardigan by hand in lukewarm water. Carefully lay flat to dry and smooth gently into right shape and measurements.
Zipper: Cut between the sewn rows at front. Sew zipper under front edge twice with thread in matching color, first from RS where edge is folded, then slip stitch edge from WS.

Chart

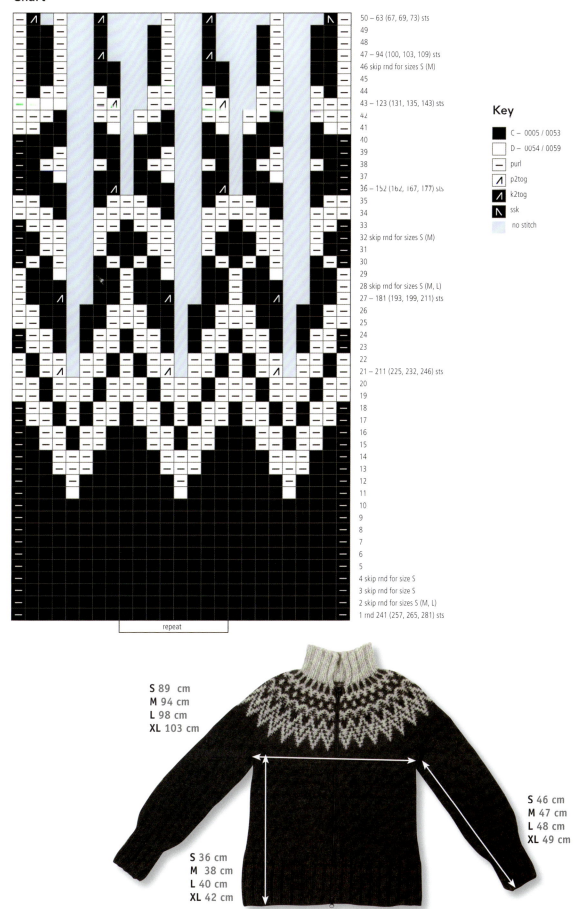

Key
- ■ C – 0005 / 0053
- □ D – 0054 / 0059
- − purl
- ◺ p2tog
- ◸ k2tog
- ◹ ssk
- ░ no stitch

Row labels (right side of chart):
- 50 – 63 (67, 69, 73) sts
- 49
- 48
- 47 – 94 (100, 103, 109) sts
- 46 skip rnd for sizes S (M)
- 45
- 44
- 43 – 123 (131, 135, 143) sts
- 42
- 41
- 40
- 39
- 38
- 37
- 36 – 152 (162, 167, 177) sts
- 35
- 34
- 33
- 32 skip rnd for sizes S (M)
- 31
- 30
- 29
- 28 skip rnd for sizes S (M, L)
- 27 – 181 (193, 199, 211) sts
- 26
- 25
- 24
- 23
- 22
- 21 – 211 (225, 232, 246) sts
- 20
- 19
- 18
- 17
- 16
- 15
- 14
- 13
- 12
- 11
- 10
- 9
- 8
- 7
- 6
- 5
- 4 skip rnd for size S
- 3 skip rnd for size S
- 2 skip rnd for sizes S (M, L)
- 1 rnd 241 (257, 265, 281) sts

repeat

S 89 cm
M 94 cm
L 98 cm
XL 103 cm

S 46 cm
M 47 cm
L 48 cm
XL 49 cm

S 36 cm
M 38 cm
L 40 cm
XL 42 cm

NOTE: See sizes on page 187 for measurements in inches

regla

The design on the yoke is a composite of several different patterns, as was the style in the early 1980s. The cardigan's edgings are worked in a color that contrasts with the main color, giving the sweater a unique look.

SIZES S (M, L, XL)
Chest: 97/38" (101/39¾", 106/41¾ ", 111/43½")
Length to armhole: 40/15¾ " (41/16", 43/17", 45/17¾")
Sleeve length: 46/18" (47/18½", 48/18¾", 49/19¼")

MATERIALS Álafoss Lopi 100g (3.5oz) balls, 100m (109yd)
A 0053 acorn heather 5 (6, 7, 7)
B 0051 white 2 (2, 2, 2)
C 0052 black sheep heather 1 (1, 1, 1)

5mm (US 8) circular needle 80cm (30in), 6mm (US 10) circular needles 40 and 80cm (16 and 30in), 5mm (US 8) double pointed needles, 9 buttons

GAUGE
10 x 10cm (4 x 4in) = 13 sts and 18 rows in st st on 6mm (US 10) needles.

NOTE
Body and sleeves are worked in the round from lower edge to underarms, then joined to work yoke in the round. Round begins and ends with a purl st at front of body. The front is cut open.

BODY

Using B and 5mm circular needle, CO 125 (131, 137, 143) sts. Work 1x1 ribbing, *k1, p1* rep from * to *, until piece measures 5 (5, 6, 6) cm. Switch to 6mm circular needle. CO 2 sts (these count as the first and last sts in the rnd and are always purled) and join in the rnd => 127 (133, 139, 145) sts. Work **Chart 1**. Once chart is complete, knit with A until body measures 40 (41, 43, 45) cm from CO edge, or as desired. Set the body aside and make the sleeves.

SLEEVES

Using B and 5mm needles, CO 30 (30, 32, 32) sts. Join in the rnd and work 1x1 ribbing, *k1, p1* rep from * to *, until piece measures 5 (5, 6, 6) cm. In the last rnd of ribbing, inc 6 (6, 4, 4) sts evenly throughout => 36 sts (all sizes). Switch to 6mm needles and work **Chart 1**. Once chart is complete, knit with A. Inc 2 sts (1 st after the first st of the rnd and 1 st before the last st of the rnd) every 8th rnd 2 (3, 4, 5) times => 40 (42, 44, 46) sts. Knit without shaping until sleeve measures 46 (47, 48, 49) cm from CO edge. Place 8 (9, 10, 11) underarm sts on a stitch holder or scrap yarn => 32 (33, 34, 35) sts. Make the other sleeve.

YOKE

Using A and the longer 6mm circular needle, combine the body and sleeve sts to form the yoke as follows: p1, knit 27 (28, 29, 30) sts (right front), place next 8 (9, 10, 11) sts on a stitch holder or scrap yarn, knit the right sleeve 32 (33, 34, 35) sts, knit 55 (57, 59, 61) sts (back), place next 8 (9, 10, 11) sts on a stitch holder or scrap yarn, knit the left sleeve 32 (33, 34, 35) sts, knit 27 (28, 29, 30) sts (left front), p 1 => 175 (181, 187, 193) sts. Work **Chart 2** followed by 3 rnds using A. Next rnd: dec 28 (28, 30, 30) sts evenly throughout => 147 (153, 157, 163) sts. Knit 1 (1, 3, 3) rnds.
Work **Chart 3** followed by 3 rnds using A. Next rnd: dec 29 (31, 32, 33) sts evenly throughout => 118 (122, 125, 130) sts. Knit 1 (1, 3, 3) rnds.

Work **Chart 4** followed by 2 (2, 4, 4) knit rnds. Next rnd: dec 21 (19, 18, 21) sts evenly throughout => 97 (103, 107, 109) sts. Knit 1 rnd. Next rnd: k2 (2, 1, 2) sts using B *3 sts using C, 3 sts using white yarn* rep from * to * until 5 (5, 4, 5) sts rem, k3 sts using C and 2 (2, 1, 2) sts using B. Knit white sts with B and black sts with C: k2 (2, 1, 2), *k1, k2tog* rep from * to *, knit the last 2 (2, 1, 2) sts => 66 (70, 72, 75) sts. Next rnd: dec 1 (1, 3, 4) sts evenly throughout => 65 (67, 69, 71) sts. Switch to 5mm needles and work 1x1 ribbing, *k1, p1* rep from * to * for 6 rnds. BO.

FINISHING

Graft underarm sts and weave in loose ends. Using a sewing machine and a short, straight stitch, sew 2 lines into each of the purled sts at the front of the sweater. Cut in between the stitches.

Buttonband: Right front, picked up from the RS. Using A and 5mm needles, pick up 3 sts for every 4 rows from the CO edge at the bottom to the BO edge at the neckline. Work 4 rows of 1x1 ribbing, *k1, p1* rep from * to *. Switch to white yarn and work 1 row of ribbing. BO in ribbing. Place markers for 9 buttons on the band; the lowest one should be placed just above the CO and the highest one in the middle of the neckline ribbing. The rest should be evenly distributed in between.

Buttonhole band: Left front, picked up from the RS. Pick up the same number of sts as for the buttonband. Work 2 rows 1x1 ribbing, *k1, p1* rep from * to *. Next row: make buttonholes opposite the button markings as follows: yo, k2tog. Work 1 more rnd of ribbing with A and 1 rnd with white yarn. BO using white yarn and ribbing. Sew buttons onto buttonband.

S 97 cm
M 101 cm
L 106 cm
XL 111 cm

S 46 cm
M 47 cm
L 48 cm
XL 49 cm

S 40 cm
M 41 cm
L 43 cm
XL 45 cm

NOTE: See sizes on page 191 for measurements in inches

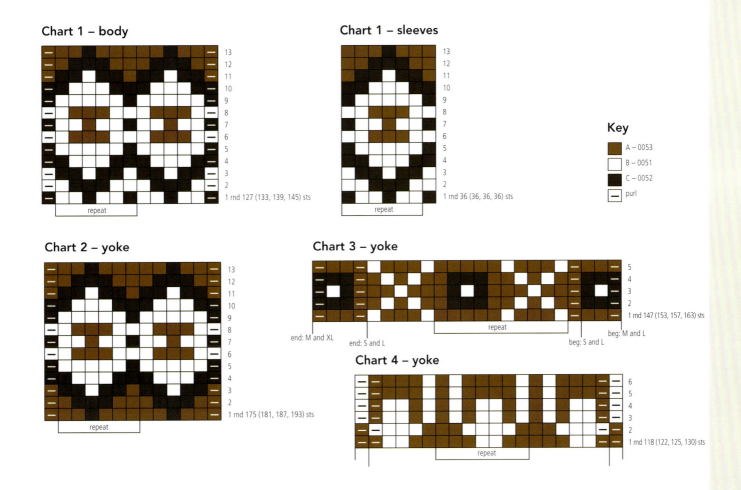

Chart 1 – body
13, 12, 11, 10, 9, 8, 7, 6, 5, 4, 3, 2
1 rnd 127 (133, 139, 145) sts
repeat

Chart 1 – sleeves
13, 12, 11, 10, 9, 8, 7, 6, 5, 4, 3, 2
1 rnd 36 (36, 36, 36) sts
repeat

Key
- A – 0053
- B – 0051
- C – 0052
- — purl

Chart 2 – yoke
13, 12, 11, 10, 9, 8, 7, 6, 5, 4, 3, 2
1 rnd 175 (181, 187, 193) sts
repeat

Chart 3 – yoke
5, 4, 3, 2
1 rnd 147 (153, 157, 163) sts
end: M and XL
end: S and L
repeat
beg: S and L
beg: M and L

Chart 4 – yoke
6, 5, 4, 3, 2
1 rnd 118 (122, 125, 130) sts
repeat

riddari

The color pattern on this sweater is lively and more complex than the usual Icelandic yoke pattern. The sweater also features rolled-up edgings for a modern look.

SIZES XS (S, M, L, XL, XXL)
Chest: 89/35" (93/36½", 98/38½", 102/40", 107/42", 111/43½")
Length to armhole: 40/15¾" (42/16½", 43/17", 44/17¼", 45/17¾", 46/18")
Sleeve length: 47/18½", 49/19¼", 50/19¾", 51/20", 52/20½", 53/21")

MATERIALS Létt-Lopi 50g (1.7oz) balls, 100m (109yd)
A 1416 moor 6 (7, 7, 8, 8, 9)
B 0059 black 2 (2, 2, 3, 3, 3)
C 0086 light beige 1 (1, 1, 1, 1, 1)
D 1417 frostbite 1 (1, 1, 1, 1, 1)

4.5mm (US 7) circular needles 40 and 80cm (16 and 30in), 3.5mm (US 4) circular needles 80cm, 4.5mm and 3.5mm (US 7 and 4) double pointed needles, markers

GAUGE
10 x 10cm (4 x 4in) = 18 sts and 24 rows in st st on 4.5mm (US 7) needles.

NOTE
Body and sleeves are worked in the round from lower edge to underarms, then joined to work yoke in the round. Each round of the body begins on the left side of the sweater, but the yoke rounds begin where the back of the sweater meets the left sleeve.

BODY

CO 160 (168, 176, 184, 192, 200) sts with A using 3.5mm circular needle, join in the rnd and knit 4 rnds. Change to B and knit 1 rnd. Work *k2, p2* rib for 5 rnds. Change to 4.5mm circular needle and work in st st patt from **Chart 1**. When patt is complete cont with A until body measures 40 (42, 43, 44, 45, 46) cm from CO edge. Set aside and work sleeves.

SLEEVES

CO 40 (40) 44 (44) 48 (48) sts with A using 3.5mm dpns. Join in the rnd and knit 4 rnds. Change to B and knit 1 rnd. Work *k2, p2* rib for 5 rnds. Change to 4.5mm dpns and work in st st patt from **Chart 1**. Cont with A and inc 1 st after first st and 1 st before last st of rnd, then in every 7th (7th, 8th, 8th, 9th, 8th) rnd up sleeve, total 11 (12, 11, 12, 11, 12) times => 66 (68, 70, 72, 74, 76) sts. Cont without further shaping until sleeve measures 47 (49, 50, 51, 52, 53) cm from CO edge. Place 9 (10, 11, 12, 13, 14) sts underarm on st holder => 57 (58, 59, 60, 61, 62) sts.
Work second sleeve.

YOKE

Join body and sleeves as follows: With A using 4.5mm circular needle, place the last 5 (5, 6, 6, 7, 7) sts and the first 4 (5, 5, 6, 6, 7) sts of body on st holder for underarm. Knit 57 (58, 59, 60, 61, 62) sts of first sleeve. Knit 71 (74, 77, 80, 83, 86) sts for front, place next 9 (10, 11, 12, 13, 14) sts of body on st holder for underarm. Knit 57 (58, 59, 60, 61, 62) sts of second sleeve. Knit 71 (74, 77, 80, 83, 86) sts for back => 256 (264, 272, 280, 288, 296) sts. Work patt and dec's from **Chart 2** as indicated. Change to shorter circular needle when necessary. When chart is complete => 96 (99, 102 105, 108, 111) sts.

NECKBAND

Change to 3.5mm needle and cont with B. Knit 1 rnd and dec evenly spaced 24 (27, 26, 29, 28, 31) sts => 72 (72, 76, 76, 80, 80) sts. Work *k2, p2* rib for 6 rnds. Change to A and knit 5 rnds. BO loosely.

FINISHING

Graft underarm sts tog and weave in loose ends. Rinse sweater by hand in lukewarm water and lay flat to dry. Let the st st edges roll up.

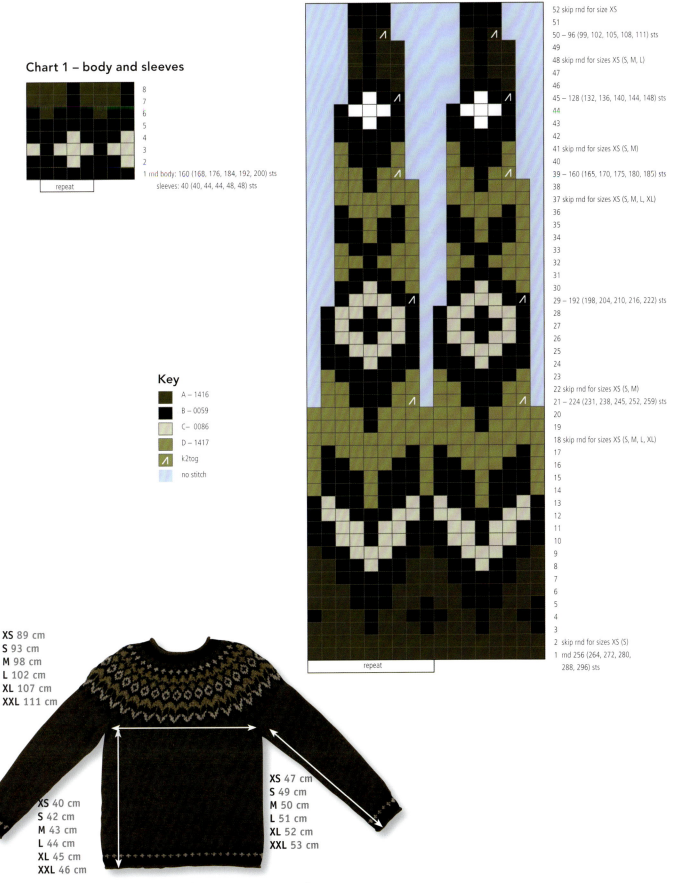

rjúpa

This pretty collar is not only soft and warm, it also instantly dresses up any outfit.

COLLAR

CO 192 sts with A using 4mm circular needle. Work garter stitch 6 rows (knit every row). Change to 4.5mm circular needle and join in the rnd. Work in st st from **Chart 1** and dec as shown. When chart is complete there are => 64 sts.
Rnd 22: *k2tog, yo*, rep from *to* to end.

Knit 2 rnds.
Turn collar and work from WS. Warp stitch to prevent a hole in the piece: Slip first st of R-needle to L-needle; bring wool between the needles to back of work, return slipped st to R-needle.

Work **Chart 2**.

Rnd 1: *k2tog, yo, k1, yo, sl1, k1, psso, k3* rep from *to* to end.

Rnd 2: Knit 1 rnd.

Repeat rnd 1 and rnd 2, 4 times.

Rnd 11: Repeat rnd 1.

Rnd 12: *K7, inc1, k1* rep from *to* to end => 72 sts.

Rnd 13: *k2tog, yo, k1, yo, sl1, k1, psso, K4* rep from *to* to end.

Rnd 14: Knit 1 rnd.

Repeat rnd 13 and rnd 14, 2 times.

Rnd 19: *k2tog, yo* rep from *to* to end.

Knit 1 rnd.

BO very loosely.

FINISHING

Sew garter stitches at beg of collar together. Weave in any loose ends.

Rinse by hand in lukewarm water and lay flat to dry. Make your own cord with color A or draw a silk ribbon through eyelets above pattern. Place beg and end of rnd behind left shoulder.

SIZE Woman

MATERIAL
Létt-Lopi 50g (1.7oz) balls, 100m (109yd)
A 0059 black 1
B 0086 light beige 1
C 0053 acorn 1
D 0051 white 2

4.5mm (US 7) circular needles 40 and 60cm (16 and 24in),
4mm (US 6) circular needle 60cm (24in)

GAUGE
10 x 10cm (4 x 4in) = 18 sts and 24 rows in st st on 4.5mm (US 6) needles.

NOTE
The collar is worked in the round from shoulder to neck, then turned and worked from the wrong side.

Key
- A – 0059
- B – 0086
- C – 0053
- D – 0867
- V lifted stitch
- ⅄ k2tog
- ⅄ ssk
- O yo
- no stitch

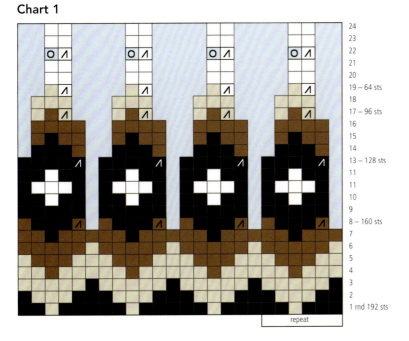

Chart 1 | Chart 2

sigur

The pattern on this sweater's yoke has a distinctive graphic look that makes a strong statement.

SIZES 10 (12, 14) years
Chest: 83/32¾" (92/36¼ ", 97/38")
Length to armhole: 34/13½" (38/15", 42/16½")
Sleeve length: 38/15" (41/16", 44/17¼")

MATERIALS Álafoss Lopi 100g (3.5oz) balls, 100m (109yd)
A 0058 dark gray heather 4 (4, 5)
B 0051 white 1 (1, 2)
C 0005 black heather 1 (2, 2)

4.5mm and 6mm (US 7 and 10) circular needles 60cm (24in), 6mm (US 10) circular needle 40cm (16in), 4.5mm and 6mm (US 7 and 10) double pointed needles

GAUGE
10 x 10cm (4 x 4in) = 13 sts and 18 rows in st st on 6mm (US 10) needles.

NOTE
Body and sleeves are worked in the round from lower edge to underarms, then joined to work yoke in the round. Each round of the body begins on the left side of the sweater, but the yoke rounds begin where the back of the sweater meets the left sleeve.

BODY
Using C and 4.5mm circular needles, CO 108 (120, 126) sts. Join in the rnd and work 1x1 ribbing (*k1, p1*, rep from * to * to end of rnd) for 5 (6, 6) cm. Switch to the longer 6mm circular needles and knit **Chart 1**. Once **Chart 1** is complete, work st st using A until body measures 34 (38, 42) cm from CO edge. Do not knit the last 5 sts of the rnd. Set body aside and knit the sleeves.

SLEEVES
Using C and 4.5mm dpn, CO 28 (32, 34) sts. Join and work 1x1 ribbing (*k1, p1*, rep from * to * to end of rnd) for 5 (6, 6) cm. Switch to the shorter 6mm circular needle and knit 1 rnd, inc 8 (8, 8) sts evenly throughout => 36 (40, 42) sts. Knit **Chart 1**. (Please note that the chart doesn't work for the 12-year-old size, see page 258). After working the chart, inc 2 sts every 6th rnd, 1 st after the first st in the rnd and 1 st before the last st in the rnd, 3 (4, 4) times => 42 (48, 52) sts. Knit until sleeve measures 38 (41, 44) cm from CO edge. In the last rnd, knit until 5 sts remain. Place next 9 (9, 9) sts on a stitch holder or scrap yarn => 33 (39, 43) sts.

YOKE
Combine body and sleeve sts on the longer 6mm circular needle as follows: Place the last 5 (5, 5) sts and first 4 (4, 5) body sts on a stitch holder or scrap yarn. Knit left sleeve 33 (39, 43) sts. Knit 45 (51, 53) body sts (front). Place the next 9 (9, 10) body sts on a stitch holder or scrap yarn, knit the right sleeve onto the needle, 33 (39, 43) sts, and knit the rem 45 (51, 53) body sts (back) => 156 (180, 192) sts. Knit **Chart 2** and remember to skip the indicated rows for sizes 10 (12) yrs. Dec according to the chart. Dec by k2tog, except for rnd 17, where every other dec is a k2tog tbl. Switch to a shorter circular needle when needed. After completing Chart 2 you will have 52 (60, 64) sts rem.

NECKLINE EDGING
Switch to 4.5mm needles and C, knit 1 rnd dec 0 (4, 4) sts evenly => 52 (56, 60) sts. Work 1x1 ribbing *k1, p1*, rep from * to * for 8cm (4cm if you don't want to fold the ribbing). BO.

FINISHING
Weave in loose ends and graft underarm sts. Fold the neckline ribbing (if desired) and stitch to the inside of the sweater. Gently block the sweater into shape.

Chart 1 – body and sleeves

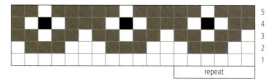

Key
- A – 0058
- B – 0051
- C – 0005
- k2tog
- ssk
- no stitch

Chart 2 – yoke

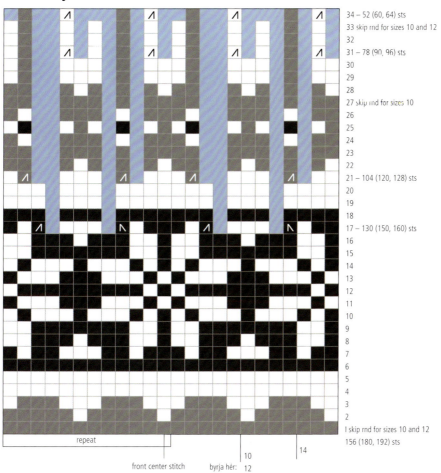

10 83 cm
12 92 cm
14 97 cm

10 38 cm
12 41 cm
14 44 cm

10 34 cm
12 38 cm
14 42 cm

NOTE: See sizes on page 201 for measurements in inches

sjónvarpssokkar

No matter the occasion, it feels cozy and warm to wear these simple heel-less socks while relaxing around the house.

SOCKS

CO 45 (55, 65) sts with A. Purl 1 row (WS) and sl1 st with the yarn in front. Knit 1 row and purl 1 row. On the WS the 1st st at the top of sock is always slipped with the yarn at the front but at the other edge the the 1st is always knit.

Next row (RS): This end is the toe and the other is the top of the leg. Inc 1 st every other row 3 times for all sizes. => 48 (58, 68) sts. After 6 rows of st st knit 4 rows in g stitch. (2 ridges). Next row (RS): Change to B. Colors can be changed as often as wished as long as it is always done on the RS. Knit 24 (32, 36) rows in garter st (12 (16, 18) ridges). Change to A and knit 4 rows in garter st (2 ridges). Finally knit 6 rows int st st and dec 1 st at the beg of each RS row 3 times => 45 (55, 65) sts.

FINISHING

There are several ways of finishing off the front seam:
- BO and sew the cast of row to the CO edge.
- Graft the stitches with the CO edge.
- Turn to the WS and BO the stitches with the CO edge, i.e. knit the st and 1 stitch from the CO edge together and the 2nd st and the 2nd st of the CO edge together then slip the 2nd stitch on the the right hand needle over the 1st and continue to the end. Sew the toe edges together and pull to create a pointed end. Weave in ends and sew a cross stitch with B from the arch up the leg to the top as in the photo.

SIZES child (teenage, adult)
Approx. length: 41/16" (50/19¾", 55/21¾")

MATERIAL Álafoss Lopi 100g (3.5oz) balls, 100m (109yd)
A 9982 lake blue 1 (1, 2)
B 9983 apple green 1 (1, 1)

6mm (US 10) circular needles or 1 pair straight needles

GAUGE

10cm (4in) = 12 sts garter st on 6mm (US 10) needles.

NOTE

The socks are knitted back and forth lengthwise i.e. the start of the row is at the toe and the end is at the top of the sock. Start above the arch then knit down the side of the foot, under the sole and then up the other side. The socks are sewn together at the top of the sock from the toe to the edge. Color changes are made on the right side.

stapi

A challenge to the traditional idea of what a man's Icelandic sweater should look like, Stapi is a cabled and traditionally patterned sweater.

SIZES XS (S, M, L, XL, XXL))
Chest: 93/36½" (98/38½", 102/40", 107/42", 111/43½", 116/45¾")
Length to armhole: 41/16½" (41/16", 43/17", (43/17", 45/17¾", 45/17¾")
Sleeve length: 50/19¾" (50/19¾", 52/20½", 52/20½", 54/21½", 54/21½")

MATERIALS Álafoss Lopi 100g (3.5oz) balls, 100m (109yd)
A 0085 oatmeal heather 5 (5, 5, 6, 6, 7)
B 0051 white 1 (1, 1, 2, 2, 2)
C 0052 black sheep heather 1 (1, 1, 2, 2, 2)

4.5mm and 6mm (US 7 and 10) circular needles 40 and 80cm (16 and 30in), 4.5mm and 6mm (US 7 and 10) double pointed needles, double-ended zipper

GAUGE
10 x 10cm (4 x 4in) = 13 sts and 18 rows in st st on 6mm (US 10) needles.

NOTE
Body and sleeves are worked in the round from lower edge to underarms, then joined to work yoke in the round. Round begins and ends with a purl st at front of body. The front is cut open.

SLEEVES

CO 34 (34, 36, 36, 38, 38) sts with A using 4.5mm dpns. Turn and knit back 1 row (making 1 ridge). WS: Join in the rnd and work *k1, p1* rib for 6 rnds. Change to 6mm dpns and set cable: knit 13 (13, 14, 14, 15, 15) sts, work cable (8 sts) knit to end of rnd. Work st st and cable, at same time inc 1 st after first st and 1 st before last st of rnd after rib, then in every 9th rnd, 7 (8, 8, 9, 9, 10) times up sleeve => 48 (50, 52, 54, 56, 58) sts. Work without further shaping until sleeve measures 50 (50), 52, 52, 54, 54) cm from CO edge or as long as preferred. Place 8 (8, 9, 10, 10, 11) sts underarm on st holder => 40 (42, 43, 44, 46, 47) sts.
Work second sleeve.

BODY

CO 123 (129, 135, 141, 147, 153) sts with A using 4.5mm circular needle. Turn and knit back 1 row (making 1 ridge). Work *k1, p1* rib for 6 rows. WS: Change to 6mm circular needle, CO 2 sts (P first and last st of rnd) and join in the rnd => 125 (131, 137, 143, 149, 155) sts.
Set cable: p1, k3, work right cable (8 sts), k 47 (50, 53, 56, 59, 62) sts, work cable center back, knit to last 12 sts on rnd, work left cable (8 sts) k3, p1. Work in st st and cables from chart until body measures 41 (41, 43, 43, 45, 45) cm or as long as preferred. Set aside and work sleeves.

YOKE

Join body and sleeves as follows: With A using 6mm circular needle, work right front (beg with purl st) 27 (29, 30, 31, 33, 34) sts, place next 9 (8, 9, 10, 9, 10) sts of body on st holder for underarm. Knit 40 (42, 43, 44, 46, 47) sts of first sleeve. Knit 53 (57, 59, 61, 65, 67) sts of back, place next 9 (8, 9, 10, 9, 10) sts of body on st holder for underarm. Knit 40 (42, 43, 44, 46, 47) sts of second sleeve. Work left front 27 (29, 30, 31, 33, 34) sts, end with purl st => 187 (199, 205, 211, 223, 229) sts. Work patt and dec's from Chart 2 as indicated. Change to shorter circular needle when necessary. When chart is complete => 65 (69, 71, 73, 77, 79) sts.

XS 93 cm
S 98 cm
M 102 cm
L 107 cm
XL 111 cm
XXL 116 cm

XS 50 cm
S 50 cm
M 52 cm
L 52 cm
XL 54 cm
XXL 54 cm

XS 41 cm
S 41 cm
M 43 cm
L 43 cm
XL 45 cm
XXL 45 cm

NOTE: See sizes on page 207 for measurements in inches

NECKBAND

Cont with A and change to 4.5mm needle. BO purl st, knit 1 rnd and dec evenly spaced 2 (6, 6, 8, 10, 10) sts, BO end purl st => 61 (61, 63, 63, 65, 67) sts. Now work back and forth, *p1, k1* rib for 8 rows. Next row WS: knit 1 row. Beige: Change to C, Blue: Change to B, work in st st for 5 rows. BO loosely.

FINISHING

Graft underarm sts tog. Weave in loose ends but pull the ends by the purl st chain to RS. Sew by machine using straight small stitches across the ends as you sew twice through each chain of purl sts up body front. Rinse cardigan by hand in lukewarm water and lay flat to dry.

Zipper: Cut between the sewn rows at front. Sew zipper under front edge twice with thread in matching color, first from RS where edge is folded, then slip stitch edge from WS. Fold neckband in half to inside at purl row and slip stitch in place, hiding the fabric end of zipper inside the neckband.

Key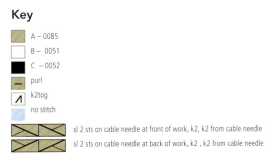

Chart – yoke

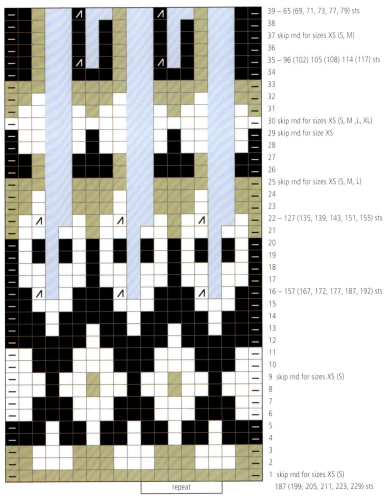

Cable – right side and sleeve

Cable – right side and sleeve

strax

A simple, masculine sweater knitted using bulky Icelandic wool. The set-in sleeves are knit separately. Without a yoke pattern, this sweater's main visual element is the tweedy flecks of color in the wool.

SIZES S (M, L)
Chest: 96/37¾" (105/41¼", 113/44½")
Body length from shoulder: 63/24¾" (65/25½", 67/26½")
Sleeve length: 49/19¼" (50/19¾", 51/20")

MATERIAL Bulky Lopi 100g (3.5oz) hanks, 60m (966yd) 1416 country green tweed 9 (9, 10)

9mm (US 13) circular needles 40 and 80cm (16 and 30in), 8mm (US 11) circular needle 80cm (30in), 8mm and 9mm (US 11 and 13) double pointed needles

GAUGE
10 x 10cm (4 x 4in) = 9.5 sts and 13 rows in st st on 9mm (US 13) needles.

NOTE
Body and sleeves are worked in the round to underarm. From underarm, body and top of sleeves are worked back and forth.

BODY

CO 92 (100, 108) sts with 8mm circular needle. Join in the rnd and work 5cm rib: *k1, p1*. Change to 9mm circular needle and work st st until body measures 41 (42, 43) cm from CO edge. Divide body in half and BO 6 (6, 8) sts at each side. Back => 40 (44, 46) sts. Front => 40 (44, 46) sts. Now work back and forth; knit on RS, purl on WS.

Back: Dec 1 st at beg and 1 st at end of next 3 (4, 4) rows. Work until armhole measures 21 (22, 23) cm. Shoulder shaping: BO 4 (5, 6) sts (RS) work 8 sts, turn. BO 2 sts, work 6 sts, turn. BO 6 sts. Break yarn. BO 10 sts at neck edge, work to end of row. BO 4 (5, 6) sts, work 8 sts, turn. BO 2 sts, work 6 sts, turn. BO 6 sts. Break yarn.

Front: Dec 1 st at beg and 1 st at end of next 3 (4, 4) rows. Work until armhole measures 16 (17, 18) cm. Work 14 (15, 16) sts, BO 6 sts (RS) for neck, work 14 (15, 16) sts. Work each shoulder seperately: Dec at neck 1 st on both sides 3 times, then once following 2nd row. Work until armhole measures 21 (22, 23) cm. BO from shoulder 4 (5, 6) sts, work 6 sts, turn and BO.

SLEEVES

CO 26 (26, 28) sts with 8mm dpn. Join in the rnd and work 5cm rib: *k1, p1*. Change to 9mm dpn and work st st. Inc 1 st at beg of rnd in every 4th rnd, 12 (14, 14) times => 38 (40, 42) sts. Work without further shaping until sleeve measures 49 (50, 51) cm. Now sleeve is worked back and forth. BO 3 (3, 4) sts at beg of row, work to end of row. Turn and BO 3 (3, 4) sts, work to end of row. Dec 1 st at beg and end of next 8 (9) 9 rows. Dec 2 sts at beg and end of next 2 rows. BO rem 8 sts. Work second sleeve.

FINISHING/NECKBAND

Join shoulder seams and weave in loose ends.

Collar: Pick up evenly from RS around neck 40 (40, 42) sts using 8mm needles. Join in the rnd and work rib: *k1, p1*. Work 11 rnds rib. BO loosely in rib.

Sew sleeves carefully to armhole from RS and weave in any loose ends.

Rinse sweater and lay flat to dry.

NOTE: See sizes on page 211 for measurements in inches

strik

A simple yet beautiful lace scarf knitted using lace-weight wool.

SCARF

Using 4mm needle, CO 39 sts very loosely. Work back and forth in garter St for 5 rows (3 ridges). Work pattern (8 rows) from chart a total of 40 times or as long as preferred. Chart shows RS rows plus 3 extra knit stitches at either edge. Work WS rows: k3, P33, k3. After last patt row, work back and forth in garter St for 5 rows.

BO: knit first stitch, *pull the stitch (so it becomes bigger) and pass the stitch back onto left needle over the second stitch on the needle, knit second st through the first stitch. Slip both stitches from left needle*. Rep from *to*. Take care to pull the stitches evenly and work the BO as loosely as the CO.

FINISHING

Weave in loose ends. Rinse by hand in lukewarm water, squeeze out excess water with towel and lay flat to dry, pinning the edges carefully.

SIZE after blocking

Length: 120/47"
Width: 20/7.5"

MATERIALS

Einband 50g (1.7oz) balls, 225m (245yd)
0047 red 1

4mm (US 6) circular needle 60cm (24in)

BLOCKED GAUGE

1 patt rep: 6 x 3cm = 11 sts and 8 rows

NOTE

The scarf is worked back and forth. Add repeats of pattern if you prefer the scarf to be longer. It will stretch when washed and blocked.

Key

- k on RS, p on WS
- yo
- k2tog
- ssk

Chart

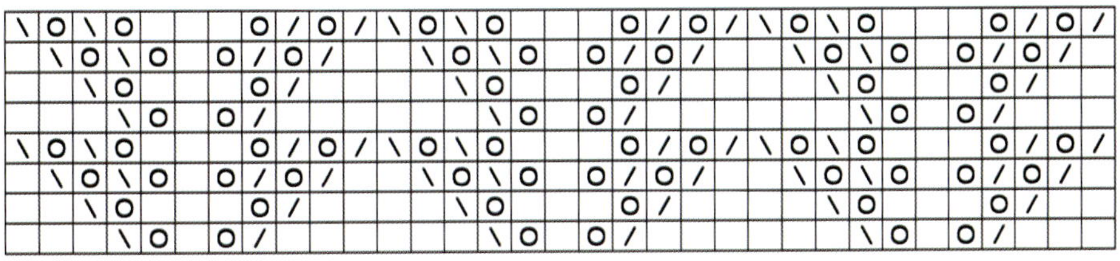

Chart shows every other row: 1, 3, 5, …. k3, knit 33 st from chart, k3
Rows 2, 4, 6, … are knit on the WS: k3, p33, k3.

strýta

This beautiful sweater's pattern has a well-balanced color pattern that can easily be adapted to suit each individual knitter's color preferences. The same pattern can also be found in the longer sweater, Astrid on page 34.

SIZES XS (S, M, L, XL, XXL)
Chest: 97/38" (102/40", 106/41¾", 111/43½", 115/45¼", 120/47¼")
Length to armhole: 40/15¾" (41/16", 42/16½", 43/17", 44/17¼", 45/17¾")
Sleeve length:
Women's: 45/17¾" (46/18", 47/18½", 48/18¾", 49/19¼", 50/19¾")
Men's: 48/18¾" (49/19¼", 50/19¾", 51/20", 52/20½", 53/21")

MATERIALS Álafoss Lopi 100g (3.5oz) balls, 100m (109yd)
A 0054 ash heather 5 (5, 6, 6, 6, 7)
B 0058 dark gray heather 2 (2, 2, 2, 2, 2)
C 0005 black heather 2 (2, 2, 2, 2, 2)

4.5mm and 6mm (US 7 and 10) circular needles 40 and 80cm (16 and 30in), 4.5mm and 6mm (US 7 and 10) double pointed needles.

GAUGE
10 x 10cm (4 x 4in) = 13 sts and 18 rows in st st using 6mm (US 10) needles.

NOTE
Body and sleeves are worked in the round from lower edge to underarms, then joined to work yoke in the round. Each round of the body begins on the left side of the sweater, but the yoke rounds begin where the back of the sweater meets the left sleeve.

BODY

Using C and 4.5mm circular needle, CO 120 (126, 132, 138, 144, 150) sts. Join in the rnd and work 1x1 ribbing, *k1, p1*, rep from * to *, for 3cm. Switch to 6mm circular needle and inc 6 sts evenly throughout the rnd => 126 (132, 138, 144, 150, 156) sts. Knit **Chart 1**. Once chart is complete, cont knitting with A until piece measures 40 (41, 42, 43, 44, 45) cm from CO edge. On the last rnd, do not knit the last 4 (4, 5, 4, 5, 5) sts. Set the body aside and make the sleeves.

SLEEVES

Using C and 4.5mm dpn, CO 32 (34, 36, 38, 42, 42) sts. Join in the rnd and work 1x1 ribbing, *k1, p1*, rep from * to *, for 3cm. Switch to 6mm needles and inc 4 (2, 6, 4, 6, 6) sts evenly throughout the rnd => 36 (36, 42, 42, 48, 48) sts. Knit **Chart 1**. Once chart is complete, contknitting with A, immediately inc 2 sts (1 st after the first st in the rnd and 1 st before the last st in the rnd) and then inc again in every 10th (8th, 10th, 8th, 10th, 8th) rnd 5 (6, 5, 7, 5, 6) times => 46 (48, 52, 56, 58, 60) sts. Knit without shaping until sleeve measures 45 (46, 47, 48, 49, 50) cm from CO edge for a woman or 48 (49, 50, 51, 52, 53) cm from CO edge for a man. Place 8 (8, 9, 9, 10, 11) underarm sts on a stitch holder or scrap yarn => 38 (40, 43, 47, 48, 49) sts. Make the other sleeve.

YOKE

Using A and the longer 6mm circular needle, combine the body and sleeve sts to form the yoke as follows: place 8 (7, 10, 8, 9, 10) body sts on a stitch holder or scrap yarn, knit the first sleeve 38 (40, 43, 47, 48, 49) sts, knit 55 (59, 59, 64, 66, 68) sts (back), place next 8 (7, 10, 8, 9, 10) body sts on a stitch holder or scrap yarn, knit the second sleeve 38 (40, 43, 47, 48, 49) sts, knit 55 (59, 59, 64, 66, 68) sts (front) => 186 (198, 204, 222, 228, 234) sts. Knit **Chart 2** and dec accordingly. Switch to a

NOTE: See sizes on page 217 for measurements in inches

XS 97 cm
S 102 cm
M 106 cm
L 111 cm
XL 115 cm
XXL 120 cm

XS 40 cm
S 41 cm
M 42 cm
L 43 cm
XL 44 cm
XXL 45 cm

XS 48 cm
S 49 cm
M 50 cm
L 51 cm
XL 52 cm
XXL 53 cm

Chart 2 – yoke

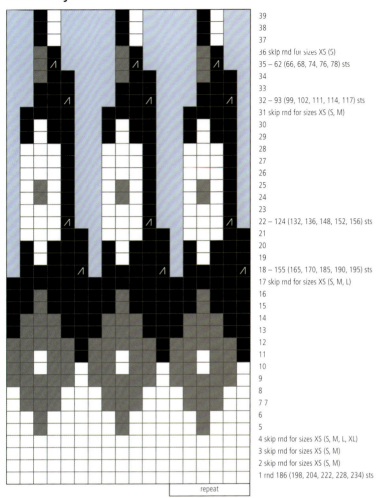

- 39
- 38
- 37
- 36 skip rnd for sizes XS (S)
- 35 – 62 (66, 68, 74, 76, 78) sts
- 34
- 33
- 32 – 93 (99, 102, 111, 114, 117) sts
- 31 skip rnd for sizes XS (S, M)
- 30
- 29
- 28
- 27
- 26
- 25
- 24
- 23
- 22 – 124 (132, 136, 148, 152, 156) sts
- 21
- 20
- 19
- 18 – 155 (165, 170, 185, 190, 195) sts
- 17 skip rnd for sizes XS (S, M, L)
- 16
- 15
- 14
- 13
- 12
- 11
- 10
- 9
- 8
- 7
- 6
- 5
- 4 skip rnd for sizes XS (S, M, L, XL)
- 3 skip rnd for sizes XS (S, M)
- 2 skip rnd for sizes XS (S, M)
- 1 rnd 186 (198, 204, 222, 228, 234) sts

Chart 1 – body and sleeves

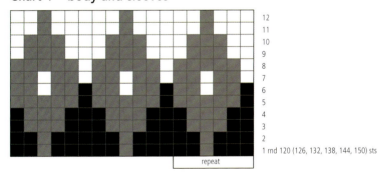

- 12
- 11
- 10
- 9
- 8
- 7
- 6
- 5
- 4
- 3
- 2
- 1 rnd 120 (126, 132, 138, 144, 150) sts

Key

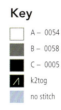

- A – 0054
- B – 0058
- C – 0005
- k2tog
- no stitch

shorter circular needle as the yoke's circumference becomes smaller. Once chart is complete => 62 (66, 68, 74, 76, 78) sts rem.

NECKLINE EDGING

Using C and 4.5mm circular needle, knit 1 rnd, dec 4 (6, 6, 10, 10, 10) sts evenly throughout => 58 (60, 62, 64, 66, 68) sts. Work 1x1 ribbing, *k1, p1*, rep from * to *, for 3cm. BO.

FINISHING

Graft the underarm sts and weave in loose ends. Gently block the sweater into shape.

toppur

Surviving centuries of Icelandic weather, the sheep have developed a unique weatherproof fleece. Hats knitted using lopi keep you warm, no matter how cold it is outside.

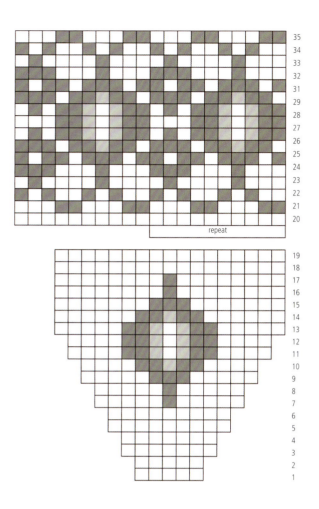

Key

- A – 0054/0056
- B – 0058
- C – 0056 (only for the pale hat)

SIZES Adult 56/22" 58/23"

MATERIALS Álafoss Lopi 100g (3.5oz) balls, 100m (109yd)
Pale hat
A 0054 ash heather 1 (1)
B 0058 dark gray heather 1 (1)
C 0056 light ash heather 1 (1)
Dark hat
A 0056 light ash heather 1 (1)
B 0058 dark gray heather 1 (1)

6mm (US 10) double pointed needles, 6mm circular needle 40cm (16in), 5mm (US H/8) crochet hook

GAUGE
10 x 10cm (4 x 4in) = 13 sts and 18 rows in st.st. on 6mm (US 10) needles.

NOTE
The earflaps are knit back and forth and then sts are CO between them for the front and back of the hat and then knitted in the round.

HAT

Earflaps: CO 5 sts with color A on 6mm needles. k2 rows in garter stitch (both sides knit). Inc 1 st at the beginning and end of every other row (1 st after the first st and 1 st before the last stitch of the row, 6 times => 17 sts. Knit in st st for 19 rows from the beg, ending on the RS. The colorwork patt can be knitted following the chart, remember to have the strand of wool at the front when knitting the WS. Knit 2 earflaps

Crown: CO 13 sts (back), knit across one earflap, CO 23 sts (front) and knit across second earflap => 70 sts. Join in the rnd and knit one rnd. Knit the stranded patt from the chart. Make sure the placement of the pattern matches the patt on the earflaps charts. Knit 1 rnd after completing the chart. Now knit the star decrease: *(k8 sts, k2tog) rep from* to end of rnd. Continue dec every other rnd until 7 sts remain. The number of stitches decreases by 1 st on every dec rnd. Break the yarn and thread it through the rem sts. Weave in ends and crochet a rnd of double crochet aound the edge of the entire hat.

upp

Knit using lace-weight wool and small needles, these wrist warmers are delicate and lovely.

RIGHT WRIST WARMER

Using three or four 2.5mm dpns, CO loosely 60 (68) sts and join in the rnd. Work twisted rib: *k1tbl, p1*, 8 rnds.
Knit 1 rnd.
Place pattern: knit 10 (12) sts, place marker, work first rnd of 10 sts pattern from **Chart**, knit 10 (12) sts, place marker at left side, knit 30 (34) sts to end of rnd. Work pattern and dec at same time:
Work 5 rnds.
1st dec: ssk , work st st and pattern as before to 2 st before marker at left side: k2tog, ssk . Knit to 2 sts before marker at RS k2tog => 56 (64) sts.
Work 11 rnds.
2nd dec: dec 4 sts as before.
Work 11 rnds.

3rd dec: dec 4 sts as before.
Work 7 rnds.
4th dec: dec 4 sts as before => 44 (52) sts.
Work 7 rnds.
Wrist rib: knit 6 (8) sts, work 10 sts pattern, knit 6 (8) sts, work 22 (26) sts in twisted rib: *k1tbl, p1*. Work total 7 rnds.
1st inc: Cont working st st and pattern. Inc after rib on right and left side: k1, M1L, work to 1 st before marker, M1R, k2, M1L, work to 1 st before end of rnd, M1R, k1 => 48 (56) sts.
Work 3 rnds.
2nd inc: inc 2 sts at left side.
Work 3 rnds.
3rd inc: inc 4 sts, right and left side.
Work 3 rnds.
4th inc: inc 2 sts at left side.
Work 3 rnds.
5th inc: inc 2 sts at RS => 58 (66) sts.
Work 12 (15) rnds.
Thumb placement: Work 29 (33) sts, knit next 8 (9) sts to piece of scrap yarn in different color, slip these sts back to left needle and work again, work to end of rnd. Work 3 rnds.
1st dec: at left side: k2tog, ssk .
Work 3 rnds.
2nd dec: Dec 4 sts, right and left side.
Work 3 rnds.
3rd dec: Dec 2 sts at left side => 50 (58) sts.
Work 4 rnds twisted rib: *k1tbl, p1*. BO in rib.

Thumb: Pick up 20 (22) sts from scrap yarn, and 1-2 sts from the strand between the rows. Divide sts to 3 needles and knit 5 rnds. Work 4 rnds twisted rib. BO.

LEFT WRIST WARMER
Work as right wrist warmer, but place thumb and dec/inc after wrist rib reversed to right wrist warmer.

SIZES S/M (L/XL)

MATERIALS Einband 50g (1.7oz) balls, 225m (245yd)
0851 white 1 (1)

2.5mm (US 1) double pointed needles, markers

GAUGE
10 x 10cm (4 x 4in) = 30 sts and 40 rows in st st on 2.5mm (US 1) needles.

NOTE
The wrist warmers are worked in the round. Each round begins at right side.

Chart

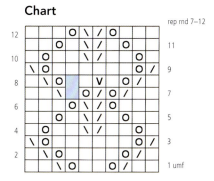

Key

knit
yo
k2tog
ssk
lifted stitch
no stitch

FINISHING
Weave in loose ends. Rinse by hand in lukewarm water, squeeze out excess water with towel and lay flat to dry.

útjörð

This simple sweater is knit using two strands of unspun Icelandic wool held together. The choice of colors evoke the sight of mountains on the horizon.

SIZES S (M, L, XL, XXL)
Chest: 91/35½" (97/38", 102/40", 108/42½", 114/44¾")
Length to armhole: 42/16½" (43/17", 44/17¼", 45/17¾", 46/18")
Sleeve length:
Men's: 49/19¼" (50/19¾", 51/20", 52/20½", 53/21")
Women's: 46/18" (47/18½", 48/18¾", 49/19¼", 50/19¾")

MATERIALS Plötulopi 100g (3.5oz) plates, 300m (328yd)
A 1432 winter blue 2 (2, 2, 2, 2)
B 0709 midnight blue 1 (1, 1, 1, 1)
C 1422 sea green 1 (1, 1, 1, 1)
D 1420 marsh heather 1 (1, 1, 1, 1)
E 1052 denim 1 (1, 1, 1, 1)
F 1053 faded denim 1 (1, 1, 1, 1)

5.5mm (US 9) circular needles 40 and 80cm (16 and 30in), 4.5mm (US 7) circular needle 80cm (30in), 4.5mm and 5.5mm (US 7 and 9) double pointed needles

GAUGE
10 x 10cm (4 x 4in) = 14 sts and 19 rows in st st on 5.5mm (US 9) needles.

NOTE
Body and sleeves are worked in the round from lower edge to underarms, then joined to work yoke in the round. Each round of the body begins on the left side of the sweater, but the yoke rounds begin where the back of the sweater meets the left sleeve.
Knit from the plates or carefully wind two strands of wool together for each color. When knitting, vary the way you carry the 2 strands to make the colors more changeable.

SLEEVES

CO 36 (38 38 40 42) sts with **A+B** using 4.5mm dpns. Join in the rnd and work *k1tbl, p1* rib for 4cm. Change to 5.5mm needles and work in st st . Inc 1 st after first st and 1 st before last st of rnd, after that:

men's: every 12th (12th 11th 11th 11th) rnd

women's: every 11th (11th 10th 10th 10th) rnd total 7 (7 8 8 8) times up sleeve => 50 (52 54 56 58) sts.

Change colors at same time.

Color changes men's:

1: Cont with **A+B**, work 17 (18 18 18 19) cm from CO edge.

2: Change to **A+C**, work 16 (16 17 17 17) cm.

3: Change to **A+D**, work 15 (15 15 16 16) cm.

4: Change to **A+E**, work 1cm or until sleeve measures 49 (50 51 52 53) cm from CO edge.

Color changes women's:

1: Cont with **A+B**, work 16 (17 17 17 18) cm from CO edge.

2: Change to **A+C**, work 15 (15 16 16 16) cm.

3: Change to **A+D**, work 14 (14 14 15 15) cm.

4: Change to **A+E**, work 1cm or until sleeve measures 46 (47 48 49 50) cm from CO edge.

Place 7 (8 9 10 11 sts underarm on st holder => 43 (44 45 46 47) sts.

Work second sleeve.

BODY

CO 128 (136 144 152 160) sts with **A+B** using 4.5mm circular needle. Join in the rnd and work *k1tbl, p1* rib for 4cm. Change to 5.5mm circular needle and work in st st.

Color changes:

1: Cont with **A+B**, work 15 (15 16 16 16) cm from CO edge.

2: Change to **A+C**, work 14 (14 14 15 15) cm.

3: Change to **A+D**, work 12 (13 13 13 14) cm.

4: Change to **A+E**, work 1cm or until body measures 42 (43 44 45 46) cm from CO edge. Do not work last 4 (4 5 5 6) sts of last rnd. Set aside and work sleeves.

NOTE: See sizes on page 225 for measurements in inches

S 91 cm
M 97 cm
L 102 cm
XL 108 cm
XXL 114 cm

S 42 cm
M 43 cm
L 44 cm
XL 45 cm
XXL 46 cm

S 49 cm
M 50 cm
L 51 cm
XL 52 cm
XXL 53 cm

YOKE

Join body and sleeves as follows: With **A+E** and 5.5mm circular needle, place 4 (4 5 5 6) last sts and 3 (4 4 5 5) first sts of body on st holder for underarm. Knit 43 (44 45 46 47) sts of first sleeve. Knit 57 (60 63 66 69) sts for front, place next 7 (8 9 10 11) sts of body on st holder for underarm. Knit 43 (44 45 46 47) sts of second sleeve. Knit 57 (60 63 66 69) sts for back => 200 (208 216 224 232) sts. Work dec's and colors change from chart as indicated. Change to shorter circular needle when necessary. When chart is complete => 75 (78 81 84 87) sts.

NECKBAND

Change to **E+E** and 4.5mm needles. Knit 1 rnd and dec evenly spaced 15 (16 17 18 19) sts => 60 (62 64 66 68) sts. Work *k1tbl, p1* rib for 4cm. Cont with one strand of plötulopi **E** and work 6 rnds in st st . BO loosely.

FINISHING

Graft underarm sts tog and weave in loose ends. Rinse sweater by hand in lukewarm water and lay flat to dry.

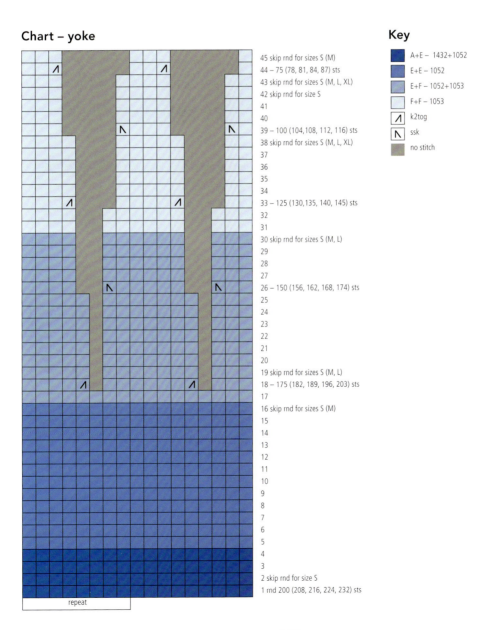

Chart – yoke

45 skip rnd for sizes S (M)
44 – 75 (78, 81, 84, 87) sts
43 skip rnd for sizes S (M, L, XL)
42 skip rnd for size S
41
40
39 – 100 (104,108, 112, 116) sts
38 skip rnd for sizes S (M, L, XL)
37
36
35
34
33 – 125 (130,135, 140, 145) sts
32
31
30 skip rnd for sizes S (M, L)
29
28
27
26 – 150 (156, 162, 168, 174) sts
25
24
23
22
21
20
19 skip rnd for sizes S (M, L)
18 – 175 (182, 189, 196, 203) sts
17
16 skip rnd for sizes S (M)
15
14
13
12
11
10
9
8
7
6
5
4
3
2 skip rnd for size S
1 rnd 200 (208, 216, 224, 232) sts

Key

- A+E – 1432+1052
- E+E – 1052
- E+F – 1052+1053
- F+F – 1053
- k2tog
- ssk
- no stitch

varmi

These socks evoke cozy moments in front of the fireplace, curled up with a cup of cocoa and a good book. They are as warm and comfy as slippers.

SOCKS

With 5 mm needles and A cast on 40 sts. Knit ribbing, *k1, p1*, for 5-6 cm. Change to 5.5 mm needles and knit the pattern from the chart. On row 33 knit the waste band across the stitches on the front of the sock, between the light colored side-stitches (see chart). Place these stitches back onto the left needle and continue knitting from the chart.

Heel: Knit according to chart. Cast off last stitches, be sure that the light side-stitches cover the dark ones. This pattern carries across the bottom of the sock.

Foot: The foot is knitted with rose-pattern on the arch and checker-pattern (alternating light and dark sts as on heel) across the sole. Undo the waste yarn and place the stitches on 4 needles. There will be fewer

SIZES S (M, L)
Foot length: 24/9½" (28/11", 30/11¾")cm

MATERIAL Álafoss Lopi 100g (3.5oz) balls, 100m (109yd)
Perfect for leftover yarn, 100 gr main color and
50 gr of contrast colors.
A 0005 black heather 1   B 0054 ash heather 1
C 0056 light ash heather 1   D 0058 dark ash heather 1
or
Plötulopi - 100g (3.5oz) plates, 300 M (320yd)
A 0005 black heather 1   B 1026 ash heather 1
C 1027 light gray heather 1   D 9102 gray heather 1

5mm and 5.5mm (US 8 and 9) double pointed needles

GAUGE
10 x 10 cm (4 x 4in) = 16,5 sts and 16 rows in pattern with Álafoss Lopi in st st on 5.5mm (US 9) needles.
10 x 10 cm (4 x 4in) = 15 sts and 14.5 rows in pattern with 3 strands of plötulopi on 5.5mm (US 9) needles.

NOTE
Knit using either Álafoss Lopi or 3 strands of Plötulopi. The socks are knitted from the top down. A length of waste yarn is knitted across the front before the heel is knitted and then undone so the arch can be completed. The pattern ends at different places on the chart depending on the length of the sock.

stitches on the sole (the heel-stitches are now upside down). Make 1 black stitch on either side (hook up the black strand, twist it and knit). In order to keep the light side-stitch continuous knit into 2nd row below. Be sure to have a black stitch on either side of the light side-stitches. The smallest sock has 3 complete rose patterns. Decrease for the toe as shown on the chart.

FINISHING
Weave in all ends and then soak and lay flat to dry.

Toe decreases depending on size of sock

Size L

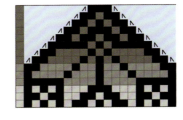

Size M

Size S

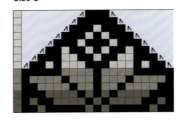

Key

Heel from underneath / pattern at front   Heel at back

beg

verur

A lightweight sweater for either boys or girls that's perfect for camping trips in the summer and school in the winter.

SIZES 8 (10 12 14) years
Chest: 80/31½" (84/33", 89/35", 93/36½")
Length to armhole: 34/13½" (37/14½", 39/15½", 42/16½")
Sleeve length: 36/14" (39/15½", 42/16½", 45/17¾")

MATERIALS Létt-Lopi 50g (1.7oz) balls, 100m (109yd)
Beige
A 0085 oatmeal 5 (5, 5, 6)
B 0052 black sheep 2 (2, 3, 3)
C 0086 light beige 1 (1, 1, 1)
D 0051 white 1 (1, 1, 1)

Blue
A 9418 stone blue 5 (5, 5, 6)
B 0054 ash 2 (2, 3, 3)
C 1415 rough sea 1 (1, 1, 1)
D 0005 black heather 1 (1, 1, 1)

3.5mm and 4.5mm (US 4 and 7) circular needles 40, 60 and 80cm (16, 24 and 30in), 3.5mm and 4.5mm (US 4 and 7) double pointed needles

GAUGE
10 x 10cm (4 x 4in) = 18 sts and 24 rows in st st on 4.5mm (US 7) needles

NOTE
Body and sleeves are worked in the round from lower edge to underarms, then joined to work yoke in the round. Each round of the body begins on the left side of the sweater, but the yoke rounds begin where the back of the sweater meets the left sleeve.

BODY

CO 140 (148, 156, 164) sts with B using 3.5mm circular needle. Join in the rnd and work *k1, p1* rib for 4 (4, 5, 5) cm. Change to 4.5mm circular needle and work in st st from **Chart 1**, inc 4 sts evenly spaced in first rnd => 144 (152, 160, 168) sts. When chart is complete cont with A until body measures 34 (37, 39, 42) cm from CO edge. Set aside and work sleeves.

SLEEVES

CO 34 (36, 38, 38) sts with B using 3.5mm dpns. Join in the rnd and work *k1, p1* rib for 4 (4, 5, 5) cm. Change to 4.5mm needles and work in st st patt from **Chart 1** inc 2 (0, 2, 2) sts evenly spaced in first rnd => 36 (36, 40, 40) sts. When chart is complete cont with A, inc 1 st after first st and 1 st before last st of rnd, then in every 9th (9th 11th 11th) rnd, total 7 (8, 7, 8) until => 50 (52, 54, 56) sts. Cont without further shaping until sleeve measures 36 (39, 42, 45) cm from CO edge. Place 9 (10, 11, 12) underarm sts on st holder => 41 (42, 43, 44) sts.
Work second sleeve.

YOKE

Join body and sleeves as follows: With A and 4.5mm circular needle, place the last 5 (5, 6, 6) sts and the first 4 (5, 5, 6) sts of body on st holder for underarm. Knit 41 (42, 43, 44) sts of first sleeve. Knit 63 (66, 69, 72) sts for front, place next 9 (10, 11, 12) sts of body on st holder for underarm. Knit 41 (42, 43, 44) sts of second sleeve. Knit 63 (66, 69, 72) sts for back => 208 (216, 224, 232) sts. Work patt and decs from Chart 2 as indicated. Change to shorter circular needle or dpns when necessary. When chart is complete => 78 (81, 84, 87) sts.

NECKBAND

Change to 3.5mm needles, cont with B and dec 10 (11, 12, 13) sts => 68 (70, 72, 74) sts, evenly spaced. Work *k1, p1* rib for 7 (7, 8, 8) cm. BO loosely.

FINISHING

Graft underarm sts tog and weave in loose ends. Fold neckband in half to inside and slip stitch in place. Rinse sweater by hand in lukewarm water. Carefully lay flat to dry and smooth gently into right shape and measurements.

Chart 1 – body and sleeves

7
6
5
4
3
2
1 rnd body: 144 (152, 160, 168) sts
sleeves: 36 (36, 40, 40) L

Key Blue / Gray

- A – 9418 / 0085
- B – 0054 / 0052
- C – 1415 / 0086
- D – 0005 / 0051
- ◢ k2tog
- no stitch

Chart 2 – yoke

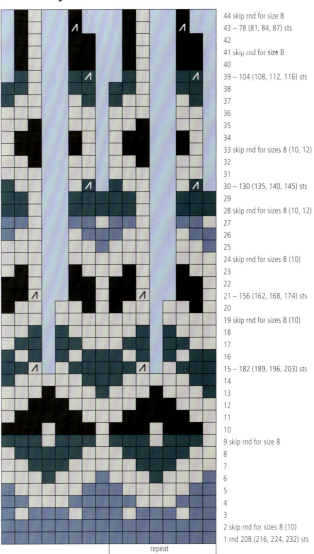

44 skip rnd for size 8
43 – 78 (81, 84, 87) sts
42
41 skip rnd for size 8
40
39 – 104 (108, 112, 116) sts
38
37
36
35
34
33 skip rnd for sizes 8 (10, 12)
32
31
30 – 130 (135, 140, 145) sts
29
28 skip rnd for sizes 8 (10, 12)
27
26
25
24 skip rnd for sizes 8 (10)
23
22
21 – 156 (162, 168, 174) sts
20
19 skip rnd for sizes 8 (10)
18
17
16
15 – 182 (189, 196, 203) sts
14
13
12
11
10
9 skip rnd for size 8
8
7
6
5
4
3
2 skip rnd for sizes 8 (10)
1 rnd 208 (216, 224, 232) sts

8 80 cm
10 84 cm
12 89 cm
14 93 cm

8 34 cm
10 37 cm
12 39 cm
14 42 cm

8 36 cm
10 39 cm
12 42 cm
14 45 cm

NOTE: See sizes on page 231 for measurements in inches

vetur

This soft, cozy sweater is knit using two strands of unspun Icelandic wool. Its all-over color pattern gives it extra warmth.

SIZES S (M, L, XL, XXL)
Chest: 91/35¾" (97/38", 102/40", 108/42½", 114/44¾")
Length to armhole: 42/16½" (43/17", 43/17", 45/17¾", 46/18")
Sleeve length: 49/19¼" (50/19¾", 50/19¾", 52/20½", 53/21")

MATERIALS Plötulopi approx 100g (3.5oz) plates, 300m (328yd)
Black-white
A 0005 black heather 4 (4, 4, 5, 5)
B 0001 white 2 (2, 2, 3, 3)

Light gray-blue
A 1026 ash heather 4 (4, 4, 5, 5)
B 1432 winter blue heather 2 (2, 2, 3, 3)

5.5mm and 4.5mm (US 9 and 7) circular needles 40 and 80cm (16 and 30in), 5.5mm and 4.5mm (US 9 and 7) double pointed needles, markers

GAUGE
2-ply Plötulopi: 10 x 10cm (4 x 4in) = 14 sts and 19 rows in st st on 5.5mm (US 9) needles

NOTE
Use two strands of plötulopi together from the plates for each color. Body and sleeves are worked in the round from lower edge to underarms, then joined to work yoke in the round. Each round of the body begins on the left side of the sweater, but the yoke rounds begin where the back of the sweater meets the left sleeve. When knitting the "lice", always carry the color across the top (over left index finger) to make it dominant. See page 251.

BODY

CO 120 (128, 136, 144, 152) sts with B using 4.5mm circular needle. Join in the rnd and work *k1, p1* rib for 6cm, inc evenly spaced 8 sts in last rnd => 128 (136, 144, 152, 160) sts. Change to 5.5mm circular needle and work in st st patt from **Chart 1**. Work 10 (10, 10, 11, 11) "lice" patterns up body or until body measures 42 (43, 43, 45, 46) cm from CO edge.

SLEEVES

CO 36 (36, 38, 40, 42) sts with B using 4.5mm dpns. Join in the rnd and work *k1, p1* rib for 6cm, inc evenly spaced 4 (4, 2, 8, 6) sts in last rnd => 40 (40, 40, 48, 48) sts. Change to 5.5mm needles and work in st st **Chart 1**. Work 12 (12, 12, 13, 13) "lice" patterns up sleeve or until sleeve measures 49 (50, 50, 52, 53) cm from CO edge.

At same time: Inc 1 st after first st and 1 st before last st of rnd in 13th (11th, 10th, 13th, 12th) rnd, total 5 (6, 7, 5, 6) times up sleeve => 50 (52, 54, 58, 60) sts. Place 7 (8, 9, 9, 10) sts underarm on st holder => 43 (44, 45, 49, 50) sts. Work second sleeve.

YOKE

Join body and sleeves as follows: With A using 5.5mm circular needle, place the last 4 (4, 5, 5, 5) sts and the first 3 (4, 4, 4, 5) sts of body on st holder for underarm. Knit 43 (44, 45, 49, 50) sts of first sleeve. Knit 57 (60, 63, 67, 70) sts for front, place next 7 (8, 9, 9, 10) sts of body on st holder for underarm. Knit 43 (44, 45, 49, 50) sts of second sleeve. Knit 57 (60, 63, 67, 70) sts for back => 200 (208, 216, 232, 240) sts. Work patt and dec's from **Chart 2** as indicated. Change to shorter circular needle when necessary. When chart is complete => 75 (78, 81, 87, 90) sts.

NECKBAND

Change to 4.5mm needles and cont with B. Knit 1 rnd and dec evenly spaced 15 (16, 17, 19, 20) sts => 60 (62, 64, 68, 70) sts. Work *k1, p1* rib for 6cm. BO loosely.

FINISHING

Graft underarm sts tog and weave in loose ends. Rinse sweater by hand in lukewarm water. Carefully lay flat to dry and smooth gently into right shape and measurements

S 91 cm
M 97 cm
L 102 cm
XL 108 cm
XXL 114 cm

S 42 cm
M 43 cm
L 43 cm
XL 45 cm
XXL 46 cm

S 49 cm
M 50 cm
L 50 cm
XL 52 cm
XXL 53 cm

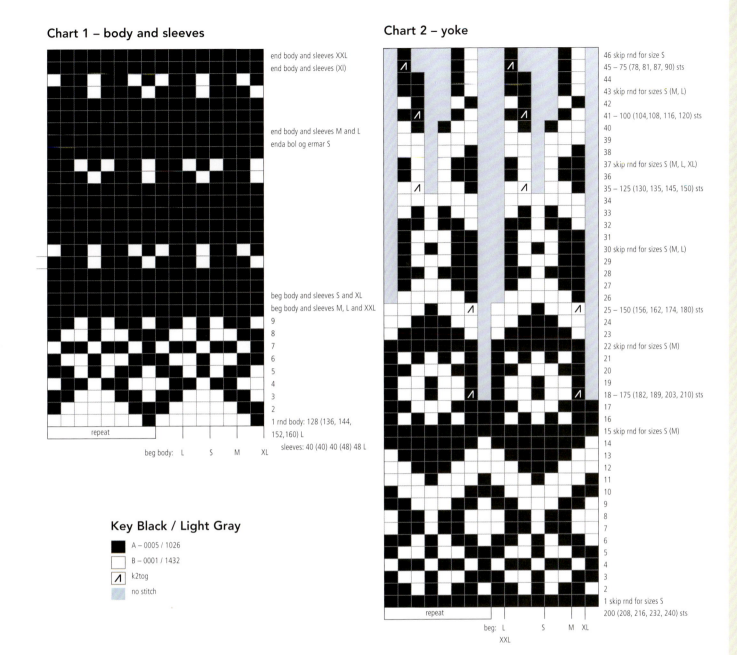

NOTE: See sizes on page 235 for measurements in inches

voff

This cozy sweater will look great on any small dog to keep him warm when the weather gets colder.

BODY

CO 24 (30, 33) sts with A using 4.5mm needles. Work 3 rows rib: *k1, p1* back and forth.

Back: (from RS) p1, k1, P1, work st st 18 (24, 27) sts, p1, k1, P1. Repeat until back measures 8 (10, 12) cm from CO edge.

Body: CO 24 (30, 33) sts, join in the rnd and work st st 24 (30, 33) sts (back), then 24 (30, 33) sts rib: *k1, p1* next 3 rnds. Work st st until body measures 14 (18, 22) cm from first CO edge. Set aside and work legs. Do not break yarn.

FRONT LEGS

CO 16 (18, 18) sts with A using 4.5mm needles. Join in the rnd and work 3 rnds rib: *k1, p1*. Work st st and inc 6 sts evenly over rnd. Work until sleeve measures 5 (6, 7) cm from CO edge. Place 5 (6, 6) sts under leg on st holder. Work second leg.

YOKE

Join body and sleeves with A. Knit 3 (4, 4) sts of body, place 5 (6, 6) sts on st holder, knit 17 (18, 18) sts across first sleeve. Knit 8 (10, 13) sts across body (front). Place next 5 (6, 6) sts of body on st holder, knit 17 (18, 18) sts across second sleeve. Knit 27 (34, 37) sts across body (back) => 72 (84, 90) sts. Work pattern from chart and dec as shown. => 36 (42, 45) sts. Change to 3.5mm needles and work 1 rnd st st with A. Work 2 rnds rib: *k1, p1*. Change to B and work 1 rnd rib. BO loosely.

FINISHING

Sleeve Gusset: Pick up 5 (6, 6) sts of body and work 5 (6, 6) rows st st (from RS). Graft to sleeve. Sew sides of inset to body. (This is done to give the sweater more mobility.. Work inset under second sleeve.

Weave in any loose ends. Rinse sweater and lay flat to dry.

SIZES S (M, L)
Chest: 27/10½" (33/13", 36/14")cm
Length of back: 20/7¾" (25/9¾", 30/11¾")cm

MATERIAL
Létt-Lopi 50g (1.7oz) balls, 100m (109yd)
A 0052 black sheep heather 1 (1, 1)
B 0051 white 1 (1, 1)
C 0053 acorn heather 1 (1, 1)

3.5mm and 4.5mm (US 4 and 7) double pointed needles

GAUGE
10 x 10cm (4 x 4in) = 18 sts and 24 rows in st st on 4.5mm (US 7) needles.

NOTE
Back is worked back and forth but body, yoke and sleeves are worked in the round. Measure dog's length and chest before starting, adjust the sweater length or width if necessary.

Chart

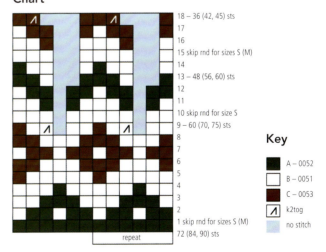

vor

This short, feminine vest will keep you at just the right temperature. It looks great dressed up with a shirt or dressed down with a T-shirt and jeans.

BODY

CO 152 (164, 176) sts with A using 3.5mm circular needle. Join in the round and work rib: *K1, P1*, for 5 rnds. Place a markers at each side. Change to 4.5mm circular needle and knit 4 (6, 8) cm. Dec 2 sts each side, then knit 12 rows and dec 2 sts each side again => 144 (156, 168) sts. Knit until work measures 5,5 (5,5, 7,5) cm. Change to B and knit 4 (5, 6)cm. Inc by 2 sts each side, then knit 12 rows and inc by 2 sts each side again => 152 (164, 176) sts. Knit until body measures 27 (29, 32) cm from CO edge. Do not work the last 6 (7, 8) sts in rnd.
Next rnd: BO 12 (14, 16) sts (last 6 (7, 8) and first 6 (7, 8) sts of row). Knit over front piece until there are 6 (7, 8) sts to marker. BO 12 (14, 16) sts and knit to end of row. Now there are 64 (68, 72) on each piece, front and back. Break yarn and work each piece back and forth.

FRONT

Bind off 1 st at the beginning of each row 7 times => 50 (54, 58) sts. Work in st st until 10 cm from beg of armhole, ending with WS row. Knit 15 (16, 17) sts, place next 20 (22, 24) sts on stitch holder and knit to end of row. Work each front piece separately. Dec 1 sts at neckline every second row three times => 12 (13, 14) sts. Work until piece measures 20 cm from beg of armhole. BO 6 sts at armhole and finish the row. Work 1 row and then bind off the rest of the sts.
Work other side the same

BACK

Work decreases at armhole as on front piece. Work until 18 (19, 19,5) cm from beg of armhole, ending with WS row. Knit 15 (16, 17) sts, place next 20 (22, 24) sts on stitch holder and knit to end of row. Work each back piece separately and dec 2 sts once and 1 st once => 12 (13, 14) sts. Work until piece measures 20 cm from beg of armhole. BO 6 sts at armhole and finish the row.

SIZES S (M, L)
Chest: 84/33" (91/35¾", 98/38½")
Body length: 52/20½" (54/21½" 56/22")

MATERIAL

Létt-Lopi 50g (1.7oz) balls, 100m (109yd)
A 0005 black heather 2 (2, 2)
X 0867 chocolate heather 2 (2, 2)

3.5 mm (US 4) circular needles 40 and 80cm (16 and 20in),
4.5mm (US 7) circular needle 80cm (30in)

GAUGE

10 x 10 cm (4 x 4in) = 18 sts and 24 rows in st st on 4.5mm (US 7) needles.

NOTE

Vest is worked in the round to armholes, then back and front are worked separately back and forth.

Work 1 row and then bind off the rest of the sts.
Work other side the same

FINISHING

Weave in ends. Sew up or graft shoulder seams together from right side.
Armhole: Pick up 74 (78, 82) sts around the armhole with A using 3.5mm short circular needle. Work rib in the rnd: *K1, P1*, total 3 rnds. Bind off.
Neckline: Pick up 84 (88, 92) sts around the neckline with A using 3.5mm short circular needle. Work rib in the rnd: *K1, P1*, total 3 rnds. Bind off.
Rinse vest by hand in lukewarm water. Carefully lay flat to dry and smooth gently into the right shape and measurements.

þel

A warm, comfortable sweater that is especially suited to the Icelandic climate. It will come in handy on chilly evenings or while on a picnic or barbecue.

BODY

CO 172 sts with A using 4.5mm needle and CO method as described. Work rib: *k2, p2* back and forth until work measures 50cm from CO edge.
Armhole: *Work 62 sts. BO 40 sts, work to end of row. Next row: Work 70 sts. CO 40 sts (over BO edge), work to end of row*.
Work 44cm. Repeat armhole from *to*. Work 50cm. BO in rib.

SLEEVES

CO 62 sts with A using 4.5mm dpn, with CO method as described. Join in the rnd and work rib: *k2, p2*. Inc 2 sts under arm in every 12th rnd 9 times => 80 sts. (Work inc sts into rib pattern). Change to 40cm circular needle when rnd gets bigger. Work without further shaping until sleeve measures 50cm. BO in rib. Work second sleeve.

FINISHING

Sew sleeves to armhole. Weave in any loose ends. Rinse sweater and lay flat to dry.
Decorations: Sew mother of pearl buttons to every 3rd ridge of rib at lower edge (15 on each side) and 3 buttons up mid sleeve.

SIZES S–XXL

Length of body to center back: 72/28½"
Sleeve length: 50/19¾"

MATERIAL Létt-Lopi 50g (1.07oz) balls, 100m (109yd)

A 0085 oatmeal 17

4.5mm (US 7) circular needles 40 and 80cm (16 and 30in), 4.5mm (US 7) double pointed needles, 36 mother of pearl buttons for decoration

GAUGE

10 x 10cm (4 x 4in) = 26 sts and 24 rows in rib: *K2, P2* on 4.5 (US 7) needles.

NOTE

Body is worked back and forth, sleeves are worked in the round. The cast on for the body is crochet cast on, which looks like a bind off edge.
a) Make a chain and put it on the crochet hook.
b) Hold the crochet hook in the right hand and needle in the left. Put the point of the needle on top of the yarn right up to the crochet hook.
c) Put the crochet hook in front of the needle and hook the yarn, pull it through the loop. Now there is 1 st on the needle and 1 st on the crochet hook.
d) Put the yarn behind the point of the needle (hold both needle and hook in right hand) so the point of the needle is right up to the yarn as it is in b.
Repeat from c) to d) until 1 st is left of the sts you want to CO. End by putting the yarn behind the needle like before and slip the st from the crochet hook to the needle.

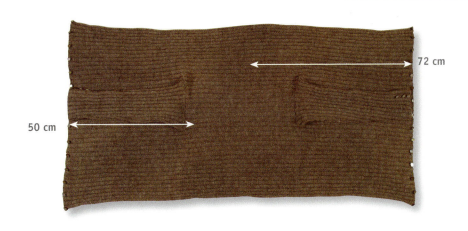

æði

One of the most popular contemporary Icelandic sweaters by Védís Jónsdóttir, who was a designer for Ístex for many years. Its shorter length, fitted silhouette, and zipper add a breath of fresh air to the traditional world of patterned-yoke sweaters.

SIZES XS (S, M, L, XL)
Chest: 84/33" (89/35", 94/37", 98/38½", 103/40½")
Length to armhole: 30/11¾" (31/12", 33/13", 35/13¾", 36/14")
Sleeve length: 45/17¾" (47/18½", 49/19¼", 51/20", 53/21")

MATERIALS Álafoss Lopi 100g (3.5oz) balls, 100m (109yd)
A 0005 black heather 5 (5, 6, 6, 6)
B 0085 oatmeal heather 1 (1, 1, 1, 1)
C 0051 white 1 (1, 1, 1, 1)

6mm (US 10) circular needles, 40 and 80cm (16 and 30in), 4.5mm (US 7) circular needle, 40cm, 4.5mm and 6mm (US 7 and 10) double pointed needles, double ended zipper, 50–55cm (20–22in) long

GAUGE
10 x 10cm (4 x 4in) = 13 sts and 18 rows in stockinette st on 6mm (US 10) needles. Check your gauge and adjust your needle size accordingly.

NOTE
Body and sleeves are worked in the round from lower edge to underarms, then joined to work yoke in the round. Round begins and ends with a purl st at front of body. The front is cut open.
Moss stitch: See page 250.

BODY

Using A and 6mm circular needle, CO 109 (115, 121, 127, 133) sts. Work 4 rows moss st. Join in the rnd and CO 2 sts (these count as the first and last sts in the rnd and are always purled) => 111 (117, 123, 129, 135) sts. Knit until piece measures 30 (31, 33, 35, 36) cm from CO edge. Set body aside and make the sleeves.

SLEEVES

Using A and 6mm dpn, CO 28 (28, 28, 30, 30) sts. Join in the rnd and work 4 rnds moss st. Switch to st st, immediately inc 2 sts (1 st after the first st in the rnd and 1 st before the last st in the rnd) and then in every 12th (12th, 11th, 11th, 11th) rnd 6 (6, 7, 7, 7) times => 40 (40, 42, 44, 44) sts. Knit without shaping until sleeve measures 45 (47, 49, 50, 51) cm from CO edge. Place 8 (8, 9, 10, 10) underarm sts on a stitch holder or scrap yarn => 32 (32, 33, 34, 34) sts. Make the other sleeve.

YOKE

Using A and the longer 6mm circular needle, join the body and the sleeves to form the yoke as follows: knit 24 (25, 26, 27, 29) sts (right front including the first purl st), place next 8 (8, 9, 10, 10) sts on a stitch holder or scrap yarn, knit the right sleeve 32 (32, 33, 34, 34) sts, knit 47 (51, 53, 55, 57) sts (back), place next 8 (8, 9, 10, 10) sts on a stitch holder or scrap yarn, knit the left sleeve 32 (32, 33, 34, 34) sts, knit 24 (25, 26, 27, 29) sts (left front including the last purl st) => 159 (165, 171, 177, 183) sts. Work **Chart**, dec accordingly. Switch to a shorter circular needle as the yoke's circumference becomes smaller. Once the chart is complete => 55 (57, 59, 61, 63) sts rem. Using A, knit 1 rnd, dec 4 (4, 6, 6, 8) sts evenly throughout => 51 (53, 53, 55, 55) sts (do not dec the first 2 or last 2 sts in the rnd). Switch to 4.5mm needles, BO the first purl st, work 1x1 ribbing, *k1, p1*, rep from * to *, to last st in rnd, BO. Work ribbing back and forth for 7cm. BO.

FINISHING

Graft underarm sts. Weave in loose ends, except as follows: pull the loose ends at the front of the sweater out to the RS and lay them down on top of the purl sts. Using a sewing machine and a straight, small stitch, sew 2 lines into each of the purl sts up the front of the sweater, sewing into the loose ends as well along the way. Cut between the sewing. Hand stitch the zipper to the front edges of the cardigan twice: first from the RS, folding the cardigan edge and securing it to the zipper and then again from the WS, securing the zipper's fabric edge to the WS of the cardigan. Fold the collar and stitch it to the WS of the neckline. Gently block the sweater into shape.

Chart – yoke

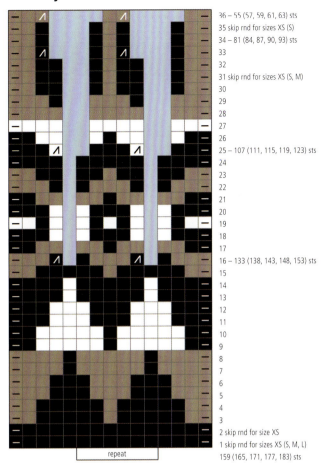

36 – 55 (57, 59, 61, 63) sts
35 skip rnd for sizes XS (S)
34 – 81 (84, 87, 90, 93) sts
33
32
31 skip rnd for sizes XS (S, M)
30
29
28
27
26
25 – 107 (111, 115, 119, 123) sts
24
23
22
21
20
19
18
17
16 – 133 (138, 143, 148, 153) sts
15
14
13
12
11
10
9
8
7
6
5
4
3
2 skip rnd for size XS
1 skip rnd for sizes XS (S, M, L)
159 (165, 171, 177, 183) sts

Key
- ■ A – 0005
- ■ B – 0085
- □ C – 0051
- ∧ k2tog
- — purl
- no stitch

repeat

XS 84 cm
S 89 cm
M 94 cm
L 98 cm
XL 103 cm

XS 45 cm
S 47 cm
M 49 cm
L 51 cm
XL 53 cm

XS 30 cm
S 31 cm
M 33 cm
L 35 cm
XL 36 cm

NOTE: See sizes on page 245 for measurements in inches

sweaters and other garments for women

- 1 x var • 21
- aftur • 25
- astrid • 29
- birta • 55
- endurreisn • 73
- faðmur • 77
- fjara (skirt) • 87
- frjáls • 91
- gjöf • 99
- hraði • 117
- keðja (dress) • 125
- klukka (slip) • 129
- kross • 137
- land • 143
- ljúfa • 155
- miðja (dress) • 163
- nost • 171
- nú • 180
- prýði • 188
- ranga • 192
- regla • 196
- vor (vest) • 246
- vormorgunn (vest) • 87
- þel • 242
- æði • 245

sweaters for men

- álafoss • 33
- árni • 41
- grein • 103
- riddari • 195
- stapi • 207
- strax • 211
- vetur • 235

unisex sweaters

- ár trésins • 37
- dalur • 63
- dropar • 69
- gefjun • 95
- órói • 179
- strýta • 217
- útjörð • 225

sweaters for children

ása • 45
bára • 51
bláklukka • 59
skotta • 81
hlökk • 111

kambur • 121
kría • 133
lappi • 147
sigur • 201
verur • 231

miscellaneous

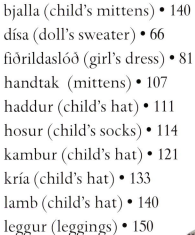

bjalla (child's mittens) • 140
dísa (doll's sweater) • 66
fiðrildaslóð (girl's dress) • 81
handtak (mittens) • 107
haddur (child's hat) • 111
hosur (child's socks) • 114
kambur (child's hat) • 121
kría (child's hat) • 133
lamb (child's hat) • 140
leggur (leggings) • 150

leistar (socks) • 152
mark (hat) • 159
rjúpa (collar) • 198
sjónvarpssokkar (socks) • 204
strik (scarf) • 214
toppur (hat) • 220
upp (wrist warmers) • 222
varmi (socks) • 228
voff (dog coat) • 238

information

THE HANDKNITTED ICELANDIC LOPI SWEATER

The Icelandic lopi sweater is designed to be worn by both sexes as it doesn't usually have waist-shaping. It's a unisex sweater and only the different sizes determine whom it fits best.

SIZES

Most of the patterns in this book are written in a range of sizes. Instructions for the smallest size are given first, with the larger sizes following. If only one figure is given it applies to all sizes. When choosing which size to make, check the finished measurements at the beginning of each pattern.

GAUGE

In order to achieve the correct measurements of the finished garment, it is essential to work to the recommended gauge given at the beginning of each pattern. The size of needles given for each pattern is only a recommendation. We urge you to knit a swatch before starting your project to check whether your knitting corresponds to the recommended gauge. Measure 10 cm (4in) horizontally across the stitches for the stitch gauge and vertically down the rows for the row gauge.

- If there are too many stitches to 10 cm (4in) try again with larger needles.
- If there are too few stitches to 10 cm (4in) try again with smaller needles.

BRIOCHE STITCH

Work back and forth:
Row 1: *k1, yo, slip 1 as to purl*, rep from *to* to end. Turn work.
Row 2: *k1 (into the stitch with the yo from previous row), yo, slip next st as to purl (the knitted stitch from previous row)*, rep from *to* to end. Turn work and rep.

MOSS STITCH

Row 1: *k1, p1* to end.
Row 2: p the k sts, k the p sts. Rep row 1 and 2.

KNITTING WITH TWO COLORS

When knitting in the round with two colors, the color not in use is carried loosely across the wrong side. Always carry the same color across the top throughout the round for an even appearance.

CHANGING TO A NEW BALL OF YARN – SPLICING

Never tie two ends together. Split the last 8 cm of each of the ends to be joined into two strands, and tear one strand off each. Overlap remaining strands and twist lightly together. Knit both strands together as one. Most knitters prefer to start a new ball of yarn by pulling the yarn from the inside of the ball rather than from the outside.

KNITTING FROM LEFT TO RIGHT

This is a way of working without turning the work: Insert left needle into back of stitch, wrap yarn down front and up back of left needle, lift right needle tip and draw new stitch through.

GRAFTING SHOULDER STITCHES OF FRONT TO BOUND-OFF STITCHES OF BACK

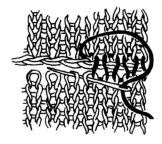

GRAFTING UNDERARM STITCHES TOGETHER

PLÖTULOPI

Plötulopi is unspun Icelandic wool or roving available as circular wool plates. Plötulopi needs to be knitted carefully and can be used 1-ply, 2-ply or 3-ply. Knit straight from the plate or wind the strands together in a ball. If the strand breaks it is easy to join by overlapping the ends and twisting them lightly together. Hand wash like other lopi garments but do not leave the garment to soak.

EINBAND

Einband is lace-weight Icelandic wool. It feels a bit rough but when it has been washed or soaked it softens up considerably. Garments knit with einband tend to be very stretchy and difficult to measure so it's essential to knit a swatch which is then soaked and blocked to ascertain the correct gauge.

CARE OF BULKY LOPI, ÁLAFOSS LOPI AND LÉTT-LOPI

Hand wash only. Use lukewarm water and mild soap or wool detergent. Soak the garment in the suds for about 10-minutes, do not rub or wring. Rinse thoroughly in lukewarm water. Wrap in towels and squeeze out as much water as possible. If necessary, spin for a few seconds to remove excess moisture. Smooth the garment out on a dry towel and pull gently into shape. If you wish, you may press the garment gently on the wrong side, with a damp cloth on top of it using a warm iron.

ZIPPER

Choose zipper for your garment after knitting and rinsing to ensure right length. Take care not to pull the knit as you attach the zipper.

FRONT OPENING

Using a machine, sew two rows of small straight

stitches up each purl stitch at body front. Cut carefully between sewn rows.

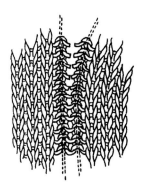

POM-POMS

Cut two identical cardboard circles that are the desired pom-pom size.

Cut holes in the center of both circles so that the cardboard circles resemble flat doughnuts. The larger the hole, the fuller the pom-pom. Place the two cardboard circles one on top of the other. Cut several strands of your chosen yarn to a manageable length. Place one strand at the center hole and wrap yarn from the center to the edge and back to the center again. Continue wrapping yarn in this manner until the center hole is packed with yarn. Distribute yarn evenly around the circle.

Insert the blade of the scissors through the yarn and in between the outside edges of the cardboard circles. Cut evenly around the circle until all the yarn has been cut.

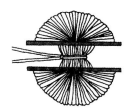

Pull the cards apart slightly and wrap a length of yarn tightly between the cards — around the middle of the yarn strands — a few times. Secure the yarn tie with a double knot. Leave a trailing end of yarn long enough to attach the pom-pom. Adjust and fluff the pom-pom. Trim away any excess yarn.

DUPLICATE STITCH (Swiss darning)

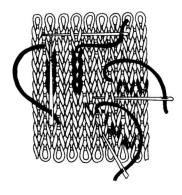

PATTERN-SIZE CHART MISMATCH

A pattern-size chart mismatch occurs when only part of the pattern on the chart can be included at the beginning and end of a row — i.e., not the full pattern or half of it. This happens when, for a particular size, the number of stitches shown in the chart does not fit within the number of stitches in the row. Put a marker at the beginning of the row and always be careful to start at the appropriate point in the pattern.

abbreviations

approx	approximately
beg	begin, beginning, begins
BO	bind off/cast off
CO	cast on
cm	centimeter(s)
cont	continue
dec	decreas(e), decreasing
dpn	double pointed needles
foll	follow(s), following
g	grams
in	inches
inc	increase(s), increasing
k	knit
k2tog	right dec: insert right needle into front of first 2 sts on left needle from left to right and knit these 2 sts together
right lifted inc	knit into right side of stitch in the row below, then knit st on needle
left lifted inc	knit into left side of stitch in the row below the stich last knitted
mm	millimeter(s)
M1L	make one left: from the front, lift strand between sts with left needle, twist strand by knitting into back of loop
M1R	make one right: from the back, lift strand between sts with left needle, twist strand by knitting into front of loop
oz	ounce
p	purl
p2tog	purl 2 stitches together
patt	pattern
rem	remain(s), remaining
rep	repeat
–	repeat instructions between asterisks
rnd(s)	round(s)
RS	right side
sc	single crochet
sl	slip
sl1,k1,psso	left dec: slip 1, knit 1, pass slipped stitch over knit 1
ssk	left dec: slip 2 sts knitwise, one at a time, to right needle, insert left needle into fronts of sts and knit them together
st(s)	stitch(es)
st st	stockinette stitch / stocking stitch
tbl	through back loop
tog	together
US	United States
WS	wrong side
yd	yard(s)
yo	yarn over
A, B . . .	color indication

resources

Alfoss Lopi
Bulky Lopi
Einband
Left Lopi

Distributed in North America by Westminster Fibers
8 Shelter Drive
Greer, SC 29650
800-445-9276
info@westminsterfibers.com
www.istex.is

Einband Plotulopi

Distributed by School House Press
schoolhousepress.com
800-YOU-CAN-KNIT

designers

26 1 x var – Védís Jónsdóttir
30 Aftur – Védís Jónsdóttir
34 Astrid – Astrid Ellingsen. Instructions Védís Jónsdóttir
38 Álafoss – designer unknown. Instructions Hulda Hákonardóttir
42 Ár trésins – Jóhanna Hjaltadóttir. Instructions Hulda Hákonardóttir
46 Árni – Astrid Ellingsen. Adaptation Hulda Hákonardóttir
50 Ása – Védís Jónsdóttir
56 Bára – Bára Þórarinsdóttir. Instructions Védís Jónsdóttir
60 Birta – Bára Þórarinsdóttir. Instructions Hulda Hákonardóttir
146 Bjalla – Álafoss. Adaptation Hulda Hákonardóttir
64 Bláklukka – Védís Jónsdóttir
68 Dalur – Bára Þórarinsdóttir. Instructions Hulda Hákonardóttir
72 Dísa – Védís Jónsdóttir
74 Dropar – Astrid Ellingsen. Instructions Hulda Hákonardóttir
78 Endurreisn – Védís Jónsdóttir
82 Faðmur – Védís Jónsdóttir
86 Fiðrildaslóð – Védís Jónsdóttir
92 Fjara – Védís Jónsdóttir
96 Frjáls – Védís Jónsdóttir
100 Gefjun – Astrid Ellingsen. Instructions Hulda Hákonardóttir
104 Gjöf – Gréta Björk Jóhannesdóttir. Instructions Hulda Hákonardóttir
108 Grein – Jóhanna Hjaltadóttir. Adaptation Védís Jónsdóttir
112 Handtak – Védís Jónsdóttir
116 Haddur – Védís Jónsdóttir
116 Hlökk – Védís Jónsdóttir
120 Hosur – Baldrún Kolfinna Jónsdóttir
122 Hraði – Védís Jónsdóttir
126 Kambur – Védís Jónsdóttir
130 Keðja – Védís Jónsdóttir
134 Klukka – Védís Jónsdóttir
138 Kría – Védís Jónsdóttir
142 Kross – Védís Jónsdóttir
146 Lamb – Álafoss. Adaptation Hulda Hákonardóttir
148 Land – Védís Jónsdóttir
152 Lappi – Védís Jónsdóttir
156 Leggur – Védís Jónsdóttir
158 Leistar – Hulda Hákonardóttir
160 Ljúfa – Designer unknown. Adaptation Hulda Hákonardóttir
164 Mark – Védís Jónsdóttir
168 Miðja – Védís Jónsdóttir
176 Nost – Védís Jónsdóttir
180 Nú – Védís Jónsdóttir
176 Órói – Védís Jónsdóttir
188 Prýði – Designer unknown. Instructions Hulda Hákonardóttir
192 Ranga – Védís Jónsdóttir
196 Regla – Designer unknown. Instructions Hulda Hákonardóttir
200 Riddari – Védís Jónsdóttir
204 Rjúpa – Védís Jónsdóttir
206 Sigur – Védís Jónsdóttir
210 Sjónvarpssokkar – Álafoss. Adaptation Hulda Hákonardóttir
86 Skotta – Védís Jónsdóttir
212 Stapi – Védís Jónsdóttir, part of pattern originates from an old Álafoss pattern
216 Strax – Védís Jónsdóttir
220 Strik – Védís Jónsdóttir
222 Strýta – Astrid Ellingsen. Instructions Hulda Hákonardóttir
226 Toppur – Astrid Ellingsen
228 Upp – Védís Jónsdóttir
230 Útjörð – Védís Jónsdóttir
234 Varmi – Hildur Sigurðardóttir
236 Verur – Védís Jónsdóttir
240 Vetur – Védís Jónsdóttir
244 Voff – Védís Jónsdóttir
246 Vor – Védís Jónsdóttir
92 Vormorgunn – Védís Jónsdóttir
248 Þel – Védís Jónsdóttir
250 Æði – Védís Jónsdóttir

picture credits

9: The Icelandic Museum of Photography / Ívar Brynjólfsson. 11: The Icelandic Museum of Photography / Drawing of Sigurður Guðmundsson, 1860-1870. 12: The Icelandic Museum of Photography / Johannes Klein, 1898. 13, left: The Textile Museum in Blönduós / Gísli Egill Hrafnsson. 13, right: The Icelandic Museum of Photography / photographer unknown, 1900-1905. 14, upper photo: Reykjavik Museum of Photography / Magnús Ólafsson 1910-1930. 14, lower photo: The Textile Museum in Blönduós / Gísli Egill Hrafnsson. 15: The Textile Museum in Blönduós / Gísli Egill Hrafnsson. 16, upper photo: Reykjavik Museum of Photography / Magnús Ólafsson 1910-1930. 16, lower photo: The Textile Museum in Blönduós / Gísli Egill Hrafnsson. 17, upper photo: The Icelandic Museum of Photography / T. Throup, 1898. 17, lower photo: The Icelandic Museum of Photography / Geir Zoëga, 1921. 18, upper photo: Reykjavik Museum of Photography / Sveinn Þormóðsson, 1963. 18, lower photo: Reykjavik Museum of Photography / Eyjólfur Halldórsson, 1945-1960. 19, upper photo: Reykjavik Museum of Photography / Magnús Ólafsson 1910-1920. 19, lower photo: Reykjavik Museum of Photography / Sigurhans Vignir, 1953. 20, upper photo: From the womens magazine Melkorka, des. 1956 / photographer unknown. 20, lower photo: Reykjavik Museum of Photography / Óli Páll Kristjánsson, 1973. 22, upper photo: The Icelandic Museum of Photography / photographer unknown, 1920. 22, lower photo: The Icelandic Museum of Photography / photographer unknown, 1920. 23: The Icelandic Museum of Photography / photographer unknown, 1920. 24: Reykjavik Museum of Photography / Andrés Kolbeinsson, 1957

notes